SOURCE OF LIFE

SOURCE OF LIFE

Léonard Lassalle

MY LOCAL MEDIA COMPANY LTD • ENGLAND

Published in 2013
by My Local Media Company Ltd

ISBN: 978-0-9576475-1-0

Cover Illustration: Léonard Lassalle
Cover Design: Laurence Lassalle
Book Design Marcus Bolt
Typeset in Palatino
Produced through www.lulu.com
for My Local Media Company Ltd, England

Contents

Acknowledgements

With many thanks for their help and encouragement:

To Mélinda, for her valuable assistance during the writing of this book.

To our children, who made it possible by offering me a speech recognition software programme called Dragon. This enabled me to talk into the computer instead of having to type the text, as my vision is now too poor for me to see the keyboard clearly.

To our youngest son Laurence, who contributed greatly to the layout of the book.

To Laurence Shorter for his pertinent remarks.

To Adrienne Campbell, for her encouragement, support and willingness to edit, along with Brianna Shepard; and to Jane Phillimore, who gave Source of Life her final editor's approval.

Thanks also to Marcus Bolt for his precious advice, for designing the layout and seeing it through to the finished product.

Léonard Lassalle,
Beaumont du Ventoux, France
August 2012

Introduction

Source of Life contains stories of my life experiences which were not initiated by the impulses of wants and desires, but by a place that comes from far beyond my ordinary self, which I'll come to call my soul.

Now, I do not want to give the impression that my whole life was inspired by something noble and high that came from far beyond my ordinary self. Be reassured, my wants and desires are truly alive, they still fill my ego and have been active in my life's unfolding process, with its ups and downs, pleasures and sufferings.

In October 1957 when I was 19, I started a spiritual training called the latihan kejiwaan* of Subud*. Gradually, through continued practice, I became aware that alongside my ordinary self there resided in me a deeper and finer consciousness.

In order for this consciousness to take root, I needed to cultivate an inner space that would only come about when I willingly let go of my ordinary egocentric self. This realisation did not come from my heart and mind, but rather through the act of abandoning them in order to become more sensitive and aware of my inner life.

In Source of Life I share my experiences, aware that at times you may find some of them a little difficult to grasp or accept as true, as they are not rational in the earthly sense of the word. They come from a different consciousness where the logic of two plus two will not necessarily make four. However, their impact on my daily life is evident, as you will discover when you read on.

As much as I am aware, these experiences have arisen from the re-awakening of my primary consciousness, which originates from the Source of Life. By doing the practice of the latihan, little by little I have come to discover in myself a new form of understanding which does not spring from deductions or additions, but rather from a global perception of the whole without the use of thought.

I find that in my being I have developed different places of understanding: creations of the mind are to be understood by the mind, feelings of the heart to be understood in the heart, realities of a spiritual nature to be understood through the embrace of the whole by the soul. I discovered in myself that each level of consciousness has its own reality and laws of existence.

Twenty-six years after my first latihan, at a meeting at London's Tara Hotel on the 2nd of October 1983, Muhammad Pak Subuh* (the man who first received the latihan and whom we call 'Bapak'*) asked me to share with others my life experiences during my years practising the latihan.

This is the main reason for writing this book: to tell the stories of these experiences as I have lived them, in all simplicity and sincerity.

* *see Glossary, page 280*

Chapter 1

First steps with the new spiritual practice, 1937–1959

My childhood was an unusual one, mainly due to my eccentric, loving mother who brought me up on a wild island off the Var coast of southern France. There were no shops or schools on the Ile du Levant and until the age of six the only children I knew were my older sister and another little girl. Most of my time was spent by myself, close to my soul, with the birds, fish, reptiles and insect life that inhabited the island and its coastline. My artistic education came mostly from the music of the movement of the sea as it gurgled into the crab holes of the rocks, from the gentle dying of the waves on the tiny, pebbled beach, or the whistling sounds of the mistral blowing through the *maquis*.

Ile du Levant

My mother, a painter, acted as a mirror, imprinting my feelings with her search to find the correct vibration of colour when painting. I used to observe her scrutinising her subject at length, before energetically mixing the bright, oily pigments with her palette knife in order to obtain the desired result. I could watch her for hours in complete silence and admiration.

Mother painting off the island

In 1942, in the midst of war,

surviving on the Ile du Levant became too difficult; food was scarce and supply boats were making the 15km crossing from the mainland less and less frequently. My adoptive father had left for the war, never to return, and mother decided to move to a small village called Dieulefit, in the Drôme region of south-east France. There, she found a private mixed school where we were accepted as the only non-boarding children. The headmistress, aware of our poverty, very kindly waived the fees.

Summerhill, in the art room

We attended this school for nine years; it gave us a basic elementary education. After the war period, in 1951, our mother had the bright idea of sending us to a revolutionary free school in England called Summerhill, run by Mr AS Neill. My sister's father and my grandmother paid the fees. This school had a profound and positive effect on my emotional development, bringing me self-confidence together with the ability to express myself fluently in English. At the age of 15, I went to Paris to study drawing for two years and learn what was then called 'advertising' – poster design and lettering.

This unorthodox, fatherless upbringing probably contributed to making me independent and self-reliant. I tend to be a very matter-of-fact person, not really believing in anything except that which I experience directly myself. I base my understanding on what I can touch, what I can feel.

While we were growing up, our mother never mentioned the word God, or told us of the existence of the Bible, the New Testament, or any spiritual practices or religions. She herself had suffered extensively from an authoritarian clergyman father who later became a colonel in the British army. Yet through much emotional suffering, she had found her individual way by being close to nature, and had brought us up in a loving and free manner. I wrote my first book, *Chestnuts, Walnuts and Goat Cheese*, about the adventures of my early life up to the end of my studies and meeting my wife, Jean.

Rationality of thought brought me a certain comfort, and gave me a platform from which to operate. My world was relatively small, but what I understood in it made sense, as what I trusted came only from the reality of my experiences. Having an artist's nature, I tended to live in certain parts of my emotions and sensitivity, rather than in my head. This helped me to steer my fragile sailing boat across the complex, wide oceans of feelings.

Discovering my life partner

It was during a two-year period when I was studying painting at the Central School of Arts and Crafts in London that I first met Jean, who later became Mélinda. At the time she was earning a little money as a model in Leslie Cole's painting classes.

On a morning in September 1956, I entered the painting studio later than usual and found to my delight a most inspiring new life model posing on a draped, tall-legged chair. Not wanting to waste any more precious painting time, I rapidly fixed my canvas on to the rickety art-school easel and, squeezing the colours out of the tubes on to my palette, kept glancing at her intently, wondering which angle would best create an attractive composition on the white board.

Jean (Mélinda) London 1956

I finally chose a three-quarter view, poured some turpentine into an old yoghurt pot and, brush in hand, was ready to start. Like a fire catching a field of dry grass, increased by a sudden gust of inspiration I became fully immersed in my creativity. I worked solidly for the first part of the morning; there were no thoughts in my mind except concentration on the subject.

While observing her intently, I noticed that this new model was different from others I had worked with in London and Paris. She seemed to be inwardly awake; there was an intensity in her distant, pale green eyes that reflected an inner awareness about something actively going on inside her. During the customary English elevenses tea break, I could not resist going up to Jean and asking whether I could sit with her; she smiled and nodded gently, affirmatively, silently.

After the usual exchanges we started to chat. "What do you do inside yourself while you're posing?" I asked, curious to know if what I had observed while she was posing was correct. Taken aback by my very personal question she answered, " ... Nothing!" I repeated the question several times and she finally acknowledged, "Well, if you insist I'll tell you: at times, I count up to 100 and at the same time from 100 down to one. Also, I try to feel the end of my toes and slowly rise my body up to my head while trying to become aware of my whole."

Now laughing, she added, "But I rarely succeed; it's difficult, you know!" Surprised, and feeling a certain admiration for her achievements, I said, "What you do sounds just like a Gurdjieff exercise." Somehow, a part of us had already fused together; both were pleased the other knew about the Gurdjieff work, it established an instant rapport. If you have not heard of Mr Gurdjieff before, he was a Caucasian esoteric teacher who bought techniques of self- development from the Middle East to the westerners; his Centre was in Fontainebleau, near Paris.

Jean told me that she lived and worked in a centre called The Institute for the Comparative Study of History, Philosophy and the Sciences. It stood in a property called Coombe Springs, near Kingston upon Thames. Its director was John G Bennett and under his guidance pupils practised the Gurdjieff work. I myself had already become interested in this work and in Ouspensky's writings through an artist friend in London. Reading these esoteric books showed me how much I fluctuated in my consciousness depending on what mood I was in. I noticed that there was nothing really permanent in my feelings or thoughts.

Jean soon became my close companion and we spent all our free time together. I started visiting her at Coombe Springs, mostly in the evenings, often staying until the early morning. She shared her life there with me, including the inner work she did through different kinds of exercises such as 'Movements' and the 'Stop Exercise'. Mr Bennett was the master while some of his more experienced pupils took the classes. Alongside the artistic student life I was living in London, I quickly developed new relationships with Jean's friends at Coombe Springs, but to me the residents and people who visited the Institute seemed complicated and somehow gave the impression of being 'stuck' in their devotion to the Gurdjieff work, as well as to Mr Bennett, their master. I was 18 years of age and too independent and self-motivated to follow anyone else's ways but my own. Probably due to my wild, unusual upbringing, I did not want to join this or any other organisation that would have authority over me.

Hearing of a new approach to spirituality

At the time I was sharing a small first-floor flat with a student friend called John Lawrence, who studied book illustration at the Central School of Arts and Crafts. The flat was in Belsize Park Avenue, not far from Hampstead Heath. John had been brought up as a Catholic and attended a public school, and our very different conditioning and upbringing had left us with different understandings on all kinds of subjects. We often enjoyed our exchanges, each striving to make the other comprehend his own point of view. On spiritual matters, he had been taught to 'believe': in God, the New Testament, the Bible, in Jesus and his miracles. My reasoning was that to 'believe' in something tends to mean that I did not know that thing I was asked to believe in, as when I know something through my own experience, there is no more need to believe in it.

"Isn't it better to trust what you know from your own experience, rather than believing in something you don't know anything about, however holy it might sound?" I would query. To that John would reply, "But you can't know God! You can only believe in Him." And so our conversations would continue, often deep into the night. My short stay at Summerhill School had taught me that there was no right or wrong behaviour – it depended from which angle you looked at it. I see now that although our discussions were interesting, neither he nor I changed our points of view.

So, I will now return to the story of how the consciousness in my soul was reawakened. One night, early in the summer of 1957, I was woken up in the middle of the night by a car hooting outside Belsize Park Avenue. I looked through one of the large sash windows to see who would be crazy enough to do such a mad thing. To my great surprise, I saw Jean and our friend Peter Gibbs waving at me from the small, open-roofed Austin 7 parked below. I lifted up the sash and said, keeping my voice down, "Shush, be quiet, you will wake the whole neighborhood!"

"Can we come up and see you?" begged Jean, giving me a broad smile. I waved them in, quickly put on a pair of jeans and shirt that lay at the bottom of my bed, and rushed down to open the front door.

They had come to tell me that something incredible had happened at Coombe Springs. I noticed their eyes were sparkling with life; they seemed elated as if touched by a fairy's magic wand. "Are you drunk? Or have you taken some kind of drug? Do you realise it's 2.30am?" I asked, keeping my voice as low as I possibly could. Peter proceeded to tell me the reason for their excitement. Mr Bennett, who held international seminars on the Gurdjieff work, had recently invited an Indonesian man called Muhammad Pak Subuh to stay, together with his family and friends. They had, according to Peter, come to Coombe Springs to bring a completely new kind of spiritual training.

The decision to invite the Indonesian gentleman had, it seems, been taken rapidly by Mr B and a few Gurdjieffites; some of the old 'Work' people were rather put out. Many of the Gurdjieff hardliners had already left Coombe Springs, though others had stayed on to receive and experience the 'contact' that Muhammad Pak Subuh had brought with him.

"He is offering us what he calls the *latihan kejiwaan*, which apparently means a kind of spiritual training," Peter hesitatingly explained. Apparently Mr B, together with a very few chosen pupils, had started this latihan a few months previously in London. It had been brought out of Indonesia by a certain Hussein Rofé, who himself had directly received it when he had stayed with Pak Subuh in Indonesia. Based on the positive results they had themselves experienced, Mr Bennett and his small group had decided to offer it to the other members of the Institute present at Coombe Springs.

Later, Mr B explained why he had decided to invite Pak Subuh to the Institute. He told them about his last conversations with Gurdjieff, just before his death in October 1949. Gurdjieff had suggested that Bennett turn his attention towards a new spiritual way that would come to help humanity from the Far East. Some time later, a wise Sufi master from the Middle East told Mr B something similar. Then Mr B convincingly affirmed that, in his short experience of the latihan, he would certainly recommend it as something entirely new and very worthwhile.

Peter explained all this in almost one breath. "So, what is the difference with what you were doing before ... these Gurdjieff exercises ... self observing and all that stuff?" I asked, not quite understanding what it was all about.

He explained: "This is completely different. With the Gurdjieff exercises people use their will and concentration. With this latihan, on the contrary, we do not use our will or concentration; we completely let go of everything and what comes out from inside is quite incredible."

Peter tried to share his new experience with enthusiasm. "Let go of what? For what?" I retorted cynically, not comprehending what he was saying.

Jean took over, longing to share with me her latihan experience; her mouth was dancing freely as she spoke, expressing much joy. "Just before the ladies started the latihan, we were asked to take off our shoes and close our eyes. Then I heard an Indonesian lady say 'begin'. Soon after, I felt movement coming from deep inside me, which I didn't resist but followed. Tears came rolling down my cheeks. I started spontaneously to sing sounds I'd never made before. There were about 10 ladies in the room and everybody was moving about freely and singing, some crying, some laughing. It was amazing; I felt so great afterwards ..."

To emphasise what she was sharing, she slowly brought down her eyelids to close her eyes, showing me the sincerity of her letting go. There was so much emotion in her voice that tears flooded her eyes.

"When did this happen?" I asked, trying to get back to a more grounded reality.

Jean replied, "Oh, just this evening around 10pm in the big house. Everyone who has started this latihan is wondering what on earth is happening to them."

I observed them both, silently thinking to myself, "These guys are high; they don't talk sense and that Coombe Springs place seems to have become a kind of madhouse."

Finally, realising that their joy and enthusiasm did not seem to be having much effect on their French friend, Peter suddenly decided, "I think we'd better go; you know, Jennifer will wonder where the heck I have disappeared to at this time of the morning!" Jennifer was Peter's wife.

I looked into Jean's colourful green eyes. In their luminosity, I saw a shadow of disappointment and knew it was because I had not been able to respond positively to their immense joy. I smiled gently and said, "Goodnight. Next time, try to come at a more reasonable hour! See you next weekend." We had arranged that I would visit her on the coming Saturday evening at Coombe Springs.

Back in bed, I listened to the purr of the Austin 7's engine slowly fade into the night. The silence that followed, instead of appeasing my mind, gave space for me to reflect on what had just happened.

No, my friends were obviously not drunk. Why had they bothered to come all that way, from Kingston upon Thames up to north London, to share their weird experience with me? Certainly, it did show a lot of care and even love for their friend, but what was the real reason for their hyper-joyful and excited state? After all, one doesn't undertake such a long journey in the middle of the night, just for the sake of it. Maybe what they had encountered was so vast and powerful, so new and sublime, that they felt an urgency to share it immediately with the person closest to their hearts.

With these thoughts came a warm feeling that spread through my chest: they had driven all that way because they cared for me. I suddenly felt bad about having said that "goodnight" so quickly and sharply.

A few days later, visiting the Institute, I noticed that there was an enormous change in the residents since the arrival of Pak Subuh. There was more lightness and smiles, as if everyone had loosened up and suddenly become happy to be themselves. The younger generation especially felt that the experience of the latihan had severed them from the umbilical cord that had tied them so firmly to Mr Bennett and the Gurdjieff work. I found the residents more talkative, as if they had been delivered from an inner tension probably caused by the concentration of thought needed for Gurdjieff's method of self-observation.

Jean's first visit to France

It was early summer of 1957 and time for us to visit my mother for the holidays. I had invited Jean to stay with us in Vallauris, where mother lived on the Côte d'Azur. We made the long journey by train and arrived in Cannes under a magnificent blue sky. It was the first time Jean had been to France and I was proud to show her this beautiful part of the world.

My mother was extremely pleased at last to meet my girlfriend and immediately felt much love for her. The contrast in the everyday life of our families was quite radical. Jean had been brought up in a very bourgeois English atmosphere, where little of what was felt inside oneself was shared with the parents. Everything was kept in, and to your mother and father, as well as others, you always gave the appearance that all was under control.

In my family, most emotions were shared instantly; I say most because the very deep ones, where suffering was involved, were not shared so as to prevent hurt to the ones we loved.

Mother's house in Vallauris

On a material level, it was different as well: in England, most houses had bathrooms with hot and cold water, sitting rooms with flowery curtains and deep, cosy armchairs. In France, we had only one cold tap in the kitchen which had to serve the whole household. There was no sitting room, no curtains at the windows nor comfy armchairs. The kitchen functioned as the sitting and work room, as the only sturdy table in the house was the dining table.

Although my new companion did not show any discomfort at the time, she told me many years later that she had been shocked to experience such a different way of living.

It was most gratifying to find that Jean related so well to my mother; they chatted together on the terrace under the grapevine, while Mum, a cigarette in her mouth, made her raffia lampshades. We swam in the blue Mediterranean sea, visited the attractive coastline and wild backcountry, riding comfortably together on my old grey Lambretta scooter.

The holiday was exhilarating for both of us but it was soon time to return to England. The meeting with my mother had been an important moment, as it had helped Jean to better understand my background. I had met her family and admired the way she was able to free herself from the strong influence of bourgeois living. Now she could understand that my background and upbringing was what had mostly formed my character and behaviour.

Afterwards, Jean went back to Coombe Springs. She was not quite clear what she should do next; the arrival of the latihan had completely changed the dynamics of the Institute and its followers. For myself, I had not quite finished my art studies at the Central School of Arts and Crafts and found it was a real pleasure to take up my brushes, colours and palette again. I was soon back in the swing of life as an art student in London.

First contact with the spiritual training

My sister, her husband Toby and I decided to share a flat in Nevern Square, not far from Earl's Court Tube station. Toby was recovering after three months in a convalescence centre in Jordan, and my sister was earning a little money being a model in London's fashion world. I tried to spend any free time I could find with Jean, often staying for weekends at Peter and Jennifer Gibbs' oast house in East Sussex.

My friends spent most of their time talking about their new experience of the latihan. I could see how much it meant to them, but I did not wish to start getting involved; I did not really feel the need. Nevertheless, I was witnessing the obvious effects and changes that the spiritual training was having on them. I wondered whether it was also having an effect on me. Although I did not practise the exercise myself, my closeness to Jean must have been influencing my whole being.

I noticed that the frail structure I had been building in myself, through the joys and suffering of my life, was beginning to crumble. It was not as stable as I had thought; doubt was creeping in. Did I really know who I was? This fellow inside me seemed never to be the same, he was always fluctuating depending on who was around. I slowly became more and more confused and when friends or family asked me a question, any question, I would reply, "I have no idea; actually, in truth, I do not know anything, not even who I am."

My sister and Toby became quite worried about me. They thought my strange behavior might be due to the influence of Jean, as I was spending so much time with her. Their supposition disturbed me; I knew deep down that the beginning of a change had started within myself, but I could not explain it clearly. What was going on deep inside was too blurred in my understanding to share with anyone, even my family. I felt vulnerable, as if all my defences were down, leaving me feeling like a very young child. I was still in this lost state when, late on a Friday afternoon in mid-October of 1957, I entered the gates of Coombe Springs. Automatically, as had become my custom, I walked straight towards Jean's bedroom, when I inadvertently met Pierre Elliot in the courtyard outside the main house.

Pierre, who was related to Mr Bennett's family, had spent much of his student life at the Sorbonne in Paris. He never missed an opportunity to speak French with me.

"Salut, François! Comment ça va?" he said, smiling, offering his right hand for a shake. When Pierre asked how I was, I felt I could open my heart to him and I answered, hesitantly, "Not terribly well, in fact not well at all; I feel that I have lost myself, or my selves? I feel that I know absolutely nothing about who I am or about anything else."

With his hands behind his back, walking slowly while looking at the ground, he listened intently. Suddenly he stopped walking and said softly, turning his head to look directly into my eyes: "Why don't you simply start the latihan?" And after a moment he added, "I could organise it for you to start tonight if you like?"

I was about to answer, "No thanks, that's not for me," when I felt a silence inside and my inner voice, that on a few rare occasions before had come from the depths of my being, said with calm authority: "Why not? You realise you know nothing; you admit that you do not know who you are; why not try it and see? What can you lose?"

This made sense, why not? How could I make any judgment on something I only knew from the outside? What did I have to lose? I looked into my friend's soft, hazelnut brown eyes that were screened by a scratched old pair of thin tortoiseshell glasses; they seemed to be laughing; his lips carried an inviting smile. "Okay! Why not? Tell me when and where," I heard myself say.

"Tonight, nine o'clock at the hut," he replied, adding, "Come just as you are." The hut was a large, temporary wooden shed. It had been built not far from the main house for the sole purpose of doing latihan, while the Djamichunatra (a large nine-sided building based on the enneagram) was being finished at the south end of the property.

Jean was not in her room; I found her in the cottage chatting to her new friend, Sheila. They were both delighted when I told them about my brief conversation with Pierre in the courtyard. A brilliance in Jean's eyes made them glitter like the sparklers one waves about at Christmas. I understood her happiness, as it would be one more thing in our close inner world that we would share together.

"Yes, I'm so lost ... I realise I know nothing and that I have nothing to lose; so why not try?" I said, feeling positive since having decided to start the spiritual training the Indonesians called the latihan kejiwaan.

A few minutes before 9pm, I walked down to the hut. My steps were slow, my breathing long and deep. The autumn air had become sharp, leaves were already falling from the trees; there was no moon and I was guided in the darkness by the feeble, shaded light bulb set above the hut's door. Pierre was standing in the narrow antechamber waiting for me.

"Just take off your coat, jacket and shoes and anything metallic including your watch and any coins; put them there, on the bench, or in your shoes," he said as he pointed to the long metal-framed, wooden slatted bench that stood to my right against the wooden wall.

As I nervously took off my moccasins I became aware that my heart was thumping and thought, "What on earth are you letting yourself in for?" It wasn't the kind of thought I needed just then, as the door of the latihan hall swung open. But there was no time for reflection; I found myself in a room more spacious than I had expected when I had seen the building from outside. It was lit by a dim light bulb that hung from the apex of the pitched roof, making it difficult to see in all its four corners. My nostrils instantly detected a strong smell of burnt paraffin oil mixed with the dampish odour of the many old woollen carpets that covered, in a higgledy-piggledy way, the creaky wooden suspended floor.

Pierre guided me to the centre and placed me under the light bulb. Opposite, standing about three feet away, was the tall, impressive Mr Bennett, his pale blue eyes looking at me kindly, his mouth smiling slightly to one side. To his left was Muhammad Pak Subuh, better known as Bapak. I noticed that he was wearing a modern pair of thick, square-lensed glasses, and that he was the only person in the room who kept his shoes on. He held his hands behind his back, looking into the distance as if absent.

To the right of Mr Bennett was Pierre without his glasses, his eyes already closed. Further into the room I recognized, in the semi-darkness, Sjafrudin, Iksan, Batara Pane and a very young man called Imran, later named Asikin.

People call the first latihan 'an opening'; I wondered what in me was going to be opened.

Mr Bennett drew me out of my thoughts by saying in a quiet voice, "Relax, close your eyes ... begin!"

I closed my eyes, thinking, "Begin what?" Then, after a short time, I started to feel that the air was moving around me and that there was movement in the room. I heard, coming from the direction of Mr Bennett, weird noises and a kind of spontaneous chanting. Intrigued, I imperceptibly opened my eyes.

Looking through my eyelashes, I saw the respectable Mr B dancing, I should say more like gesticulating; he reminded me of a large orangutan loosely expressing his happiness. Keeping my eyes semi-closed I turned my head towards the other sounds. In the far distance of the room I saw Iksan doing some strange Javanese martial art dance, his legs and feet pointing outwards, his hands flat like choppers moving briskly as he made sharp jerky calls. Pierre had disappeared, but then reappeared, circling the room with large, slow steps. Each one present, except me, was making his individual expression, totally independent from each other.

I felt out of place in this room with these strange people. I wondered whether I should just run to the door and get out. Did I really want to be in here, amongst this peculiar lot, doing weird things? I did not feel part of this training exercise; I did not know what to do to get into it. Had I been too quick in agreeing to come tonight? Yet they had all come to do a latihan with me. I couldn't just walk out, could I? I was now feeling very awkward, not in the right place emotionally or physically, and was wondering how long it would go on for when suddenly, from close behind me, came a large, clear burp ...

"Why not?" I thought, "why not fart while they're at it too? That would also come from God," I continued, amused by my dribbling thoughts.

While these critical reflections were bubbling in my head, another colossal burp came rolling out. This time it was as if the bowels of the Earth had opened up and the rumbling sounds were coming out completely freely, with no resistance whatsoever.

I had been brought up in the country; I had always observed with some admiration how relaxed goats, cows and horses were when they let their gases escape from their bodies. Intrigued and curious to know who had the ability to belch with such natural relaxation, I gently turn my head to see who it was.

Just behind my right shoulder was Bapak, his eyes closed, his body swaying gently. He seemed to be in a faraway place, yet I felt entirely enrobed by his awareness. I suddenly became self-conscious; what was I doing? Was I a kind of a voyeur? Then I felt myself melting inside, and closed my eyes feeling tremendously humble as I found myself diminishing into a tiny being. It was as if my ordinary self, with all its many 'Is', had vanished; there was just consciousness in stillness.

A moment of deep silence and peace grew from inside, followed by an awareness that there was much life and presence in my hands and arms as they slowly rose up, just by themselves; the only 'will' needed was the letting go of the self to give them their freedom of movement. They were now fully out, suspended in space without any effort on my part and a smile of wellbeing shone on my face ...

"Finish!" Bennett's voice came down like a massive chopper. "Finish now!" I felt irritated by this brusque interference and protested, "What do you mean finish! I have only just started!"

"Oh no, you've done over half an hour, and that's enough," he answered in the manner of a father who knows what is good for his child.

There was nothing further to say; the experience, although rather short, had been deep and completely new to me. I felt great peace inside as I walked slowly towards the door of the hut. I did not feel like talking to anyone. I rapidly put on my shoes and coat as the others were slowly coming out talking and laughing. As I walked in the darkness towards the cottages, my mind was empty as if my thinking had been temporarily disconnected from the source of my thoughts.

Walking in the cool darkness felt wonderful. I noticed how I felt different inside compared to earlier. As I reached the cottages, I enjoyed a moment of nothingness, just feeling present in my being, and stopped at the bottom of the steps, waiting to find the initiative to start climbing up to Sheila's flat.

Finally, I heard laughter coming from the kitchen; its positive vibes carried me up the steps and I entered the room with a beaming face. "Oh there you are, we were wondering where you were," said Jean with a happy grin. She went on, "Quick, tell us, how did it go? Who was there?"

Sheila stopped stirring her saucepan and turned round, holding her wooden spoon; she was smiling too. In truth, I was not quite ready to share the experience that had seemed to last just an instant, but upon seeing their thirst to know what had happened to François in the latihan, I surrendered and let my clowning nature take over.

How we laughed as the story unravelled; I mimicked Mr Bennett dancing like an ape; Iksan doing his martial dancing in the semi-darkness; Pierre walking round in circles with his hands behind his back, face down as if looking at the ground ... Then the majestic burp and the sudden awareness that Bapak was standing just behind me. I became serious again when I told them of my realisation of how stupid I had been, being a voyeur, and how I had melted down to nothing, feeling so deeply humble. It was then that I had become conscious of an inner awareness that I had not experienced since I was a child, but different because I was now an adult.

I woke up early next morning and, lying in bed next to Jean's warm body, wondered, "If I were to die now, which François would I be?" As my thoughts quieted, I instantly became aware of a peaceful, timeless immensity in which there was consciousness that that's where I was now. In that moment, I hoped I would be able to access that place at the time of my death.

It was a most comforting realisation, to feel close to the source of my origin, the 'being' before the 'word', in full awareness of my living self in what felt like eternity. I had the feeling I would now be able to reconnect to it by simply letting go of my ego.

At that time I was only 19; the word soul was not yet part of my vocabulary.

I was longing to do my next latihan; this time, I would not sit on the fence and watch the others, but would go into the arena with all my sincerity and completely let go, observing what would come.

Two days later I came up from London to join the 9pm men's general latihan (as a rule, men and women were advised to do the latihan separately). There was a queue outside when we arrived; the foyer was tiny and it took a while for everyone to remove their shoes, coats and metallic objects from their pockets. Many were chatting to each other as if they were on their way to the movies; others seemed already to be in their bubbles, absent in their own world.

Peter looked at me, smiled and said, "See you later," before disappearing into the poorly lit hall. I followed behind. Some men were already doing their latihan; others were sitting quietly on the floor, their backs against the wooden walls. A few had finished and were slowly returning to their physical presence.

I found a place to stand where I had enough space to move without disturbing anyone. Now, with my eyes closed, my arms relaxed by my sides, legs and feet slightly apart, I stood there in silence, sincere in my keenness not to resist whatever arose from inside. It felt as if I was in front of an invisible gate, waiting for the impulses that would make me move into the unknown grounds of my inner world.

Shifting my attention outside myself, I realised that the room was now filled with other men, each one deeply involved in his own latihan. The mixture of sounds and movements produced by all these men was dense and surprising. Closing my eyes blocked my vision to the outside world, but I could not close my ears to the strangely harmonious yet chaotic tumult that surrounded me. How could I be standing there so quiet, so peaceful, in a place that sounded more like a madhouse than a place of devotion? I allowed my being to be permeated with the vibrating resonance of the whole room, similar to rushing water flowing through reeds.

I noticed in myself a certain detachment from my body and from what was going on around me. My consciousness shifted into a different level of being; it was clearer yet more embracing.

My attention was drawn to a discordant voice that my ears could not help selecting from the general hubbub; it seemed to be coming closer until it was so near I half-opened my eyes. There, standing bang opposite me less than a foot away, was a short bearded man in his late thirties, his wrinkled forehead frowning over tightly closed eyes. The unpleasant sounds came from an invisible mouth hidden in a bushy beard. I moved back slightly thinking, "Where do I go from here? How do I cope with this?"

Then I suddenly realised I had popped out of my inner self into the outer François. There I stood, self-conscious and not feeling the latihan at all. I waited, and after a while as nothing came, decided to abandon myself in depth, away from the uncomfortable presence of my thoughts about the man. The answer to the above questions did not come from my mind in words, but through completely letting go of the unpleasant feelings my thoughts were entertaining. It was interesting to notice that as soon as I detached myself from the source of my disturbance (which was actually in myself), the noisy bearded man moved on and I reconnected to the finer vibrations of the latihan.

I became aware that my whole body, especially my hands, seemed to have become larger, as if full of vibrating life. My arms were lifted weightlessly, as though pulled up by some magic force. I recognised what had started to happen on the evening of my first latihan. Aware of the rising movements, I let them continue freely. I felt I was the spectator to a happening within my body. The impulse come not from my will, as that part of my being seemed not to be active, but from somewhere else; where, I could not tell. Yet I felt that these movements were in harmony with my whole being. The wrists of the hands followed, undulating slowly, similar to large kelp that follow the swells of the cool oceans. Now my whole body was following the slow, harmonious rhythm. Not only was I seeing my relaxed body move, but also my consciousness had become broader. At the same time, I was fully aware of the others doing their spiritual training around me.

Distance, time and will, together with ego, vanished. My presence seemed to be in a different dimension where ordinary awareness was not present. Therefore I was surprised when I heard, coming from somewhere in the room, Bob Wiffin's gentle voice saying, "Finished for now." Indeed I noticed that the noisy hullabaloo of the latihan had come to an end; a profound silence filled the large space of the wooden hut.

I found a corner where I could sit; the feeling inside was so good that I did not want to disturb it. I stayed there for some time, sitting on the carpeted floor, savouring the peaceful consciousness. Men were getting up and leaving the room. I noticed how gently I was parachuted down into my ordinary self again; thoughts came back into my mind. I saw my friend Peter Gibbs walking out of the room, and followed him. Before slipping his shoes on in the foyer, he looked at me with his pale blue eyes that were brilliant with joy as if to say,

"Now you understand why we are so excited about this incredible latihan!"

How to share the experience

Bapak recommended doing the spiritual training two or three times a week, but no more; apparently at the beginning it was not good to practice too often as it would tend to make you lose your connection with the material world. I chose to do it twice a week, as it was expensive for me to get to Coombe Springs from London.

Something in me was elated by the experience. This contact was so simple; there were no words needed to receive it, no technique, no musts, no oughts, no exercises to do or learn, no need for a master or guru. All that was needed was to let go of one's ordinary self completely and in full sincerity; that was all.

In the weeks that followed, I regularly joined the other men to do latihan in the wooden hut. I noticed how the experiences never repeated themselves; each time was different as if I had come into a continuously evolving and growing awareness. The movements present in my being were now accompanied by sounds that emanated from deep inside. Some of them were pleasant and harmonious, others crude and discordant. I have to say though that I wasn't in complete deep latihan for the whole half hour. I found I kept escaping back into my mind, suddenly finding myself mechanically thinking about this or that. This was somehow disturbing; why wasn't I able to turn the spiritual tap on for the whole half hour?

I realised, some months later, that this was part of the process; that's why it is called a spiritual training. It was taking one's consciousness into a different level of being, where the ordinary mind and thoughts have no access. But whatever the quality of my latihan, I always experienced the same at the end: being immersed in a peaceful feeling that lasted for quite some time.

Of course all this was exciting; it was completely new to me and there was nothing in my previous life experience to compare with it. Often through the day I would feel light and happy, as if something in me had been liberated, but I could not say what, or understand from where it came. I wanted to share this light, happy feeling with my friends and close family – and even with people in the streets. At times I felt like climbing on to the low roof at the entrance to Earls Court Tube station and shouting to the people passing below, "Hey, you guys over there! It has arrived! It's for all of you, come!"

But I jolly well knew that if I did, I would be seen as a mad hatter. How could I share this enthusiasm with others? How could I explain it clearly? What words could I use to share its simplicity, its accessibility? It was all too new … I didn't have the vocabulary, self-assurance or understanding then to explain it.

One Sunday evening, I had come back from Coombe Springs to the Nevern Square flat feeling light and happy after having had a particularly energetic latihan. My sister Sylvette and her husband Toby were there as we had decided to have supper together. During the meal she asked me, "Why are you so bubbly and happy lately? What is happening to you? You're different."

I felt cornered, searching for the right words to explain what was happening as indeed something was changing. They were both looking at me inquisitively, waiting for my answer.

"Well, it's this incredible latihan. It is this, er ... spiritual training that I have started doing; it's just amazing!" I tried to share the enthusiasm but the words were coming with difficulty. "Men and women do it separately, you see, one simply stands there as relaxed as one can be, and things start to happen ... I do movements or even sometimes dance, sing or make funny noises. All these things happen spontaneously; none of it is done intentionally. It lasts about 30 minutes, then afterwards one feels very clear and peaceful inside."

Toby was looking at me with doubt and suspicion; his eyes full of concern, he said, "To me, it sounds quite dangerous; how do you know where this latihan comes from? The whole thing sounds bizarre and if I were you, I would keep well away from it!"

I thought, "Oh no, I am giving them the wrong impression. Isn't me feeling happy enough proof that it's okay?" Sylvette pushed me further into despair, saying, "Yes, Toby is right; it's crazy. You have no idea where this thing comes from. Anyway, you have been behaving oddly lately. It is because of that girl you go out with, isn't it?"

I was now in agony inside, feeling completely misunderstood; the pain was considerable. Why had I let myself get into this situation? I loved them both so much and knew they were concerned about me. Yes, I was changing, but how could I not change when I discovered in myself such space and blissful immensity, such acute awareness, which I had not known before. It reminded me of being a young child, when I would see things, understand things, feel situations, but wasn't able to express them in words.

The adults used to misinterpret then what I was trying to explain, and I felt there was no point sharing my Subud experiences with Sylvette and Toby any more, as they were not in the frame of mind to listen objectively. They must have felt my feeling since, after that evening, they did not ask me about the latihan and its effects for many years. Still, I could understand their reaction: I was Sylvette's little brother and she was trying to protect me from something unknown to her. She did not really recognise at that time that I was capable of being responsible for myself.

As the days went by, I became aware that there was another presence within my many selves; it was in my finer inner feelings, as compared to the everyday awareness that resided in my ego, my ordinary 'I'. This inner presence seemed to be there constantly, as if watching in the background, not judging or weighing things out like the ordinary 'I' normally does, but just observing quietly. The closest comparison I could give to this presence was what the Tibetans call 'the third eye'. I had just read Seven Years in Tibet. I liked this analogy as it described an awareness and vision that is above ordinary awareness and the act of seeing through the ordinary eyes.

All these realisations were very new to me; they did not come about because I had learnt or read about them in books, but they were part of my most recent experiences, of my newly discovered inner world.

I came to know some of the Indonesians who resided at Coombe Springs, especially one called Sjafrudin. He was tall and thin, with large, kind brown eyes and a nice smile that revealed irregular teeth. He was very approachable and probably the most at ease with the Europeans; he spoke some English. I often chatted and joked with him after the latihan; the subject of our exchanges did not matter, we just enjoyed each other's company. Often Peter, Robin or Tom joined in; the atmosphere was light and pleasant.

The meeting with the beast

Something unusual happened to me about two months after I started my new spiritual venture. I became ill. I had rarely been ill enough to take to my bed – sometimes I had the odd cold or sore throat, which I always dealt with myself and never called a doctor. But a violent pain, in the region of my heart, suddenly developed in the middle of the night on a Friday in late November.

The pain was so sharp and intense that it made breathing difficult and forced me to curl up and then stretch in all directions, as if manipulated by some badly-intentioned string puppeteer. By the early hours of Saturday morning I was delirious and my mind, uncontrollable and hyperactive, was full of black thoughts. Yet, that deeper consciousness I had recently become aware of in myself was still present like a good companion, keeping an eye and telling me that all would be okay, there was nothing to worry about. At least, these were the messages I was getting from the deeper part of my being but, most of the time, the agonising pain brought me back into the black reality of my physical body, floating in a space where there was only obscurity.

On Saturday morning, Jean arrived for the weekend as we had previously arranged. When she saw me at the door in such pain, unable to stand straight, she immediately settled me back into my untidy bed. Sylvette and Toby had gone to Paris for two weeks, and I had been greatly relieved to be alone in the flat while going through this unexpected painful phase.

"What is happening to my squeak?" Jean asked. For some reason, I still do not know why, she loved to call me squeak. The intense pain disorganised my thoughts, but I managed to give her a brief summary of what was going on.

"I must call a doctor to come see you. I don't know of any around here..." She looked concerned then murmured thoughtfully, "Oh, I know, Dr Courtenais-Mayers; he is apparently very good. He is in the Gurdjieff work. I'll ring Coombe Springs to get his phone number," and disappeared into the sitting room.

She came back sometime later with a big smile on her lovely face; her presence in the flat had brought me much comfort and simply to watch her attending to me so kindly was soothing. "Great! I've talked to Dr Courtenais-Mayers and he will be coming to see you this evening at 6pm." The doctor arrived punctually; Jean led him into my bedroom. In his late 40s, elegantly dressed in pale grey Prince of Wales tweed jacket, white shirt and a burgundy red bow tie, he sat beside the bed. As he asked me questions, I realised from his accent that he was French. He pulled his left arm forward revealing a pair of flashy gold cufflinks, and looked at his watch while feeling my pulse with the fingers of his right hand. He was certainly not a man of many words and I wondered what he would diagnose. Without a murmur, he opened his leather briefcase, pulled out a stethoscope and listened intently to my heart.

Looking concerned, he said, "Your heart condition is very poor; you must take it easy for the next two weeks. I'll give you an injection of camphor right away. From tomorrow take these pills twice a day; ring me in 10 days." He scribbled something illegible on a piece of paper and left the flat as speedily as he had arrived.

The pains in my chest started to diminish, but I was too weak to stand up yet. Jean cared for me that weekend and cooked enough soup to last me a week. She left on Sunday evening to go back to Coombe Springs.

In bed, eyes closed, I let myself drift into strange, nebulous spaces of abstract shapes and vivid colours. As if a bird flying without a body, my consciousness moved in and out swiftly through these shapes and colours, feeling their different surfaces and contents. Sometimes there were pleasant feelings of bliss, joy and love; other times, the feelings were dark and disagreeable, creating anxiety; then they returned to blissful freedom again. Sometimes the travelling was slow, at other times it was fast; but my bird never landed. This condition was not related to time; large chunks of my day were spent discovering these strange worlds.

I think it was early Monday evening on the fifth day I'd been in bed that I woke up with my hand detecting something weird. My fingers were lightly stroking my cheek when I discovered with astonishment that they were going across very rough terrain, as if my skin was covered by rugged volcano-shaped bumps. Feeling a bit anxious, I touched my lips to find them much bigger than usual and very rough. My teeth seemed bigger and felt longer too. I could not believe what I was touching. Needing some proof of this frightening and intriguing situation, I struggled up and staggered to the bathroom, switched on the tubular light over the mirror, brought myself up by resting my hands on the washbasin and dared to look up into the mirror.

I discovered an unbelievable scene: my reflection was that of a strange beast. Horrified, I looked behind me to see if it might be there, but there was no one. I looked at the mirror again and there the beast was facing me; I could not believe it, and had to touch my cheek to make sure I was not dreaming. My face was rough, bumpy and covered in prickly, bristling hairs. The dark red-brown lips were thick and cracked, the canines slightly overhanging the lower lip. The eyebrows were thick and bushy; I ventured bravely to look into the gold-orange eyes; they were the eyes of an angry wild animal. I felt the detached animal force looking at me. A ripple of shivers went down my spine. Looking further into the darkness of the pupils I found a presence that seemed strangely familiar. With some difficulty, I murmured my name through the stiff lips: "François?"

I experienced their rigidity at the same time as a low raucous voice came vibrating out of my chest, echoing up through my throat. I hit myself with the flat of my hand, felt the prickly surface at the same time as the slap. "What's all this about?" I ventured, hesitantly, as I had difficulty pronouncing the words smoothly.

A swell of deep anger rose from my chest; I felt furious, angry! The rage inside gave me tremendous force; it was pure animal. Yet very deep somewhere, near the source of my inner being, there was a detached tranquillity that was not at all affected by this incredible happening.

"How am I going to go out? I can't go on the Tube like this. I'll terrify people," I thought, as I watched the beast going to the telephone, picking it up and dialling the office at Coombe Springs.

Olga de Nottbeck, who was the secretary at the time, picked up the phone and, recognising the unusual urgency in my voice, said in her soft, Norwegian accent: "Hello François, yes, I will look for Sjafrudin right away; just wait a minute."

The waiting seemed to take ages, though finally I heard the gentle, barely audible voice of my Indonesian friend say: "Hello, what is the problem, François?"

"It's more than a problem Sjafrudin, I've become a wild beast, a monster! You must come at once to help me out of this. Maybe we can do latihan together? I don't know, it might help?" I shouted loudly down the phone, not hiding my anger.

The same gentle, monotone voice answered kindly: "It will be all right, do not worry, just go to the kitchen and make yourself a cup of tea." This was too much for the angry beast I was, and I exploded, "A cup of tea? You must be joking. You can't leave me like this. I tell you, I've become a horrific monster; it's no joke! You have to come. Peter Gibbs will bring you in his car. I am sure he'll agree to it!"

After a long hesitation Sjafrudin broke his silence and his soft, regular voice came back through the phone: "It's very, very foggy outside, actually it's rather thick; we cannot see..." That really was too much! You don't bother about a bit of fog when a friend is in a fix, that's irresponsible, I thought, fuming. In exasperation I slammed the phone down, feeling slightly ashamed. My breathing was fast and wheezy; I circled three times round the room letting the steam out of my anger, then went back to the mirror over the washbasin and looked ...

I could now recognise my deformed features in the beast that seemed somehow less wild. I gave the monster a shy smile. My eyes seemed to have become more grey than the previous flaming gold. I walked into the kitchen, did not feel like a cup of tea as my fog-frightened friend had suggested, but saw an attractive orange in the wooden bowl, which I promptly cut in half, squeezing its juice into a glass. The aroma of the orange escaped, invading the kitchen. I breathed the scent deeply as I held the glass to my nostrils and glanced out of the window.

I observed the small park; there was a thickish fog that diffused a dim and grim orange light that came from somewhere across the leafless trees. I took a small sip of juice and thought, "Honestly, dear Sjafrudin frightened of the fog ... I suppose what I was shouting down the phone sounded completely mad."

I stood leaning against the tall sash window frame for quite some time sipping the richly perfumed drink and looking into the night sky.

The wild feeling and anger dissipated; I wiped my forehead and brows with my palm to discover that my face had changed again. I rushed back into the bathroom and saw that, although my face was still swollen and slightly deformed, the wild beast appearance had become the gentler physiognomy I was used to seeing every morning when I shaved in front of the mirror. I noticed I wasn't so tired and did not feel like going back to bed. I walked back into the kitchen to warm up the soup that Jean had so kindly prepared. The powerful experience had somehow shaken my rational mind. I tried to understand it but did not know where to start. All I knew for certain was that it was not a dream but real; what I mean is that I was fully conscious while it lasted. The experience was too weird to share with anybody except Jean and Peter Gibbs; I felt that if they did not understand its meaning, they would at least not criticise it as something coming from my imagination.

I decided not to try and understand this experience but to leave it open, to accept it as something that really happened yet something I did not need to analyse.

I recovered more quickly than Dr Courtenais-Mayers had predicted; in fact, the next day I woke up feeling clear, positive, happy and strong. After breakfast I decided not to take the heart pills any more, and went back to the Central School of Arts and Crafts to pursue my studies.

The wild beast experience quietened my desire to 'announce' the coming of the latihan to the world at large, as well as to my close friends. So I decided not to share the experiences I encountered through the spiritual training any more, except with Jean.

However, I did apologise to Sjafrudin for having put down the phone so rudely that foggy evening. He laughed and said, "It's no problem, François, you will understand the meaning of this experience one day."

Growth in consciousness

The latihan became more and more part of myself; it was no effort to do it and it became a natural thing to follow and harmonise with my life. But I stopped talking about it outside the group of people who practised it.

At each session the practice was different, both the sounds and movements that occurred inside my ordinary self and also the subtler feelings. I had not been clearly aware before I started the latihan that it was possible to perceive different degrees of awareness within myself. It was many years later, through living some powerful experiences that I discovered there were different levels of consciousness within my being.

Coombe Springs had become like an active beehive: people from all over the world came, stayed for a while then went back to their homes with the latihan. Pak Subuh, his wife Ibu and some of their family started to travel round the world, to places where they had been invited. Mr Bennett, who often followed the Indonesian party, learnt their language rapidly and, on their first world tour, became the principal translator.

When speaking to us, Pak Subuh always expressed himself in Indonesian mixed with a few High Javanese words. I found that in the many talks he gave in his lifetime and in his revealing book, *Susila Budhi Dharma,* he explained most clearly the interactions of the life forces that reside in each one of us and their direct influence on our behaviour.

The simple way in which he explained the whole potential of human development, from physical to spiritual, fitted my rational mind harmoniously. I rapidly got used to this new form of language and it became part of me. Similar to a baby who starts to discover the attractive and intriguing material world that surrounds him, after I started the latihan I began to discover, through my inner self, a growing awareness of the spiritual world within its gigantic diversity. Groups started to appear, not only in England, but also on different continents. On his journeys Bapak always gave talks, but only to people who had already experienced the latihan. His explanations were very welcome as they helped us understand what was going on in each of us. He would often use an analogy when describing a spiritual realisation: "When you come across a new experience, for instance the taste of sugar, then I'll tell you this taste is called sweet."

When talking about the spiritual experiences we would be going through, he often used Arabic words to explain the more refined states of being within our inner life. This was a because of the Indonesian Muslim culture he had been brought up in, but also because these words do not exist in everyday Indonesian language. It was interesting for me to notice that our ordinary Latin-based languages did not have the abstract words to describe specific states of awareness either. Mr Bennett, when translating, had to use the Arabic word Bapak was using, as he could not find a replacement in our European tongues. Little by little, a kind of Subud language developed. We could only understand the Arabic words once we had lived the experience of their content. For instance, for a long time, Bapak used the word *jiwa* to express the word 'soul', but for many years it was more often translated as 'inner feelings' or sometimes 'finer feelings'.

When Mr Bennett first heard the word jiwa, he probably would have asked what it meant, and Bapak would have explained by using several other words, which Mr Bennett would then have employed. I found it easier to use the word jiwa until many years later, when my field of spiritual experience had broadened and I was able to use the word 'soul' more freely. In this book I will use plain English and not the Indonesian or Arabic terms that were customarily used by Bapak, except, forgive me for this, the Indonesian word 'latihan' that I find most useful. The experience is so new and unique that I don't know an English word to replace it accurately. Of course if I talked to an Indonesian, I would not use this word, which plainly means training, but would add to it the word 'kejiwaan', which means spiritual.

One evening when I could not go to Coombe Springs, I decided to do the training at home by myself. To my great satisfaction, I noticed that through my usual 'letting go' action, the latihan started coming outwards from within. It was wonderful to become aware that I did not need anyone else in the room to connect to my inner self; simply by a sincere letting go of my heart and mind, the latihan would start to flow.

Now I could carry on with my spiritual development even when I was not able to join the large group at Coombe Springs or elsewhere. Yet it is true to say that my ability to let go completely was much easier when surrounded by other men than on my own. When alone, somehow my thoughts would incessantly come back and interfere with my inner peace. It became clear to me that when I intentionally used my thoughts, my latihan would immediately stop. To find it again I had, so to speak, to restart the training by completely letting go again of my thoughts into a space where there was nothing but peaceful quietness, when the flow of the latihan would start again spontaneously.

Realisation about my origin

Sometimes I spent a long weekend at the Gibbs's oast house, where I met Jean who came from Kingston upon Thames by car with Peter. On such an occasion, a bright Saturday morning in the early spring of 1958, a hitched ride dropped me off the main road near the junction with Chillies Lane, not far from the village of Crowborough in East Sussex. I was feeling light and happy as I walked towards my friends' house when, spontaneously, my awareness lived through an inner realisation.

My mind was totally quiet at that moment when my chest was unexpectedly filled by an enormous amount of love, so big I felt its presence well beyond my physical self. Directing my attention to my inner space, I saw within myself a colossal explosion like a big, silent bang. There were no colours at that point, and from the deep darkness nebulous clouds, lit by the energy of the bang, were growing outwards. There was a quietness in my inner self, and the only sounds I could hear came from my feet hitting the road and the pure whistle of a blackbird in the nearby chestnut wood. As the love explosion expanded, a delicate, fine awareness came of the presence of a new world with its own very delicate colours emerging.

In this spiritual awareness, I felt the physical creation of my being. The colours were beautiful, from the deep ocean blue to light ochre pinks. Within its centre, in constant expansion, I noticed a spot of brightness that soon became like an embryo. Then in a galactic movement of growth, I recognised myself as a foetus in the placenta waters of the universe. The feeling was sublime, and difficult to put into words, which are so crude compared to the refinement of the experience.

The floating spiral unfolded harmoniously – the New World. The child was slowly being fitted with the elements required to face what its soul had prepared in order to cope with this earthly planet. Exhilarated by the experience, I was suddenly filled with the understanding that this was similar to the Big Bang scientists had recently told us about when describing the beginning of the universe. I realised that this experience was connected to the creation of my own being.

As I walked along the small lane that led to Chillies oast house, my whole being was now actively savouring what I had just lived in myself. "Yes, each of us is a world in its own right, with its own laws of cause and effect orbiting around the empty space of its original Big Bang," I reflected in clarity, as I reached my friends' house.

I did not share this experience with Jean, Jennifer or Peter at that time; it was too tender, too young, to take out of the fragile pod of my new consciousness.

Coincidence and reality

Bapak had started to give talks more frequently; this was new to us and we soon took to the taste that was so enriching, trying not to miss any of the talks if at all possible. One Saturday afternoon as we arrived at Coombe Springs for latihan, we – Peter Gibbs, driving, and two other friends – were told that Bapak had gone to Manchester to give a talk to members in the north. Although it was late to start such a long journey, we jumped back into the car without hesitation and drove up the M1 at great speed.

As we entered the city, we asked if anyone knew where Bapak was giving the talk. Looking at each other blankly, we realised we had no idea where it was to be held. Stopping the car by the side of the road, we exploded into laughter as the situation was so funny: we had driven all that way without knowing where we were going. I was sitting in the front, eyes wet with tears of laughter, when I saw a middle-aged woman walking towards us. I wound down the window and addressed her: "Excuse me madam, you wouldn't happen to know, by any chance, where a talk will be held in a few minutes by a man called Bapak?"

She answered, looking quite staggered, "Oh, how amazing, you're Subud members, are you?" With broad smiles we acknowledged by nodding. "Well, I'm late myself; could you possibly give me a lift? I'll show you the way. It's not far from here."

We entered the hall just as Bapak was starting his talk. I do not know whether Manchester had one million citizens at that time, but that night it was a one-in-a-million chance that had presented itself to us.

Living my independent character

During the 50s and early 60s, military service in France was compulsory. In early spring of 1954, I had to go to military camp to attend a preliminary assessment of my soldiering abilities. The camp was near Tarascon in Provence. Many young lads from the south-east region were thrown together in the large barracks. For three days we were put through all kinds of psychological, intellectual and physical tests. Out of that contingent, they selected about ten of us to stay an extra two days for further tests to assess our intelligence. On the results of these experiments, the Camp military officials decided to make an officer out of me; I would be in the Radar Army Mobile Services Corps.

Thanks to my art studies in Paris and later London, I had been allowed to stretch my student years and defer my obligatory army commitment. Finally on the 18th of March 1958, I was called up by the French military authorities to Carpiagne military camp, high up in the hills behind Marseilles. I had been hoping that day would never come, but it had and I told Jean I was obliged to go. I also told her I did not intend to stay long, but to do all I could to get out very soon, as I had no intention of fighting in the north African war that was raging at the time.

As I was leaving Coombe Springs, my mind busy with intrusive military thoughts, I walked by Olga de Notbeck's office and heard her calling, "Oh, hello François, by the way, Mr Bennett wants to see you; could you possibly go up to his study now?"

I was surprised, but climbed two by two the stairs that led up to his office. "Good morning Mr Bennett; you wanted to see me?" I said hesitantly, popping my head around the open study door. The small room seemed to be bulging with his imposing presence. "Yes, come in, take a seat," he offered, pointing vaguely to the worn leather armchair opposite his desk.

I sat down and, while waiting, looked around the bare small room, searching for something interesting to look at; finally my eyes settled on Mr Bennett's large stature. His thick flocks of grey hair were thrown back negligently; his large, straight forehead expressed intelligence and a strong will. His handsome nose was straight and landed on a short moustache. He suddenly stopped writing and looked up, staring absently at me with his electric blue eyes. I became self-conscious, then realised he had closed his eyes and seemed to be in deep concentration. I waited ...

"Do you know that Bapak advises we should follow the law of our respective countries?" he said in a soft voice, opening his eyelids slowly and looking at me intensely. "Er, yes, I do," I answered, wondering where this was leading. "I would like to advise that you do your French military service and then, when it is all over, marry Jean." He said this in an authoritative tone of voice that stirred me up. How on earth did he know that I was going to try to get out of the army? I had no intention of fighting an Algerian war to kill Arabs; first of all I had become a pacifist and secondly had no wish to separate myself from Jean for the next two years. And how could he have the cheek to give me his advice when I had not asked for it?

I felt angry about Mr Bennett's intrusion into my private life; after all, I was not his pupil and did not need to be told what to do. "Thank you for your advice, Mr Bennett," I said with determination, "but I have decided to try and get out of military service and come back to be with Jean as soon as possible." I got up from my seat, and added cheekily as I reached the door: "It is kind of you to be concerned with our future, but really I can only follow what I feel is right for us. Thank you." As I walked down the staircase, I passed Olga's open office door. "How did it go?" she asked, obviously keen to hear the result of my brief meeting with her boss. I stopped, rested my shoulder on the glossy white door frame and answered, "Whatever the laws of my country are, I do not want to join in the killing of people who are fighting to liberate their own country." And upon saying that, I walked down the corridor and out of the building.

I realised from Olga's keenness to know about the future of her 'Gin and Tonic', as she called us, that it was she who had probably mentioned the matter to Mr Bennett in the first place. Anxious about my military call up, Jean must have shared her feelings with Olga who was very fond of her, and always ready to lend a sympathetic ear to anyone in need.

I arranged to be in Vallauris for the 1st of March 1958, so as to give myself time to prepare before going to the Carpiagne military camp. Jean came to Victoria Station to see me off. She was crying as I hugged her, standing on the platform by the waiting train. "I will get out of it, do not worry, and will ring you as soon as I am out," I said with much conviction, but thought to her anxious eyes it might seem as if I would never come back.

It was hard to let go of each other, but the train whistle had been blown. I gently terminated our hug, freeing myself to get into the carriage. "How could she possibly believe me?" I wondered as I looked through the window at her beautiful long face, framed by her straight jet-black hair. Her lovely lips were now drooping at the corners, reflecting deep sadness. Jean made a big effort to give me a last positive smile; but her goodbye wave carried the feeling that she would never see me again. Indeed, the brother she had so greatly admired and loved had left similarly, on a train that had taken him to join the British forces fighting Rommel and his army in the Libyan desert. He had never returned, blown up in his tank.

First encounter with the military

As the train moved away from the station, I started to work on a plan to get out of military service. First, absolutely no one should know of my intentions, except my mother, of course, as I would be staying with her for the first two weeks.

I decided to use the physical benefits that nature had already given me to facilitate my discharge. My Parisian friend, Pierre Münz, had told me when he came out of the army where he served as a male nurse, that there was a magic number to see whether one was fit for the army or not. He told me that by taking my height, weight, the circumference of my chest while breathing in and out, and using a certain order of adding and subtraction, if I came under the magic number 45, I would absolutely not be fit to wear the uniform.

My height was 1.87m, my weight was around 65kg, my chest was narrow and to get below the magic number I had to lose 10 or 11 kilos. When breathing in and out, I should try to make the chest circumference less than one centimetre. In addition, it would make things easier if I could find a way to measure 1.92m or 1.93m.

I decided to stop eating completely two weeks before going to Carpiagne military camp. When I told my mother she was very upset but, after trying without success to make me change my mind, she accepted it totally, carefully hiding her anxiety. My only oral intake was to be water, black coffee or tea without milk or sugar, and of course I would continue smoking Gauloises cigarettes.

I had never done such a drastic fast before. The first three or four days were hard, but I noticed that gradually I was detaching myself from food. Also I saw that I had much easier access to my inner, finer feelings where I could find peace and quiet. My latihans, which I continued to practise twice a week, were getting more ethereal, less earthy. As the days went by I noticed how difficult it was to think clearly about everyday matters; my mind tended to float away and I had to make a special effort to sort out the things I needed to do, such as organising my trip to the military camp.

I went for long walks round the back of Quartier du Devens; the early spring on the Côte d'Azur was already buzzing with insect life, the sun was hot, yet the air was cool due to the snow that covered the majestic Alps behind Nice. I filled my lungs to the brim with the crystalline air. I wanted to take in all the beauty that surrounded me before going to the dreaded army camp.

The big day came; I had taken an early train from Cannes to be in Marseilles by 11am. Six other young lads and I were met by an army 2CV van and taken up to Carpiagne's military camp.

The plateau of Carpiagne stands about 600m above sea level; it is a place where the mistral blows violently, where there are no trees to offer shelter, and where as far as the horizon one sees only sharp, sun-bleached rocks and stones scattered over a rough land of hard couch grass and a few short-stalked flowers.

We were dumped outside an enormous warehouse where a hundred or so young men were queuing by a long wooden counter. We were given our military equipment including a khaki kit bag and were asked to take off our civilian clothes and put on military uniform instead. Everything seemed to be heavy; the helmet, gun, boots and all the other bits that dress up a soldier. I found it very difficult to find my ordinary self. I was acutely feeling the effects of two weeks of fasting. I finally managed to get dressed in the woolly khaki uniform, then put my belongings into the kitbag and acted as if I could not lift it up. A short wiry guy with a gentle face saw my struggle and offered to help: "My name is Alain. Here, let me help you, rest your bag on my left shoulder and I will carry it for you."

He carried our two bags on skinny, bent legs forced to do fast, short steps under the accumulated weight. As he walked ahead, he reminded me of an Asian farmer going to the fields.

The kilometre-long stony road finally led us to the main camp where there were many barracks, and we were taken to a long wooden shed that was to be our dormitory. Covered in sweat and breathing fast, Alain dropped the bags and said, "Well, here we are!" I thanked him profusely as we entered the barracks. Each soldier dumped their kit bags on the metal bed they had chosen; being rather slow in my movement, the only one left was right next to the smelly, dirty-looking toilets.

I did not go to the refectory building for the evening meal, but wandered around the camp, trembling with cold. Now that the sun had gone down the temperature had dropped below zero. I decided to go back to the dormitory, snuggled into bed and tried to build some warmth.

At what seemed the middle of the night, I heard the sound of a bugle, then the door of our barracks was violently flung open and the lights were switched on. I peered over my sheet to see what the noisy fuss was about. A tough-looking sergeant was standing, legs wide apart, hands behind his back, shouting as loudly as he could; "I want everyone up and outside the barracks in five minutes!" He looked around fiercely and seeing that some of us were not moving, pointed a shaking finger and yelled, "Hurry up, you big asses!" I looked at my watch; it was 4.30am. To be ready in five minutes was no easy matter as there were fewer cold taps than lads in the room and only one loo. I decided to be last. As I came out of the barracks my breathing was stopped by the cold mistral wind. I slowly went towards the 'soldiers to be' who were standing in a line in front of this unsympathetic sergeant. We had understood, through his spasmodic shouts, that we were going on a five-hour march through the mountains. I walked up to him to say that I was not capable of doing such a walk, that I was ill and wanted to see a doctor. He yelled angrily, pointing at a small building not far from our barracks, "Dr Colonel Aubri will be there at nine; wait until he comes. And don't go wandering around, I warn you!"

Trembling like a leaf, speared by the cold mistral wind that blew without respite, I waited till nine o'clock when finally Dr Colonel Aubri arrived. His practice was in a small, well-insulated hut. The single room was sparsely furnished: a worn-out wooden desk, a metallic swivel chair with a worn-out cushion, a large filing cabinet and an overheating radiator. The stifling heat immediately comforted my shivering body, yet I felt absolutely clear and peaceful inside myself. The army doctor did not offer me the only chair that stood opposite his desk; instead he made me wait while he absently went through a pile of files. "This must be his morning ritual, keeping an eye on the health reports of all his men," I thought.

"What's your name, soldier? And tell me why you are here," he snapped dryly, looking up at me with distant pale green eyes.

"Lassalle, François, but there must have been some mistake in your notes; I'm certainly not strong and fit enough to be in the army," I answered, shyly.

He responded immediately, obviously irritated by what I had just said. "First of all, young man, when you address an officer, you must say 'my colonel'. Secondly, you have to understand that we do not make mistakes in the army!" he barked rigidly.

He turned to the filing cabinet and, after a brief search, pulled out a file. After looking at it for a while, he raised his eyebrows and said, "I see from your excellent records that you are perfectly healthy and intelligent; in fact, because of your good report, we are to make an officer out of you."

Amused by the situation I had got myself into, I decided to act a little simple; "I want my Mummy, you see Colonel," I whined in a pitiful voice. Looking exasperated, he took out a piece of paper and scribbled something on it.

"You want your Mummy, do you? ... Here! Take this to the infirmary; they will give you a full physical examination." He said that almost gently, but suddenly his voice became hard again, "Turn right out of here, four barracks down, you'll see the hospital; it's a stone building."

Without looking at me, he gave me the paper that carried his tiny, tight signature and I walked out of his office feeling relieved. I thought he had probably been in the Algerian war and had witnessed and been through some pretty awful stuff. I concluded he must be quite a good fellow.

At the infirmary I was placed in a tiny room with a north-facing window. The only furniture was a metal bed on which was laid a neatly-folded khaki blanket and a striped pillow without its cover on a dirty, equally striped mattress. I threw my kitbag on to it.

Later in the afternoon, a very short lad wearing white overalls came in and asked me to follow him. He ordered me to take off all my clothes except my pants and to stand on the scales. He then wrote down my weight on the medical form he was holding. He told me to stand absolutely straight with my back against the graded post to measure my height; as he was too small to read the measure over my head, he was obliged to climb on to a small stool. As he did so, I took the opportunity to quickly go on tiptoes to extend my height.

"Well, you are tall!" he exclaimed as he announced the 1.92m he had just read off. Then came to the chest measurements: "Breathe in fully, good ... Now breathe out completely ... Can't you do better than that?" he questioned, surprised, and added as he read his measuring tape, "Only one centimetre! That's really a pretty poor difference."

I was satisfied and thought that from now on at each examination I would have to raise myself five centimetres to repeat this strange saga. A short time later, I was examined by the military hospital doctor. While waiting to see him, I had decided to breathe very fast so as to make my heartbeat speed up. I did this for 15 minutes; as I stood up when I heard my name called, I felt very dizzy and toppled into his practice. It smelt of disinfectant, all the equipment seemed to be made of scratched and marked white painted metal. After a quick examination, he asked me, "Do you suffer from any heart problems?"

"According to my homeopathic doctor, I have a strange, long-shaped heart; I have not much endurance, you see," I hurriedly answered. The doctor made his assessment and sent me back to my unwelcoming, cold bedroom. What would be the future of my stay in this camp? I had no idea.

I took my off my shoes but stayed fully clothed, covered with the blanket, on the creaky, rusty metal bed. Extremely tired, I soon fell into the heavenly moment of going to sleep, which took me away from my earthly realities.

I was woken up by shouts and laughter, and opening my eyes looked in the direction of the window where I saw a number of distorted, grimacing faces squashed against the glass trying to get my attention. When they saw I had noticed them, they mockingly started to point their fingers in my direction to attract more of their colleagues to take part in the joke. I realised they were queuing up for medical check-ups and that the extensive queue unfortunately happened to be alongside my window. I felt like an animal must feel in the zoo when its sheer presence entertains the passing crowds. It was not a pleasant experience, but my inner state was so quiet and peaceful that it did not disturb me. Actually, I felt sorry for them as they were being prepared to become cannon fodder in the Algerian war. Although they were fooling about mocking me, I felt love towards them, as if they were young children, completely unaware of the atrocities that were awaiting them.

I heard the bell in the corridor calling for supper in the canteen but snuggled more deeply under the thin khaki blanket and waited ... Some time later, the door flew open and the boy who had measured and weighed me came in: "Come on, it's supper time, you'll miss it!" he said, invitingly.

"No, I can only eat the food that my mother cooks me; I have a very fragile liver; could I have a glass of water, please?"

He came back a few minutes later with the glass of water and a plain yoghurt saying, "Here, eat this yoghurt, won't do you any harm." I refused it, and he left the room looking concerned.

I lay in this uncomfortable bed all day except to go to the toilet. The only book I had with me was a pocket leather-bound Bible that had been given to my mother at her birth in 1903 by her godmother. I had never read the famous holy book and thought this a good opportunity to discover at last its mysterious contents.

The effects of the fast were now very strong. The lack of food was making me feel very weak, and I noticed how my mind, feelings and ego had become practically non-existent. I did not feel any power in the singularity of the 'I'. It was as if I was in a wider awareness while my ordinary self was dozing: I seemed to be residing in a peaceful consciousness. Reading the Bible in that state of consciousness brought me to realise how my ego normally tended to filter subjectively the information it received.

I had not done a latihan since arriving in the Carpiagne infirmary and I felt an urgent need to free myself from accumulated tensions. I thought that if I did a latihan in the main corridor of this small military hospital, I would free the painful constraints in my being and also maybe the staff and doctors would think I had completely lost my mind. I would, in their eyes, be not only weak and fragile but also mentally unstable. This would surely add negatively to my military record.

I rose from my bed, stood quietly and let the latihan come. I started swaying gently, feeling extremely happy. Sounds came out from the depths of my chest; I let them escape into the surrounding space. Then I walked slowly towards the door, opened it and, still singing, turned to the right, facing the long corridor at the end of which was a French window leading on to the bright, sunny, rocky, arid landscape. The inner feeling of joy was immense and I let my body spin like a whirling dervish; still singing I whizzed around, moving fast down the corridor. After a matter of minutes, I heard a door open and saw, intermittently as I spun around, a young male nurse shouting for help. An instant later another came to his rescue through a different door. They jumped on me as if they were catching a thief, bringing me to the ground and holding me there firmly.

My singing was now mixed with amusement at this unusual scene. I was completely aware of what was going on and decided to go on with it. Suddenly, I was hit violently in the face by a wet towel, splashing one side of my face then the other. It was painfully unpleasant and I asked them to stop. The doctor who had arrived was now leaning over me listening to my heart that was beating fast; as he forced some pills into my mouth I smelt the disagreeable odour of his large, rough, nicotined fingers. I did not spit the pills out immediately, but tucked them under my gums and cheek. They carried me by my legs and arms as if taken off a battlefield and dumped me back on my crooked bed.

When they left the room, I heard the doctor say to the young lads, "Just give him two of these every morning." Once silence had returned to my bedroom, I spat the two little white pills into my handkerchief. This latihan had certainly been 'special', but the first part had been extremely liberating and had reinforced the bounds of awareness with my soul. Of course the second part had not been very pleasant but there was something highly amusing and the thought of it made me chuckle in the bed.

I stayed two weeks at Carpiagne military camp, then was asked to be ready on Monday morning to be taken to a Recruiting Council of Doctors, Generals and Colonels in Marseilles' military headquarters. It was now over a month since I had started my complete fast from food, and when I looked at myself in the mirror, I noticed how my cheeks had melted into my jaws, leaving my cheekbones highly apparent and giving the impression that my eyes were sunk deep into my head. I felt very weak standing up, yet the place where I resided within myself was limpid clear; I felt at ease.

As soon as we arrived at the immense military building near the centre of the large city, I was asked to join a group of young recruits waiting in the enclosed courtyard. We were then directed into a small windowless chamber. Soon, a sergeant came in, ordering us to take off our clothes, apart from our underpants, and queue up against the wall of the adjacent room.

Again we were weighed and measured, this time in front of the severe-looking army officials who sat on one side of a long table, holding their ballpoint pens ready to scribble on their notepads. One of them cracked a feeble joke when seeing me enter the room; it was about when he had witnessed the freeing of the Jews from the camp of Buchenwald; an explosion of laughter followed from the uniformed officials.

As I was measured, I rose very slowly on to my tiptoes, hoping that I would stop at the correct height. To my great relief my trick went by unnoticed and I was asked to get dressed and go to the office to collect my military book.

As soon as the little brown book was given back to me over the worn wooden counter, I looked into it to find with great disappointment that, across the front page, were printed in two red large letters R/T. It meant 'Temporarily Discharged'. How painful it was to learn that although I had been released from duty now, I would have to go through the whole rigmarole again the following year.

However, once out I felt free; I wanted to run in every direction even though my body was not fit for a sprint. I started walking to find a café while the red letters R/T kept flashing in my mind like a warning lamp.

Reconnecting with the life forces

I found a quiet café where I sat at a round, burgundy Bakelite table. Now, at least for one year, time had become mine again; I could move, think, be in my own space and time and follow my own decisions. There I was, looking absently at the passing crowd feeling strangely free. I felt as if I was sitting on a rock, looking at the sea, a sea of feelings, and that I was about to take the plunge.

It was an important moment as, after having spent over 30 days with no food whatsoever in my stomach, I was now about to go back into the pleasures of the physical life, including eating. I knew that all my passions would eagerly come flooding back into the vast space I had been in over the last month.

I was suddenly torn out of my reverie. "And what can I bring you sir?" A young waiter stood beside me. I could not help but look into his eyes to see if I could discover whether he had yet served in the army. Yes, he must recently have suffered, as his eyes seemed hard and not readily present, as though they were looking somewhere else.

I had forgotten that one sits in a café to consume and was not ready for an immediate answer. It took a while for my mind to associate itself with food, yet alone to know what food I would desire. I replied with effort, ordering a Gruyère cheese sandwich and a light ale.

The crusty split baguette arrived, with yellow cheese and lettuce leaves sticking out from its sides. I smelt the powerful, appetising odour of fresh French bread. I held it with both hands so as not to lose any of its contents and opened my mouth wide, while closing my eyes. At that moment, the presence of Jean filled my inner space; I saw her looking at me, smiling hesitantly; a delightful feeling of love for her invaded my heart. But what was wrong? Why was her smile not free? Had she tied her heart somewhere else? I decided to stop playing this painful guessing game and passionately crunched into the surrendered sandwich, creating a myriad of golden crumbs that scattered on to the round table.

Now my whole consciousness was in my mouth. What a strange feeling it was to have a mouth full of food, to chew up and down, up and down, mixing, reactivating the saliva glands. The first swallowing was a true act of will; it was as if I had forgotten how to send the food down my throat. My jaw muscles and the upper parts of my teeth were in pain and I wondered whether I could finish the sandwich. However I noticed how quickly the whole process of action and reaction brought back earthly awareness into my being. It flowed back in, as the sandwich diminished, like a dam that had burst, flooding the plain below. It took me half an hour to finish the sandwich and beer; I felt tired from the exercise of eating.

"After all, I haven't used my jaw muscles for a long time; it's normal that they should hurt like this," I thought as I walked away from the café towards Marseilles central station. I was looking forward to being with my mother again, smelling her sweet perfume, hearing her soft voice and eating her delicious food; a large smile beamed on to my face in anticipation.

It must have been around 4pm when my train arrived in Cannes and the first thing I did was find a phone box. I could not wait any longer to tell Jean the good news about my release. "Hello? Are you there? Jean? Yes, it's François, I've just come out of the army! You can come down now!" I said with a voice tight with joy, so happy to be in contact with her again.

"What? How did you manage that?" was all she replied.

"You know ... I fasted ... I did not eat, then became too weak to be good for the army; please, come down here now!" I firmly reminded her of what I had said when we had parted on the platform at Victoria Station.

"But I can't, I have to go to Oslo tomorrow!" she answered, her voice sounding uneasy.

"Oslo? What on earth for and who on earth with?" I shouted

down the phone, horrified by what I was hearing.

Her voice had become frail, almost tearful. "With Canute." Canute was a Norwegian student of psychology who had studied in London. He had helped her through a deep depression, just before she joined the Gurdjieff work. This was some time before I had come into her life. I had met him at Coombe Springs briefly once and had not been too impressed by the red-haired, freckled Scandinavian.

"Canute? But this is crazy! I can't believe it?" I exclaimed.

"I am sorry, but it's true, I've already got the ticket," she confirmed in a sad voice.

Ignoring whatever feelings she might have had for Canute, I heard myself say with authoritative conviction: "Come down tomorrow, or I'll come up and fetch you now!" Probably moved by my sincerity and eagerness to be with her, she realigned her feelings and said, "Okay then, I'll try to arrange the tickets and come down to Cannes tomorrow evening."

Surprised by her ability to change her mind so rapidly on such an important matter, I felt secretly overjoyed by her decision, and said, "Great! I'll be at the station in Cannes on Thursday morning. Will you have enough money to get your ticket?"

"Yes, don't worry I think I have just enough in my purse. I am sorry about the confusion; somehow I did not think that I would see you again so soon. I must go now; see you on Thursday morning."

I heard traces of happiness in her voice and felt reassured by her decision to be with me; after all, she had probably thought she would never see me again as the war in north Africa was raging fiercely and France was sending more and more troops to fight the Algerian independence movement. My mother, too, was greatly surprised when she saw me, walking down the steps leading to the terrace where she was sitting making a raffia lampshade, surrounded by her cats. "No! I can't believe it! You're here already, how wonderful!" she exclaimed with tears in her eyes as she got up to hug me. "My darling, you're looking so, so thin; quick come and have something to eat," she added after our long embrace.

I told her all the details of my two weeks in the military camp of Carpiagne, not missing any of the incongruous and funny details. She was delighted to hear that Jean would be with us on Thursday morning. She adored Jean and was excited at the thought of seeing her again.

On that memorable, wonderful morning, Jean was on the train at Cannes station holding a rush basket and a small suitcase; these were all her belongings. As we hugged each other tightly, I could feel the warmth from the glow of her sincere happiness created by our reunion. I looked into her eyes and saw that our month of separation had been difficult for her.

New life in France

And so this is how our life together began, from that Thursday in April 1958. We would never be separated again...

We did not know what life had in store for us, but we were so happy in each other's company that the immediate present was all that counted. Although my mother's house was small, it was just big enough for us three; she was as delighted to be with us as we appreciated being with her.

For Jean and me, the latihan had become part of our life and we felt the need to organise ourselves so that we could practise it on a regular basis. There was no room in this tiny house to move freely, so we decided to do latihan in the clearing of a large pine forest that covered the hills behind the village of Vallauris. We found a beautiful grassy spot where, while one of us was doing the spiritual practice, the other would watch out for anyone walking by. The family whistle was used as a warning if an intruder was seen.

I have to say to the reader who has not experienced this type of spiritual training that although we practise this exercise of complete letting go for half an hour twice a week, the awareness of its presence within oneself does not leave you, but is continuously, delicately, quietly present, like the flame of a candle. Although at that time I had not been aware of it, this awakening of our souls had brought an entirely new perspective to how our life would develop together. Paris Match, a French weekly magazine, had written a long article with many photographs about Pak Subuh, who had miraculously healed the actress Eva Bartok and her newborn child. This article created many enquiries at the Subud office in Coombe Springs. Pierre Elliott, who was at that time actively working for the budding Subud organisation, had sent us a list of 30 people in our region of France who were interested in hearing about the latihan. The name Charles Parsons was underlined in red with a note saying that he might be the one who could help us to gather these people together at his house to answer their many questions.

We contacted Mr Parsons and his wife Psyche; it was arranged that we should visit them. Their large house was at the tip of a picturesque medieval village called St-Paul-de-Vence, which stretched over a hill that dominated the ultramarine blue of the Baie des Anges. The 180 degree view from Nice to the Cap d'Antibes was truly breathtaking. The Parsons lived in this impressive mansion that Charles had inherited from his father.

Saint Paul de Vence, 1959

Using the elegant, heavy, wrought-iron medieval door-knocker on the colossal walnut doors, we announced our presence ... Mr Parsons opened the door, "Come in!" he said with a husky voice, looking at us over his worn glasses.

It was cool inside the entrance hall; the walls were covered with attractive Impressionist paintings and before I could say anything about them our host said, "Oh, by the way, these were painted by my father." He said this nonchalantly, with a strong, drawling Californian accent. "Come on up, we'll go to my office and type the letter for the French."

It took several hours to type the 32 letters, making carbon copies, addressing the envelopes and so on. Mr Parsons was a writer by profession, specialising in paranormal phenomena, and seemed familiar with his temperamental archaic typewriter, in which the red part of the tape insistently popped up instead of the black. The letter invited the interested people to come to the St-Paul-de-Vence property on a Sunday in the first week of May 1958, at 3pm.

That Sunday came rather rapidly. I felt unprepared and wondered nervously what I would tell these people coming from all the different parts of the Côte d'Azur. Retrospectively, I realise that I knew very little about Pak Subuh or the latihan, which I had only practised for just over seven months. Jean, who had lived at Coombe Springs, worked with John Bennett and started latihan three months before me, did not speak a word of French and could not be of any help except by bringing her beautiful self and inner support.

We put on our best clothes and set off on the Lambretta for the hour and a half journey to the Parsons' house. "Quick! They're all here; they've been waiting for you. Follow me," said Charles Parsons in a low voice as he closed the heavy door behind us. He led the way down through the cellars, through a small arched door that gave on to a brightly sunlit walled garden. This lovely area was planted with lemon and orange trees, some still producing blossom.

All 32 people had responded to our letter and were present. We stood by the door looking at them smiling timidly; they had obviously been chatting to each other, and as we appeared an inquisitive silence floated in the strangely-scented atmosphere. I could see that there was disappointment on their faces as Charles Parsons introduced us. They obviously expected to see an old wise-looking man, maybe with a bushy white beard and long hair. Instead, a 19-year-old boy stood before them with his girlfriend, both with untidy hair from the windy ride on the scooter. Charles Parsons, feeling a little bit embarrassed by the situation, said hurriedly in his poor French:

"Come on, let's go to the room where Mr Lassalle will give his talk."

The room had been laid out in traditional conference manner, with rows of chairs facing a table with two chairs behind it. I felt most uncomfortable about this arrangement and asked the visitors to help me move the chairs into a large circle. While we were doing that my mind kept pestering me with questions: "What are you going to tell them? How will you start? They're all much older than you and probably well-read in spiritual matters; how are you going to handle that?"

Jean sat to my left, Charles Parsons and Psyche to my right, and the others completed the circle. I knew very well that if I used my mind to give a talk about Subud I would get into a tangle. So, just as I started latihan, I closed my eyes. I found inner quietness and asked inside myself: "What do I do next?" An answer rose from the depth of my being: "Only talk from your own experience of the latihan kejiwaan of Subud." I noticed embarrassment coming from some of the people present; had my silence been a little too long? I opened my eyes slowly and smiled broadly, looking at them all without focusing on anyone in particular. And, as if a tap had been opened, words started to flow freely out of my mouth. I felt as if I was listening to the stories I was telling. Actually, many changes and things had taken place within me since I started the latihan, and that was what I was talking about.

We had been together for almost two hours when suddenly the fast-running flow of words came to an end, as if the tap had been turned off. Nothing more was coming; I felt I had no more to share.

After a brief silence, I said, smiling, "Do you have any questions?" A lady in her late 50s asked: "How does Subud, or this latihan you have been telling us about, deal with the astral body and astral travelling?" Although my ego was very tempted to give an answer about the astral body from the little I had read about it, I went back to the quiet place inside myself and followed what came: "So far, in my short latihan training, I have not experienced anything about the astral body or astral travelling. If I talked about this, I would only be referring to books I have read. I don't feel I came here to do that, but more to share with you the realities of my experiences since I started the practice of the spiritual training."

No more questions were put forward, so we asked them to raise their hands if they were interested in starting the practice of the latihan. All raised their hands, apart from the middle-aged lady who had asked the question, and her husband. We told the others that we would let them know, in writing or by phone, when they could meet Pierre Elliott who would give them contact with the latihan.

Charles and Psyche Parsons were delighted by the meeting and suggested inviting Pierre and his wife Vivian to St-Paul-de-Vence. He and Psyche were very keen to start the latihan as soon as possible, and Charles kindly offered to give Pierre and Vivian the use of their property.

Pierre and Vivian arrived in the summer of 1958 and most of the people who had been at the meeting started the spiritual training. We hired a large hall in Nice where we met twice weekly; the first Subud group in France had been formed! Pierre and Vivian then went to Paris to start another group, leaving Jean and me to look after the new members in Nice.

It is interesting to note that since the birth of the Nice group, a new space had appeared inside our feelings, where Jean and I became aware of the group's presence within us. We witnessed their first latihan and this had undeniably created a strong link between each one of us; we found that we cared for the regularity and smooth development of the latihan and agreeably went out of our way to attend to the newly-interested people. Twice a week we set off happily on our Lambretta for the 90 minute journey from Vallauris to Nice.

Some time in the autumn, a telegram came from Pierre to say that Bapak had appointed us his 'assistants'; it meant that we could now pass on this spiritual contact to whoever desired it. The term assistant was used to signify that we assisted Bapak in the spread of the latihan, as the task to carry out what he described as his world mission would have been too much for one man alone. It could also be explained that this new role was to assist people during their first steps, witnessing their sincerity in connecting with what we felt was the great life force.

So our lives became rather busy as enquiries about Subud came from all kinds of places, from Menton to Marseilles and even along the coast to distant Carcassonne, near the Pyrenees. Much of our time was spent tending to new members who wanted to receive the contact. This was not an effort for us; we just followed naturally what was asked of us. We felt that we were doing the right thing in making the latihan as accessible as possible to people who were interested in it.

We had of course to make some money to survive, so we started a small silk batik business, designing and making silk shirts and scarves, which we sold in exclusive fashion shops along the Côte d'Azur. Although we followed our spiritual training regularly two or three times a week with the group in Nice, the awareness of the latihan inside was constantly present. Unusual states of consciousness were happening spontaneously: for example, once in the early hours of the morning as we were merging our feminine and masculine into one fine vibration, I found myself in a deep unifying peace. Jean, opening her eyes wide, exclaimed, "You are surrounded with brilliant lights, it's amazing!"

This unexpected announcement took me right out of my angelic state back into a more physical reality, and she said; "They have gone now; I can't see them any more."

Another time as we were coming together I felt very uneasy, as if we were being watched by some not very well-intentioned men. The feeling became so real and strong that I opened my eyes and looked around to see that six or seven men were standing around my beloved Jean, looking strangely at us. I knew right away that they were her past lovers, each filled with their own passionate fantasies of her; they were looking at me with unpleasant, envious expressions. This was a most detestable experience; I did not know how to handle the vision; it had the effect of completely cooling down my passionate impulses.

"What's the matter? What's happening?" Jean asked, worried by the very sudden change in my physical and emotional state. I did not know what to answer, as I felt it might upset her if I told her what I had seen. So I waited a while, then explained gently, "I felt other presences in the room, as if we were being watched. I opened my eyes and saw your past lovers standing all around our bed. They had unpleasant grins on their faces."

"I am not surprised, really ... Oh, I am sorry," she sadly murmured, as if it were her fault. This powerful experience had the effect of completely cutting off my sexual desire for Jean. I still loved her deeply, enjoying every moment of her presence, but the sexual attraction had vanished. This situation was unusual for me as I tended to be rather the other way. I suddenly found myself freed from spending a great part of my time occupied with sex and was amused by the thought, "It would be easy to be a monk feeling like this. Not being sexually attracted to women has some positive points!"

I asked Jean not to worry about this lack of sexual desire, explaining that it was nothing to do with her, but was something happening in me. I assured her that my sexual feelings would reawaken once I'd dealt with the situation. I felt I was going through a necessary process of cleansing, caused by the spiritual training. I felt we should not be too preoccupied by it, but trust it was temporary and give it the space in which to evolve.

The understanding of this experience came to me a few years later: these three months without sexual activity showed both of us that our loving closeness remained untouched. I noticed that the process had transformed my resentment towards so many parts of Jean's past life. I found an understanding and acceptance of who she was, with all her past experiences contributing to make her the person she was now, whom I loved so much.

Levitation experience

Around Christmas 1958, I was doing my latihan in rented premises called Salle Marie-Christine in Nice with five or six other men. The room was very large, with a worn and dusty wooden floor. At one end was a stage about a meter high on which stood a tall, fully decorated Christmas tree. Next to it, but on the floor, was a black upright piano. I was standing with my back to the piano, swaying gently, eyes closed and singing, lost in a total surrender.

I noticed that I had become weightless, my singing stopped, my arms away from the sides of my body. I felt my body rising; my feet were off the wooden floor. It was a strange sensation. Then I found myself going backwards over the piano and remember thinking, "Oh, I am going directly for the Christmas tree!" At that moment, I tensed up, the latihan stopped, and I felt the effect of gravity, crashing into the tree's glittering branches and finally landing on the stage.

I lay under the tree for some time, stunned by what had just happened, my body now feeling very heavy as if it was going to sink through the wooden platform. I said to myself, "This was a levitation, weightlessness, but now I've become heavy as lead!"

Before that experience I had been very dubious, even critical, of people who wrote or talked about levitation. Now this experience helped me understand that gravity is relative to where my awareness is; in other spheres of being the laws are different and adapted to that sphere. Was this what some people call the spiritual body, the body that can take you places with no sound or weight?

After this latihan, while we were putting our shoes on, one of the men raised his head and said jokingly, "Hey! What were you doing up there on the stage under the Christmas tree?" The other guys laughed at the thought of François on his back, legs in the air, lying under the tree. But because the experience was too fresh in my feelings for me to want to share what had actually happened, I just smiled broadly back.

Letting go of fear

A young Vietnamese lady called Marie, who lived in Cannes, had been doing the latihan with Jean for a few months when she asked if her boyfriend, André, could start the training too. Usually we met interested people a few times beforehand to inform them about Subud and the latihan.

During our chats, André told me that he had been a commando in the front lines of the French army in the Indochinese war; he had read many books and dabbled in different spiritual movements. He had also had connections with a group of Gurdjieff people somewhere on the coast. André was the kind of guy who knew it all; when I shared the little I understood about the Subud experience, he straight away found some analogy to a book he had just read. For some reason I wasn't happy about him starting the latihan; I felt him unstable, nervous and fidgety. I wasn't sure that I could look after him if he flipped into a crisis. I delayed, but wasn't clear enough in myself at that time to put words to this instinctive feeling.

Finally, as he kept insisting, I agreed and he started the latihan. One day, we received a telegram asking us to phone Marie urgently. "Come to my flat quickly; Andre has been beating me and is behaving aggressively. I need your help! Quick," cried Marie down the phone. It was not the first time that she had mentioned his violent tendencies.

Around 8pm we drove the Lambretta to Cannes, parked the scooter in the street and walked up the concrete steps to the first-floor flat. We entered the small kitchen and immediately felt an extremely tense atmosphere. Marie was shaking all over, she had a bruised cheekbone and had obviously been crying for a long time; she kindly offered us a cup of jasmine tea. I sat at the end of the table, my back to the stove, Jean to my left, Marie opposite. André was dishevelled, his blue tie undone, looking aghast as he walked rapidly around the room, his fists clenched tight. He was talking incoherently and swearing loudly, blaming Marie for his unhappiness and misery; it was all because of her that he could not sort out his life.

He was talking repetitively and going round in circles; after a long time listening to this, I attempted to talk quietly to him. Using what I thought was common sense and simple psychology, I tried to bring him to a more reasonable state of mind. At first it seemed to work;

he gave the appearance of understanding what I was saying; that he had within himself all the resources he needed to cope with his life. That he could choose within himself which way to go; but for this, he would have to be quiet inside and listen to his deeper inner self for guidance.

André's rage seemed to be contained for a while, yet his eyes were still wild, suggesting that another eruption was about to occur. He started walking around us again, tense and silent. I felt him standing behind me, and a frozen silence descended as I noticed, in the corner of my eye, the glittering blade of a long kitchen knife. Then I felt its sharp point coming to rest in contact with the tender skin of my neck.

"So!" he exclaimed, "I understand at last that you are the secret agent of Mr JG Bennett; you are working for him, are you not?" he shouted in my ear, pressing the knife point a fraction further into my flesh.

For the next few hours the kitchen became complete torture and hell; the tension reached its maximum. Outrageous language, unimaginable allegations about my involvement with the British Secret Service, mixed with accusations of co-operating with Mr Bennett who had the power to control the esoteric world and so on ... I could feel the pressure of the blade lessening or intensifying whenever André gesticulated.

It is easy to imagine what was going through my mind and feelings during these difficult hours. I realised that I had been acting too much like a father, trying to reassure André and giving him advice. This had probably contributed to bringing him into this uncontrollable state of violence. I remember thinking that he must have hated his father, who had probably been very violent with him when he was a child. No doubt my patronising words had actually done the opposite of what I had intended.

André did not want to listen to me any more, and he was now telling me how happy he was to discover that I was the secret agent of his worst enemy Mr Bennett, and that he had no choice but to kill me. Jean crossed her fingers that were resting on the table, her head leaning to one side. She was staring at her thumb slowly stroking the other. Marie was looking down, unable to say a word; her face was as white as the Formica kitchen table.

What a strange situation to be in, I thought; we came to help them and now find ourselves on the edge of drama under the horrific threat of a kitchen knife. I knew that the situation had gone too far for me to appease it through wise words. André was at the wheel and had taken command; he had caught the spy and felt in power controlling the situation.

I realised that the only thing left for me to do was to abandon my emotions together with my ego, and turn completely to my soul to let it show the way. As I did so, words bubbled up from inside me confirming my thoughts, "Put aside your heart and mind and stay close to me."

I then relaxed completely, letting go of my wish to save the situation, as well as my fears. I had a sense of hovering down into myself, like a feather slowly reaching the bottom of a well, until I found perfect stillness, where neither plus nor minus existed, only presence.

The whole situation miraculously changed. I was now feeling surrounded by love and light, cradled by an angelic awareness.

André's voice became distant now; it sounded less menacing, and the pointed pressure on my neck lessened until it disappeared altogether. My eyes were closed when I heard an explosion of tears, and André melted down heavily into the chair on my right, his forehead buried in his arms over the Formica. The kitchen knife now lay lifeless next to him.

I looked at my watch. It was 4.30am. I rose slowly to my feet, Jean and Marie followed; we all looked exhausted. As I walked by André who was still sobbing like a child, I affectionately rubbed his shoulders with my left hand. I kissed Marie goodbye; with her eyes loaded with tears she said softly, "Thank you both for coming." Jean gave her a long, affectionate embrace and we left the small flat.

The cool, early morning air together with the dawn rising, pushing away the dark night sky, contributed greatly in appeasing our emotions and tired bodies. Jean, her head to the side against my back on the Lambretta, was hugging me tightly as we meandered back along the winding road to Vallauris.

This strange event disturbed me for quite some time; why had we had to go through all that when our intention had been to help Marie? Now, in retrospect, I see that this experience took me to the limits of my fears, where I learned that the only solution had been to change my inner state to a higher level where love and trust reside. However, some questions remained in me. Should I go on caring for André and encourage him to go on with the latihan? I could not find an answer and decided to write to Pak Subuh in Indonesia to seek his advice.

Bapak replied, "This man André is an alcoholic. Neither the latihan nor you can do anything for him until he himself decides to stop drinking." The message was absolutely clear.

What was interesting was that, after the event at the flat, André never came back to the latihan and never bothered Marie again. Later, she told us that he had gone into a mental health care home in Nice. Two years later, I came across him in the streets of the city and over a cup of coffee he told me that he still felt the latihan and that it helped him, but he never came back to do the training with the group.

Our wedding and the first Subud World Congress

Jean and I were living happily together in the Quartier du Devens in my mother's tiny house. Our silk scarf business was doing well; I managed to find enough time to paint and the Subud activities kept us very busy. The idea of marriage had not occurred to us; we did not feel it was necessary as, in our eyes, we had been married before God by our sincere union. We wanted a big family with lots of children, but for some reason it had not happened yet.

Jean's mother, Winifred Orton, wrote often to her daughter, mostly to tell her about the latest plants that had joined her well-attended garden, or about a new bloom that had appeared. But in her recent letter she was now suggesting, with some insistence, that Jean and I should get married with an official church wedding in England.

Winifred and Poppa, as the family called them, suggested that the wedding could be held in the grounds of their house sometime in August 1959, and that they would pay for and organise everything. It was understandable that Jean wanted to please her parents, so we decided to take up their offer.

Wedding in Cowden, Kent, 1959

Honor, my mother, was delighted at our decision and we fixed the wedding date for the 1st of August, with the reception at the Orton's house near the delightful Kentish village of Cowden. The date fell 10 days before the first Subud World Congress, which was taking place at Coombe Springs; we decided to go there after our short honeymoon.

The wedding took place in the small, elegant 17th-century stone Anglican Church, into which squeezed 120 guests. The reception was held in a large white marquee in the grounds of the house. Beside Jean's family and mine, most other guests were our friends from Coombe Springs, including Mr Bennett and his wife Elizabeth.

Mr and Mrs Orton, with their attention to detail, had hired a Rolls-Royce for us to depart in for our honeymoon. I had politely refused it, saying that it was not my style and that we would prefer to leave on the scooter that a friend of ours, Robin Mitchell, had lent us. Nonetheless, the Rolls-Royce, together with chauffeur, cap and all, were waiting for us. But we preferred to hop on to Robin's Lambretta in our wedding outfits and drove off, waving to everybody amongst much amusement and laughter.

Our honeymoon went well, although it was cold and raining.

Being officially married gave us both a positive feeling. It wasn't because we were now closer to each other or that our sex life had heightened, no. But there was a difference, in that the acknowledgement and witnessing of all the people we loved and felt close to had acted as a kind of stamp of recognition from the outside world of our love to each other.

Just to put the reader in the political picture of the time: during the late 50s and early 60s there was an unsettling feeling of insecurity in the world, mostly due to the Cold War. The threat of atomic weapons was hanging over our heads, along with the destructive war in Vietnam and the French/Algerian fighting in north Africa. Freethinking Western society was longing to be re-awakened to a new spiritual reality. Up until then, most spiritual paths were based on ancient religions. Now, with the coming of the latihan, we could put aside our traditions and spiritual ideas and start something completely new within ourselves.

It was an exciting thought to have the possibility of connecting to our souls without the intermediaries of religions, priests or gurus. How refreshing it was to leave all the politics and old spiritual ways behind and turn ourselves to something completely different, to start discovering the path that was already latent within ourselves, where our individual, original programme was in waiting, longing to wake into action.

Jean and I arrived in Coombe Springs where the first Subud World Congress was to start the next day, on Monday the 10th of August, in the wonderful nine-sided building called the Djamichunatra, which had been built in late 1957. The weather turned to a perfect summer blue sky. I had taken some of my paintings and was organising a small exhibition, and everybody seemed happy rushing about, bringing the last finishing touches before the opening of Congress.

In less than two years the latihan had spread rapidly from Indonesia to the West. In that time many people had received what was then called the 'contact', sometimes in rather chaotic ways. For instance, in Sydney over 200 men had started their first latihan together in a large concert hall. Reporters and photographers, who were present with their cameras, had the next day displayed their photos and articles in local papers, giving quite the wrong impression of what Subud was about.

At this first World Congress, Bapak laid down a few guidelines to help us make the spread of Subud more harmonious. A Subud world organisation was established, with a simple structure that could be used in any part of the free world.

This first World Congress was a memorable experience. I had never assisted at a gathering of so many smiling people from all parts of the world. We came from different ethnic groups, languages, cultures and religions. Having the constant presence of Pak Subuh among us as well as doing many latihans together in large numbers created a powerful feeling of unity; we were living the oneness in a feeling of humanity.

Being together in the latihan, where all the shields of the ego had come down and where the divine orchestrator was guiding the sounds, movements and feelings in each one of us individually, made a harmonious whole and had a most uplifting effect.

The Djamichunatra, with its nine-sided shapes rising up to meet high at the top, created a wonderful space for doing the latihan. It was in that building that for the first time I briefly experienced my soul expanding into the universe. Although I was aware of my body moving and singing on the floor of the building, my awareness grew out of it, taking me out over Coombe Springs, over Kingston, then over England and Europe. Now looking towards my tummy I saw the earth; it was as if I had grown so big that our planet had come into a part of me. I turned my attention to the universe and felt immediately drawn into it; but then came the feeling that I wasn't capable of going further on this journey, I did not have enough trust. "I might not come back," I thought ... I became frightened and as soon as the fear overtook me, I was back on my feet, firmly grounded on the floor of the latihan hall. This brief experience confirmed to me that there was a window in myself through which I could let myself go; but for this, I knew that my fears could not be part of the journey.

The word 'training' to explain the latihan is, I find, a good one: each time I practise the training, I let go of my ordinary self, which implies the ego with all its fears, wants and desires, likes and dislikes. Of course I am not able to do this completely all the time; therefore, by practising the latihan regularly I am trained, little by little, to become more permanent and sincere in my surrender.

Throughout the whole of Congress, Jean and I attended all the meetings, talks and most of the latihans that were held. Sitting on the floor, listening to Bapak's explanations about the latihan was tremendously enriching. We did not mind being cramped and uncomfortable in the Djamichunatra as Bapak's powerful presence created such a feeling of love and oneness amongst us. The love that poured out of him, as he talked to us, made each one of us feel loved and love him in return. I had never experienced before such love and respect for a man.

Sometimes when he talked, I felt that he was talking to me personally; he would look at me and smile while kindly explaining things, using a language that I understood, answering the questions that were popping up in my mind. Others too had a similar experience of feeling that Bapak was answering their own questions.

The resonance of his gentle powerful voice vibrated through my being. Although he was talking in High Javanese mixed with Indonesian, I often understood what he was saying well before the translation came from Mr Bennett. I found it very easy to relate to his use of words to describe the life forces that inhabit us and the world around us. The material life force, the vegetable life force, the animal life force, the human life force and the others above that which, at the time, I did not have in my field of experience, were a good way to explain the interplay of forces on this earth as well as in ourselves.

There were always a lot of keen admirers around Bapak and his party, and I felt I did not want to go too close to him, but to respect his space with discretion. So in a way, I pushed down the feelings that popped up inside me of wanting to be next to him and able to talk with him in an ordinary way. A few times I had the opportunity to say something, but I always felt that his consciousness enveloped me so much, that he knew exactly what was going on inside me, and I had no more wish to talk but just to be in his presence.

Chapter 2

Encounters with an exceptional man, 1959–1988

Bapak's first visit to France

In this chapter, I will tell you some of the stories I experienced in the close presence of Bapak, or when Bapak's presence became part of my Subud experience. Through this book, the reader will find that Bapak is often mentioned. The reason is not because he acted with us like a teacher or a guru, no, not at all: he did not give us formatted exercises or mantras to follow. He was more like a grandfather who was always ready to explain and share with us his wide spiritual experience of the latihan. His constant love and care for us bought us to love him in return.

At the end of the first World Congress in 1959, it was arranged that Bapak and his party would come down to St-Paul-de-Vence to spend a short, restful holiday in the Parsons' home. Arriving on a flight from Geneva on the 21st of December 1959, they were taken directly to the house.

Jean and I stayed there with them for the two weeks to attend to their needs. Our job was to do the necessary shopping, organise meetings and latihans, and arrange a timetable for the numerous people who wanted to see and meet Bapak. Jean spent much of her time with the Indonesian ladies helping with the food and cooking. Early in the mornings, I went shopping and on my return would attend to the visitors, making sure that they did not invade Bapak's space.

One Subud member, Dr Ropars, who had recently received the contact, had a very nice black Citroën DS 21. He kindly offered to drive Bapak around, and became his chauffeur for the two weeks, taking the party to Nice for talks and the latihan and to visit Marseilles where a small group had just started.

Although the weather was sunny with blue skies, it was cold for the Indonesians, and one of my tasks was to make sure that the apartments were well heated. So, many times a day, I would pop down the cold stone staircase into the cellar of the old property in order to fetch the coal needed to fill the large boiler. The one-meter thick walls of the cellar had perforated rectangular holes at regular intervals to bring a little light into the different arched rooms.

I was singing happily, holding the bucket close to the ground and dragging it up to fill it with coal when, surprised, I felt the hairs on my head stand up; it was as if I had come into contact with a cobweb. In the semi-darkness, I raised my hand and felt the hairs on my forearm rise too as I slowly moved my hand through the air. I checked – there were no cobwebs. I felt a presence, yet it was obvious that I was alone, as I could see no one around.

When I walked back up into the Great Hall with the loaded coal bucket, I met Dr Zakir, who was at that time Bapak's personal secretary and translator. Knowing that Indonesians are quite comfortable with the invisible world, I asked him to come down to the cellar with me, telling him that I had experienced something I couldn't quite explain, and that he might understand. I said it hoping that as a Javanese, he might be able to take this strange event seriously. He agreed, and we both went down to the place by the coal pile.

"It was around here," I said, showing him vaguely with the back of my hand the space where I had felt the strange sensation.

He laughed, and said, "No, I can't feel anyone here; but you know, these spirits do move about."

So we both meandered hesitantly, each in his own direction, down into the dark rooms of the vaulted cellar in search for the invisible presence. "Dr Zakir? It's here, I found it, come!" I exclaimed quietly as I felt the strange presence on my skin, which immediately goose-pimpled.

"Yes, I can feel it too; he wants to be noticed; he's probably come to see Bapak," he added, bursting into laughter.

When I was a very young child, I had had on several occasions connected with an invisible world, but this was the first time as an adult that I had witnessed something so real, something of which my mind could not make heads or tails. Being very rational, this experience did not fit my pattern of understanding. I decided not to think about it – not to ignore it, but to leave it where it was, as simply another irrational but nonetheless real experience.

In the afternoons, people would come to see Bapak or Mr Bennett. One of my other roles at the Parsons' house was to let in visitors, and to announce their presence, providing they had previously made an appointment.

One morning, I heard a discreet knock on the big walnut door. As I opened it, a very old man with a slightly hunched back, long white beard, long white hair and piercing pale blue eyes looked straight at me and said as he walked in, "I've come to meet Pak Subuh and Mr Bennett."

Before I could ask him who he was and whether he had made an appointment, he was in the Great Hall sitting on the long bench with both hands resting on the walking stick that stood erect between his knees. I sat next to him and started to explain, with my youthful ignorance and enthusiasm, how Subud had come to the West. I felt it necessary to explain what I knew about Gurdjieff, about Mr Bennett, and the coming of Bapak. While I was talking, our eyes crossed and I saw in an instant that he was amused.

I suddenly felt very embarrassed, realising that this old man, who had not yet said a word, probably knew much more about Gurdjieff, Mr Bennett and Bapak than I did. "I do apologise. I am just realising that I should be listening to you rather than you listening to me! Did you know Yann Ivanovitch Gurdjieff then?"

"That rascal? He was truly a thief!" he replied, and began to tell me this fascinating story:

His name was Mr Zoun; he was unsure of his date of birth as he had been found unconscious, completely naked, in a forest in eastern Turkmenistan by a group of Sufi monks. They took him to their monastery and cared for and educated him. In 1924, in Italy, he played the part of Leonardo da Vinci in a film made about the great artist. Indeed, if I had to describe his physiognomy, I would simply say look at Leonardo's self-portrait drawing, imagine light blue eyes, and you have the man.

He told me how Gurdjieff had one day arrived at this monastery, had been welcomed and given food and lodging and had stayed with them for over six months, studying their secret documents. Then one night, he had suddenly left like a robber. He also said that he, Mr Zoun, had no passport or proof of his identity and that he travelled mostly on foot. When he came to a frontier he would walk backwards as if he came from there and when the custom officers saw him, thinking that he had just walked into their country, they would hurriedly take the unwanted paperless character over the border, and dump him there.

He then told me that he wanted to meet Pak Subuh. As it was time to do a general latihan, I briefly explained how we approached the training by taking off our shoes, watches, coins in the pocket and so on, stood there in total surrender and followed whatever came from within. In view of his advanced age and obvious wisdom I felt that it was right to let him come into the latihan room.

During the latihan, I briefly glanced at him to see how he was doing; there he was with his hat on, his stick hanging off his bent arm, his bag strapped round his shoulder, his sandals still on standing there looking relaxed and happy. Bapak was in the room and I remember thinking, "What better way to be meeting Bapak than in the latihan." When the latihan finished I presented Mr Zoun to Mr Bennett and they disappeared together into the upper floors of the big house.

I met Mr Zoun again unexpectedly in Paris two years later at a friend's flat where Jean and I were staying. He had come to Paris to study a rare ancient esoteric book in the National Library, and was now waiting to gather enough money to go to Reykjavik in Iceland. Our friend Richard who was lodging us told me, "Mr Zoun appears in different parts of the world. He spends much of his time studying rare books. He is not a guru, has no followers, but is seen by many as a very wise man who is probably on earth for a very specific spiritual task."

As I entered Richard's sitting room one evening, Mr Zoun was sitting by the fire in an armchair, his same friendly worn-out bag leaning against the seat. I sat in the opposite armchair and looked into the flames absently. Then I asked: "Mr Zoun, I would be very interested to know more about the reality of flying saucers; where do they come from?"

He looked at me, amused, and picking up his bag, started flicking through it mumbling, "Flying saucers ... Let me see ... Oh yes! There it is, it's all in there for you," and leaned over to hand me a neatly folded piece of paper. I opened it with curiosity: it was a black and white cut-out from a comic strip, showing little Martians coming out of a flying saucer! I heard myself swallowing loudly in embarrassment, and thanked him inwardly for the lesson, that was to find the answers inwardly and not in everyday world happenings. He was looking at me now very amused, his small blue eyes sparkling. I leaned over with the folded comic strip and gave it back to him with a shy smile.

"Thank you, Mr Zoun."

I had been wondering what his thoughts were about Bapak and just before I asked my question, he answered it by saying, "Yes, Muhammad Pak Subuh has found the centre."

Soon after this encounter, Zoun did get to Reykjavik on a one-way ticket. And the wise old man was never seen again.

One day back in St-Paul-de-Vence, I came to light the fire in the large stone inglenook fireplace in Bapak's sitting room. As I entered the room I said, "Hello, Bapak," but could not say any more than that; my heart was thumping too hard, my throat had seized up. I remember thinking: "Why do I have to be like this? Why can't I just be with him as I am normally and enjoy his presence?"

A few minutes later, three ladies came in; an Indian lady who was ill and was following Bapak's party around the world with an English friend of hers, and Rohanawati, the daughter of Bapak's wife Ibu.

They were laughing as they gathered around Bapak to ask him about palmistry. The Indian lady asked with her charming, rounded accent, "Bapak, is there any truth in palmistry? And does it also apply to feet?"

"Oh yes!" Bapak replied. "Here, look at Bapak's palms ..."

He opened his left hand wide and with his right index finger pointed to its different mounts and rivers. I could not resist watching; I stood behind Rohanawati looking over her shoulder, which had the delicate scent of sandalwood. Bapak's palm was large, square and generous, with extremely few but well-defined lines; his fingers were long, well-separated and slightly curved backwards, showing great suppleness.

"This is the head line and this is the heart ... and right in the middle here is the sun! It shows that I have come from beyond through the sun," said Bapak with a soft voice that carried amusement. I was astonished as I saw the perfect small circle with its rays surrounding it. Then he opened up his right hand, stretched it right out and said, "Look, you see? This means that when I go, I will go back through the sun just as when I came." His voice was clear, with no hesitation. There was not a doubt in me that he was talking from his direct experience. Indeed, the centre of his right hand was, too, marked by another radiating sun.

Bapak had not forgotten the Indian lady's request and, flicking off his moccasins, proceeded to pull off his socks. With great ease and flexibility, he displayed the sole of his left foot and, resting it on his right knee, explained, "Similar to the lines on the palm of the hands, the lines of the foot will talk to you just the same... Here! This is the life line and across here is the heart... There is the head line; the traits of one's character are all there." At that point, I felt rather guilty, as I was meant to be lighting the sitting room fire. I discreetly left them and went back to the chimney, where I lit the already prepared kindling.

During Bapak's stay on the Côte d'Azur, the latihan had spread and we had about 120 members. He had given two talks in Nice and in one of them had predicted that the group of that city would not last long, as the members were too argumentative. He had explained that in some cities it is difficult for Subud to grow and expand. Paris, Manila and a few other cities were mentioned. I remember wondering why he had said that, as the group seemed to me at the time a reality; I could not imagine it disappearing.

At that time, Jean and I had been married for over four months and we wondered why she had not yet conceived. We both very much wanted to have a large family; although Jean thought that she was not capable of becoming a good mother, I knew that was mostly due to her lack of self-confidence. I was somehow certain from inside that this instability in her feelings would disappear as soon as she had our baby in her arms.

One late afternoon in January 1960, as she happened to be in the presence of Bapak somewhere in the apartments, Jean asked him why she had not yet conceived. He replied with a wide smile, "Do not worry, you will conceive as soon as Bapak and his party leave St-Paul-de-Vence ..."

My new name

Soon it was time for Bapak and his party to leave and many of us accompanied them to Nice airport. To Jean and me, their visit had been a powerful experience and we felt sadness at the thought of them going, yet we both looked forward to the future that lay ahead of us. When we arrived at the airport we were told that the plane would be delayed two hours. The authorities kindly offered Bapak and his party a VIP lounge; its large glass windows gave a direct view of the runway.

From an early age I had not felt really comfortable with the name François, and when I saw Bapak standing by himself looking at the rain falling gently over the now dark grey sea, I could not resist walking up to him and saying, "Bapak, I do not feel comfortable with my present name François. If it is possible, could you give me a name that is more appropriate to my true nature?" Obviously, my query pulled him out of some distant place, as it took a few moments for him to turn his head and look at me from behind his thick glasses.

"L."

He uttered the letter clearly as he turned his head back towards the rain, now falling more fiercely against the glass. I was standing two meters away from him; my body shaking slightly, my heart thumping. I thought at the time, "Why have I asked him for a new name? Now he probably will choose Louis! Or Lucifer, why not? Oh dear me, how can I handle this?"

I felt confused, caught in the web of my feelings and thoughts. Bapak slowly turned his head towards me again and said with unexpectedly perfect French pronunciation, "Léonard."

Instantly, my whole confusion evaporated; I felt as if my old clothes, which had been full of complications and stiffened by the suffering endured during my 21 years of existence, had fallen at my feet. A colourful new garment was now on my shoulders; it felt cool and comfortable. I was at peace in myself and immensely happy.

"Léonard, could you show me where the men's toilets are?" Bapak then asked. He was the first person to use my new name and, as I heard it, I felt at one with myself.

"Yes, Bapak, please follow me as I need to go myself," I replied, overjoyed that my emotions were now completely tranquil. As we walked down the wide steps I asked again, "My initials have been FX, X for a Xavier, should I use FXL or just simply LL, for my initials?"

"Just LL," he replied.

"What changes will my new name bring me compared to François, my old one?" As we walked back towards the steps leading out of the gents, Bapak explained in his broken English, "François, very heavy, yah!, for you to carry the heavy past of France. Léonard bring you ..." He was looking for the right word ... "Yes! Bring you fighting spirit, yah! Like a lion."

I introduced my new name carefully amongst my family and friends. But every time I met somebody new who asked for my name,

I would give them the choice: either François or Léonard; invariably they would choose Léonard.

"Why did you call me François Xavier?" I asked my mother shortly after receiving my new name. She replied with a hint of an apology in her voice: "It was because when you were born, you reminded me so much of my brother Frances, whom I loved dearly and who died at the age of 10 with meningitis. And Xavier was the name that Marcel Lassalle chose for you." Interestingly enough, some time later my mother wrote to Bapak and he named her Olivia, which suited her much better than Honor, her previous name.

From this experience I became confident that Bapak knew the inner meaning of names; each name reflects an individual vibration in the form of sound, and when given to the appropriate person it vibrates correctly in harmony with his/her whole being. Most parents, it seems, give names to their children through an association with a family member or with a person they love or admire; in other words, it is subjective. With Bapak it was different, he was aware of the person's inner nature and heard the corresponding sound vibration, which harmonised with his or her inner and outer self; he then expressed it in the form of a letter and then a name.

A month after Bapak's departure, Jean and I left my mother's house, happy to move to a tiny stone built cottage set amongst a grove of orange trees which we rented from a lady called Mlle Blanc. And to our great joy, Bapak's prediction had been realised: Jean was pregnant.

Consciousness with the angels

Subud had become a worldwide organisation and Bapak, together with members of his family, would regularly visit countries to give talks to explain the latihan that we practised. He had a particularly soft spot for England, as it was there that Subud had really taken root in the West, and from where it was able to branch out to all parts of the world. We were now well-organised and could easily look after the Indonesians' needs when they visited our different countries, finding a place for them to stay, usually in a member's home, hiring large conference halls for Bapak to give talks, or conference centres for the four-yearly international congresses.

At one UK national Congress, held at the Swanwick Conference Centre in the Midlands, I had been given the responsibility of being Bapak's driver. His family was staying at a member's house in Leicester, and I had been asked to drive him up the M1 to the conference centre, while Bapak's family and party went in a different car. I had rented an extremely comfortable black Rover, with leather seats and walnut interior. Bapak sat in the back behind me, and by 9am we had set off for the hour's journey north. I was feeling excited by the thought of being entirely alone with Bapak for an hour or so. "What an occasion to have such a wise man in the car," I thought as we drove off, "I will be able to ask him all kinds of questions ... "

I have to explain that this chapter spans from 1959 to 1988, and as this moment was in the 60s or early 70s, Jean was now called Mélinda and we lived with our five children in Frant Road, Tunbridge Wells. I was already running my antiques shop.

The day was splendid, the sky was high and blue, the roads not too busy, and we soon picked up speed on the motorway. "Now, what important questions shall I ask him? Am I doing the right thing continuing to sell antiques, or should I go totally into interior design? Or maybe, actually, start painting again? And change my life altogether?" These questions were piling up in my mind. I couldn't ask them all, so which one should I choose? I looked into the rearview mirror and saw that Bapak was somewhere else – his eyes were half-open behind his thick glasses, but he was far away, probably in his vast world. He looked serene, eternal.

"Léonard, how on earth can you be so insensitive and selfish to think of asking him personal questions?" I reproached myself. "What right have you to disturb him with your problems when he's probably doing, in another sphere, things which are much more important." I decided to put all my questions away, and be close to my soul. I started singing quietly from within, and felt tremendously serene and peaceful, just enjoying driving.

After some time, I had a strange sensation that we were being followed by some kind of divine presence. Intrigued by the feeling, I looked up into the blue sky and was startled to see that it was filled with thousands of colourful angels, all close to each other. They seemed to be hovering high up over the car, as if travelling with us. Doubting what I was experiencing, to test that it was not a dream, I decided to drive towards the middle of the motorway lane; they immediately followed. I steered back to the left side of the road and they moved back as if one with us. Their presence filled me with a most delicate and refined sensation. I understood that I had just become conscious of another of Bapak's dimensions and felt full of gratitude for having been able to have this enriching moment. I thought later on, "Thank God that I did not ask him my personal questions. Otherwise there would have been no room for this enlightening experience to take place!"

I'd like to explain here that what I witnessed was not at all like a dream: the immaterial reality of the angels was entirely as authentic as the material reality of the action of driving the Rover. I understood that being close to my soul was the key to travelling into different levels of consciousness; in this case, it was in an angelic level. It was not like seeing a picture of angels in the sky – no, it was more as if my whole being was raised to the angelic dimension. Seeing all these very pure creatures with wings symbolised that I was part of that dimension. Indeed, while the experience lasted, there resided in my inner feelings tremendous peace and acute consciousness.

Meeting the Prophets for the first time

One year, Bapak gave a talk in the conference hall at Leicester University. I was driving, and had taken him to the entrance where the organisers met and accompanied him into the building. Bapak was always perfectly punctual, which left me, the driver, very little time to find a place to park the car and find a seat before his talk started. However I could not find a place to park, as all the spaces had been taken. As I found myself in a state of anxiety, I decided to completely let go of it and connect to my soul.

Bapak in Leicester

Now I was looking with different eyes. I held the steering wheel more lightly and found myself guided round the back of the building where there was one large space just waiting for me. I even found a little brown metal door, which I opened and entered into a narrow corridor that led me to the back of the stage. I went down a few steps and found that there was one seat remaining in the first row. The hall was packed and as if he had been waiting for me to sit down, Bapak started his talk. "How strange," I thought, "to be sitting in the front row, bang opposite Bapak." Usually, I would have sat somewhere at the back, leaving the front row to others, being too shy to put myself forward.

I had been listening to his musical voice for some minutes, when I witnessed something that an ordinary mind might have found hard to accept. There, in the seat where Bapak was sitting, was another man! He was young, probably in his 20s, extremely attractive and healthy looking. His hair was longish, black, with large, generous curls. His body, though elegant and slender, was muscular. Although I recognised that it was Bapak's voice, it sounded younger and more monotone; his mouth and body movements flowed harmoniously with the words.

Now, I'm not the kind of man who daydreams or normally has visions. I think I've mentioned before that I am a rational person; I only believe what I can feel, touch and see. So I wondered, "How should I handle, in myself, this situation?" I pinched the skin of my forearm with my nails until it hurt. No, I was not dreaming. Now the young man was laughing, showing two rows of perfectly white teeth. I suddenly remembered that in my jacket pocket I had my glasses for long-distance vision. I pulled them out, positioned them on my nose and curiously scrutinised: I could see the young man even more clearly. "How strange," I thought, and asked myself, "and who is that young fellow then?"

The answer came up from the depth of my consciousness: "Adam."

"Adam, why not? Maybe next time I'll see Eve!" I said to myself sarcastically. It was difficult for me to accept this reality, but what could I do but just sit and see how it would develop.

What followed surprised me even more. Adam turned older; in fact it was no longer the same man sitting talking in the armchair. This speaker was taller, he had long peppery grey hair falling untidily on his wide shoulders; thick bushy eyebrows were partly hiding his gentle yet piercing dark brown eyes; two protruding cheekbones framed his strong-featured face, the hooked nose had well-defined nostrils. His mouth was hidden by a long, curly, dark grey beard. His movements were sudden, then became ample and generous. What I noticed was the thickness of his bone structure, especially of his hands and forearms. His whole body expressed authority and power, I found him most impressive.

"I suppose this is Abraham?" I said to myself with cynical amusement. Then I heard the voice that came up again from my inner depth: "Yes, you are right. It is Abraham." The image became blurred. I realised that I could not contain my emotions with this weird situation; and I was crying. But not wanting to miss any part of this incredible event, I removed my glasses, dried my eyes with my handkerchief and went back to the show, wondering how it would develop.

After a while listening and watching Abraham, I noticed that Bapak had transformed into yet another person. This time he was definitely older, shorter, plump and somehow sophisticated and refined; he had a crescent of white hair round the back of his head, and a well-groomed beard framing his round, kind face. His eyes seemed to be of a greeny-grey blue and continuously scanned the audience as he spoke slowly in a warm, clear voice. He was standing, moving about on the stage; he was stressing a point with body movements and made the audience laugh. "I suppose," I reflected, "this must be the Prophet Moses in person!"

"Yes, it is," confirmed my inner voice.

This unexpected reality was fascinating. Not only was Bapak's talk captivating and instructive, but along with it I was being given a lively insight into who Bapak was, with the perspective of the Prophets from the cradle of our religious history. Amazement and wonder brought another flow of tears to my eyes when I saw, there on the stage in front of me, another being whom I immediately recognised.

This man was quite different from the others, as femininity and peace emanated from him. The three previous characters were undoubtedly very masculine in their gestures, body movements and in the masculine force that emanated from them. I knew that this man was the Prophet Jesus. I watched his tall, straight-backed body move about the stage; there was in him a quiet elegance, which highlighted his gentle femininity. I felt that he had his masculine and feminine natures harmoniously balanced.

Although he was an unusual-looking person, with his long aquiline nose, large eyes and evenly formed brows, I noticed that there seemed to be no ego in him; an atmosphere of love pervaded the hall, and in my inner feelings. I felt loved by him and instantly loved him in return. Rivers of tears flooded my eyes once again and I thought, "Why is it that I am so emotional; why can't I just stay cool?" I dried my eyes with the now damp handkerchief and discreetly blew my nose.

After his demonstration, the Prophet Jesus returned to his armchair and sat in it majestically, his spine not touching the back of the seat. Each forearm was resting on the supports of the armchair, his fine long hands dropped down, completely relaxed. Everything about him seemed to be connected; every so often one of the attractive hands would leave the elbow rest and move about freely, expressively. It was as if the attendance of the whole conference hall was cradled by his love and gentleness.

I shifted into a more open sitting position with my legs apart, my hands resting on them. When I raised my head to focus back on the stage, it had once again changed completely; the young person I was now seeing was of middle height, and he wore a *taqiyah* (black felt triangle-shaped hat worn by some Muslims) on his well-cut, short black hair. His roundish face was centred by a thin moustache; his very large black eyes crested by well-defined eyebrows gave him the appearance of being in constant wonder. He moved his arms and hands rapidly to affirm what he was communicating. He talked fast, but with great clarity, and expressed much humour.

"This must be Prophet Muhammad," I deduced. "Bapak must have within him the five Prophets; that is why he knows so much about each one of them. He must actually be the five of them all in one Being ... that explains why he can act as if he is one of the five Prophets in person," I finally concluded.

Bapak often explained to us that every wise word of truth that he said, or advice on good behaviour he had given, had already been spoken or written in the holy books by the Prophets. What people needed now was direct contact with the power of God (or, for the reader who finds the word 'God' difficult to come to terms with, the source, or the origin), so that each individual can be guided directly from within, and start to experience within themselves what the Prophets said in the distant past. The Prophet was now explaining that, although Jesus had demonstrated how to find the way to harmony through love, mankind had once again fallen backwards, and had not been able to put into practice these wise words. While Muhammad was speaking, Bapak was puffing on an Indonesian cigarette and suddenly a tiny explosion occurred. Bapak, laughing generously, was looking in my direction, obviously very amused by my perplexity. He was smoking an Indonesian cigarette called a *kretek* that was made of a mixture of tobacco and cloves, hand-rolled into a conical shape. The paper contained a lot of saltpetre, which every so often when the chemical was too condensed, would flare up, creating a tiny explosion.

We reached the end of Bapak's talk, but before he got up from his armchair he gave me a long look, carried by a gentle smile, as if to say, "Now you know a little more about who Bapak is."

I was finding it difficult to ground myself back into immediate reality, but gently my legs lifted me up and took me back through the narrow dark corridor, and out the small metallic brown door. As I sat in the driving seat of the Rover, I breathed deeply several times to fully regain the consciousness I needed in order to be his chauffeur. Once I felt back in my ordinary self, I drove the car round to the front of the conference hall where Bapak and his party were coming out. At the time, the only person I felt able to share this experience with was my wife Mélinda. It was somehow too incredible, too colossal to talk about; I would have felt embarrassed to put myself in the position of saying that I had seen and heard the Prophets. Even in 1983 when Bapak asked me to share my Subud experiences with my brothers and sisters, I still found it difficult to do so, and it was only four years later, in 1987, at a ceremony of the 100th day commemoration of Bapak's death, that I was confident enough to be able to tell this experience to a large Subud audience.

Bapak, Jesus and Muhammad

At the end of August 1969, we were visiting Alexandra Palace in north London. It was a lovely sunny Sunday and we had taken our six children to see Bapak. Our youngest, Dahlan, was only two weeks old; I remember because Bapak had invited families to bring their children so he could meet them.

Each of the five older children were presented, and when it came for Mélinda to show him our number six, Bapak laughed and, looking surprised, said, "Another? Ah yes, Dahlan!" He remembered, having recently chosen the name from the list we had sent him.

Alexandra Palace was like a huge chalk-white painted greenhouse, with a glazed iron-framed dome, which had been partly whitewashed to lessen the impact of the heat of the sun. The dusty palace seemed enormous for our small gathering of fewer than 100 adults; rows of uncomfortable chairs had been arranged opposite the grey wooden stage where Bapak gave his talk.

Unexpectedly, as often was the case with Bapak, after a few words of welcome, he asked to remove several rows of chairs in front of the stage to create a space where the ladies were asked to do the latihan. Most of the men present were surprised, as normally the latihan was done in separate rooms. Hesitantly, the ladies got up and stood in front of Bapak. Bapak asked the men to simply sit quietly. Then he said to the ladies, "Stand relaxed, close your eyes ... Begin!"

And the ladies started their latihan. I felt very touched when seeing these ladies of all ages move about so gracefully and hearing their feminine voices intertwine. All the men seemed to be as captivated as I was. I looked for Mélinda ... There she was, to the left near the stage, her beautiful voice reached my ears, and a wave of love flew towards her.

I noticed how during their latihan a few of the ladies, whom I knew to be stiff and awkward in their bodies, became supple and free in their voices and movements as their latihan developed. It is difficult to describe accurately the atmosphere that was created by these ladies who had let go completely of their egos and selves and were now moved by the life force of their origin. Although the dance, movements, sounds and songs were different for each individual, together they made a harmonious whole that lifted me high up into a finer state of consciousness.

After 20 minutes, Bapak leaned forward to the microphone and said, "Finished for now, finished."

Slowly, the ladies came out of their latihan and stood in front of Bapak, who gave clarification on the latihan then talked about what he called 'testing'. During testing, a question would be asked, and each of us would receive, through the latihan, some answer expressed by sound and movement. Previously, these testing sessions had been done more privately with very small numbers. Now, in retrospect, I understand that the testing sessions with Bapak were actually helping us to check how our own latihan had developed in each one of us. Also, Bapak could see for himself where we were in relation to our inner growth. So the word testing was very appropriate, as we were able to test our sincerity in our letting go, and see whether or not we were receiving answers to the questions that Bapak was putting forward.

He explained to us that we were to listen to the questions, but not to register them in our mind, and especially not to think about them; in other words to hear the questions from the inside, not with our heart and mind. Our finer feelings would then respond freely to what was being asked. For readers who have not experienced the latihan or the testing sessions, it might be difficult to imagine what was going on. The questions being asked seemed, to the heart and thinking mind, rather simple: for instance, "How does a Mexican walk? An Englishman? A Frenchman? An American?"

If you thought, for instance, "How does a Mexican walk?" and followed that thought, you would mimic a Mexican walking. But here, Bapak asked us not to follow our thoughts, but to receive the answer from inside. When it came from deep inside, one's whole being became Mexican, with all that implies.

After the ladies, it was time for the men to do their latihan and testing; the ladies became the witnesses to our receiving.

Then, late in the afternoon, as everybody was beginning to leave, Bapak asked some of the men assistants, or helpers, to stay behind with him.

When the hall emptied, 12 of us found ourselves alone with Bapak. He invited us to come up on to the stage with him and arranged us into a large circle. Then he spoke about the last two Prophets: Jesus and Muhammad. As he talked, I realised that he wanted us to witness the differences between the two Prophets. I will not try to remember word for word what Bapak said, but rather will share with you the powerful effect this session had on my whole being.

I had my eyes closed, as I found Bapak's beautifully clear voice flowed more penetratingly into my being that way; he had been talking about Jesus and Muhammad when he suddenly said, "Look at Bapak now. Bapak will show you how Jesus made his followers feel and become aware of the power of God."

I slowly opened my eyes and saw the strangest of things.

I have talked to you before about my reluctance to believe in what I could not directly witness, but here is a real account of what I saw with my own eyes, heard and felt in my being, on that late afternoon in August 1969.

What I saw and heard was not the Bapak whom I knew so well. No, it was a physically different person. Slightly taller, slimmer, in fact similar to the Jesus I had seen at Leicester University. His slow movements were graceful; his voice was of a higher, clear tone. He proceeded to walk around and stop beside each one of us, holding his hands very close to our chest but without physically touching us.

I was fifth or sixth in the circle and, as Jesus came closer to me, my heart started thumping louder and louder. It felt as if it was about to explode, and I was angry with myself for not being able to stay cool. Jesus had reached my friend Laurent to my left, and in the corner of my eye I could see that he too was very moved and somewhat nervous.

My whole body was shaking now; my turn had come and quickly I closed my eyes to try to find some inner quiet. Jesus was now standing in front of me. Slowly he raised his right hand to the region of my heart and said in a comforting and soothing voice: "Yeah, yeah... There is much fire in the chest, it is burning, isn't it?"

I timidly nodded in agreement, not able to swallow my saliva.

"Passions are hot, peaceful feelings are cool, can you feel now the coolness?"

I started to feel a loving and appeasing energy coming from his hand. The change in my inner state was immediate and impressive. Suddenly, as if a miracle had happened, I was feeling whole, relaxed, peaceful and contented, filled with love for the man who was able, apparently so simply, to alter my inner state. My whole body and being were fully conscious and aware. I opened my eyes and saw him looking at me, giving me a gentle smile, which I returned timidly with appreciation. I felt the loving power that emanated from him as he moved slowly past me to my friend Lambert Gibbs on my right.

A huge feeling of respect for this extraordinary man filled my whole being. I was now able peacefully to follow the attention he was giving to each of my six other brothers who had waited for their turn. After he stood with each of us, he said a few words to describe how Jesus worked: "Yah, yah, now you have experienced how Jesus, with his hands, passed on the 'contact' to his disciples.

"And now, Muhammad," Bapak said laughingly as he metamorphosed into the Prophet whose actions brought Islam to a large part of the world.

I recognised again the man I had seen in Leicester. He moved about quickly, and talked rapidly, making gestures with his hands, which made us laugh. It was clear that the words Bapak was expressing were a direct receiving and were not coming from his thoughts. As the words flowed out of his mouth, they were soothing and refreshing to hear. They came out in the form of poetry and had a cleansing effect on my being. The words of truth that were spoken were like vessels carrying wonderful victuals and scented flowers and I noticed, as I listened, that they had carried me into a different level of awareness, where I felt at one with my soul and the creator.

I had just witnessed the different ways of the last two Prophets. With Jesus, besides his soothing words, it was the proximity of his holy presence that healed and changed people, so that they could wake up to a new way of being. With Muhammad, it was more through receiving his prose that listeners became conscious of the power of God.

Of course, this is only my experience; in no way do I want to claim that Jesus and Muhammad are as described above. I am perfectly aware that this is my own relative reality and truth.

During these privileged moments, all my attention was turned not to the features of their physical appearances, but rather to the spiritual reality of their presence and the effect it had on my whole being. Love and compassion for their fellow men radiated from them; it enveloped and penetrated all parts of my consciousness, which soothed and appeased my being in depth.

When Bapak finished his demonstrations and explanations, he asked us not to share this moment spent with him, until after his death. As we drove away from Alexandra Palace, Lambert and I did not speak as we normally did when travelling together in a car. Instead, we both needed to savour the incredible experience in silence.

The peach

Once, in Leicester, around 8.30pm, I was asked by the ladies, who cooked for Bapak and his party, to go out and buy a white peach that Bapak had asked for.

In 60s' Leicester at that time of the evening, one would have thought it impossible to find such a fruit, especially as it was not yet in season! All the shops were shut and I went off wondering which direction to take, as I did not know the city well. I decided to drive round and see if I could find a shop that was open. There was no way I could follow my mind, so I decided to feel my way, and as I drove through the streets, I thought: "How strange that Bapak is asking for a peach this time of the night." Suddenly to my right, across the road, I saw a small grocer's shop whose proprietor was closing the shutters for the night. I rapidly parked the car and ran across the road.

"Excuse me, sir, it's one in a million, but would you happen to have a white peach, by any chance?" I asked tentatively.

The dark-haired man smiled, showing me all his large teeth. I noticed a gold one amongst them. "He must be Greek," I thought.

"Yes! I think I can help you. Come in," he said as he closed his last window shutter.

We walked into the tiny shop, and to my amazement there, in a wooden straw hamper, was a lonely but magnificent white peach. It was preciously wrapped and carefully put into a paper bag.

A few minutes later the peach was promptly delivered to the ladies in the kitchen who joyfully expressed their delight at seeing the beautiful fruit.

It was not uncommon to hear such unusual stories that brought much colour and spice to one's life when working for Bapak. Although it is not my intention to write too many pages of anecdotes concerning Bapak's unique ways of being, I will just tell you one or two more that I directly experienced and which contributed to making me aware that Bapak lived and moved from a different place than most of us, which is normally either from the heart, mind, stomach or the sex.

The shoe shop

"Léonard, would you mind taking Bapak to a shoe shop?" This request came from one of the people who were looking after Bapak and his party at a Subud member's house also near Leicester. The owner of the house had suggested that I take the motorway to Coventry were there was a gigantic shopping centre. Parking would be easy and we would find many, many shoe shops there. Mas Usman, who was the Indonesian translator of the party, came with us.

The vast shopping centre stood on three levels and the link from the motorway delivered us to the top floor where we immediately found a parking place. I wanted to go ahead so I could find the shoe shops and then take the small party there, so that people would not have to walk too far. So I suggested my plan to Mas Usman.

"No!" he categorically answered, "One doesn't walk ahead of Bapak. Just follow him." Taken aback by the blunt reaction, I concluded that this must be an Indonesian custom, a sign of respect to an elder.

We had arrived at lunchtime when many office employees were looking for places to eat, and the third level was densely crowded with people rushing about in all directions. So I just let go of my ideas and followed, looking with interest at Bapak's hands that were holding each other behind his back. They were well-groomed, powerful yet delicate; I would have called them artistic hands. The left one was holding the right wrist and I remembered the occasion in St-Paul-de-Vence when he had shown us the sun that radiated from the centre of his palm. There was no need to protect Bapak from the crowd, as it moved away from his path by itself, always leaving a few meters of clear space ahead of him; it was fascinating to see how the crowds never came close to him and how he passed completely unnoticed.

Bapak aimed towards the centre left where there seemed to be less activity. We walked into a covered passage that led to a long balcony where a staircase took us down to a deserted second level. We followed Bapak along this lower balcony until he came to a shop window. He stopped, suddenly smiling, pointing his finger at a very nice pair of deep Nile green fine leather moccasins that were displayed in the corner of the shoe shop.

Looking amused, he said simply, "Bapak's shoes here."

There were no other customers in the large shop, and Bapak walked straight towards an armchair and sat down. I took the shopkeeper out to the balcony to show her the desired green shoes. I told her the size we wanted and she disappeared behind a curtain into a storage corridor. After some time the young lady came back, apologising sadly, "I am awfully sorry, sir, but the last pair is the one in the window and they are the wrong size."

Mas Usman translated the news to Bapak who looked surprised and said, "But they are here. Ask her to look again."

The embarrassed clerk went up to the shop manager, who was standing on a high stool behind the till, to consult her for help. Looking slightly irritated, they both went into the maze of shelves and boxes. We could hear the rumblings of cardboard boxes, and the crisp sound of paper wrappings amongst subdued grunts and moans. Finally the young clerk reappeared, saying, "I told you, sir, you see, these shoes are not in stock. Sorry!"

Bapak looked completely unmoved by the situation and peacefully continued waiting. Suddenly, we heard a victorious, muffled voice coming from the depths of the storage space: "Here they are! I found them!"

Looking quite perplexed, the manager came back into the shop and went straight to Bapak carrying the box of the right-sized green shoes. She knelt down hurriedly at Bapak's feet; he looked into the distance over her head without focusing. In a flash, with her expert hands, she had taken off the old shoes and replaced them with the new ones, and they fitted perfectly.

Bapak got up, giving a large smile to the shop attendants and started walking towards the door. We rapidly paid for the shoes and proceeded to follow him to the car.

Driving blindly in the rain

I had been asked by the organisers of Subud Britain to find a large car, which would not be too costly, to take Bapak's party to the airport. Bapak's three granddaughters, Ismana, Asikin and I piled into the large Austin Maxi (an oversized mini) and followed the leading car that carried Bapak and Ibu on to the motorway. The weather was uncertain, and looking south one could see an accumulation of threatening dark clouds. The car we followed was an old-fashioned Rolls-Royce where each of the circular backlights and indicators was less than two inches across. Bapak liked his cars to move fast and my friend Lambert Coles, who was driving, was going at around 90 miles an hour.

Ten minutes later, we found ourselves in heavy rain and it became extremely difficult to follow the fast Rolls-Royce. My Indonesian passengers were telling jokes and laughing and there was a light happy atmosphere in the car, while all my concentration was on the road.

Suddenly, to my horror, the windscreen wiper to my right shot off and disappeared into nowhere. "At least I've got one left!" I said confidently to myself. But with no warning whatsoever, a few minutes later the other wiper shot off its arm as well!

"Ho là là!" I thought aloud in French, "Where do we go from here? I have to stop."

My Indonesian friends were not laughing and joking any more. They were now all fully attentive to the situation. "You must always follow Bapak, Léonard," said Ismana, quietly. She was sitting on my left and looking at me with her wide beautiful brown eyes.

I was now extremely tense, gripping the driving wheel, my nose almost touching the inside of the windscreen that had fogged up, desperately trying to follow the two tiny vibrating red dots of Lambert's car. The roads were flooded, and the downpour had increased, creating funeral march-like drumming sounds on the body of the Austin. "Sorry, but this is crazy, I have to stop, it's too dangerous!" I said desperately.

With a cool determination, looking at me with peaceful intensity, Ismana replied, "Relax, do not worry Léonard, just follow Bapak and sing now with us." On this, she started singing with a clear Olympian voice completely free of fear. The three granddaughters and Asikin joined in.

I could not join in the singing with my friends, but I did manage to relax my grip around the driving wheel and sat back in my seat, disconnecting myself from my fear. Then I connected to the place where I had been before when driving Bapak, allowing the angelic vibration to take over my anxiety. The most awkward moment came when my friend Lambert, who was not aware of the angels versus devils battle that was going on in my feelings, suddenly overtook a lorry, creating waves of fine spray that completely obliterated the vibrating tiny red dots of his backlights.

This extraordinary situation of driving without seeing went on for 45 minutes when, unexpectedly, I faintly saw the Rolls-Royce's tiny orange indicator twinkling to the left as it suddenly slowed down.

"Why do you slow down now?" Ismana queried.

"Because Lambert Cole has just come off the motorway, Ismana," I said with slight irritation now that I was concentrating with my will to stay on whatever road we were on. At the same time, inwardly, I threw a prayer out into the invisible universe: "Please God, make this awful car break down."

The Rolls-Royce had now completely vanished out of sight; the exit lane came to a small roundabout over a bridge just as our engine stopped. All became completely silent. With the momentum left in the car I managed to negotiate the curve of the roundabout and hopped on to a grassy bank by the side of a road.

"Why have you stopped the car, Léonard?" asked one of the Indonesians. "I did not stop the car! God did!" I answered happily with a big smile, feeling so relieved to be out the stressful situation.

The rain had magically stopped and a hot ray of sunshine greeted us. I turned my face into it, grinning, with both forearms resting on the wheel. In a flash, my five passengers were out of the car and stood by the road while I took note, on the back of my cigarette packet, of the number and direction of the road we were on.

Within less than a minute, a dilapidated old Volkswagen camper van pulled up out of nowhere and the driver happened to be a Subud member. Smiling, he asked, "You're having problems?"

"Could you take us to Heathrow airport? Please, it's urgent," replied Asikin.

The driver kindly agreed to take them to the airport and they were off, in a cloud of black smoke. All were happily waving goodbye and joyfully laughing through the window as the car moved away. As if by enchantment, a telephone box stood there by the car. I rang the car hire company and told them what had happened and where the Austin Maxi was situated. I went back to the spot on the side of the road where the old Volkswagen had pulled up and started singing inside, feeling so free and thankful, so relieved that nothing drastic had happened.

A large Volvo estate slowed down and I recognised the lady driver, as she had been at one of Bapak's talks in London. "Léonard, what on earth brings you here? Can I be of any help?" she asked kindly.

I told her of my unusual adventure and she drove me straight to Heathrow airport. The large space seemed empty, and while looking around for a Subud crowd, I spotted Bapak sitting alone on a bench. As I came up to him, he looked at me with a surprised expression and asked, "Where are Ismana, Asikin and my granddaughters who were with you in the car?"

"I do not know, Bapak, they went into another car because my car broke down."

I tried to explain, feeling responsible for not having them with me. I told him that the Volkswagen camper van of a Subud member was bringing them along. Bapak's English was not so good and I saw that he hadn't quite understood my explanation. "How is it you're here? Before the others?"

"I do not know why, Bapak. When my car broke down they went into another car and there was no more room for me in it. Maybe their driver got lost?" I replied putting my hands out and slightly shrugging my shoulders.

I felt relieved when, 20 minutes later, my five passengers arrived, explaining in Indonesian to Bapak, with much laughter and gestures, that the very kind driver of the Volkswagen camper van did not know the way to the airport!

Bapak unexpectedly changes his plan

Talking about the airport reminds me of another event that occurred during the late 50s. Bapak and a large party of around 15 people were booked on a flight to Spain. They were waiting in the main hall of the airport for the call to the departure gate when, for no apparent reason, Bapak spoke to the person who was responsible for the passports and tickets and said, "Bapak and his party will not be taking that flight. Could you please arrange to change the tickets for the next flight to Spain?"

With some difficulty and extra cost the tickets were changed; the next day, newspaper headlines told us that the plane the party were meant to take had crashed over the Pyrenees. There were no survivors.

Becoming conscious of the spiritual side of the material world

I will tell you now how I first consciously encountered within myself the powerful influence of the material world on our delicate, fragile and easily-influenced nature. The word 'material' is something very concrete; in other words, when you think of material it is to do with the creation of the mind together with matter. I experienced a situation where I understood that the material world has its own spiritual entity, its place on its corresponding level, in the spiritual world.

The first time I had this clear realisation was in a VIP lounge at Heathrow airport, sometime in the 60s. Bapak and his party had been visiting England and it was time for him to continue his world journey. The flight to America had been delayed by two hours and the VIP lounge we had been given was rather small for our large group. It was often the case that Subud members would come to wave Bapak goodbye, or indeed welcome him on his arrival. This time there must have been 35 of us, excluding the travellers.

It is in my nature to be discreet and stand back, letting others be physically close to Bapak. He and his family were sitting in the few large leather armchairs facing the wide bay windows, while the Subud members were sitting on the carpeted floor around him; the ones who did not have enough room to sit were standing, resting their backs against the walls. I was standing by the only door in the room, feeling I should be there to check that no one but Subud members could enter.

Bapak had been talking to us and wanted to demonstrate that what one is saying can also be received through melody, and he proceeded to sing. He had a gentle, captivating voice, and what he was saying was poetic and beautiful. Every so often, he would stop and what he had sung would be translated into English. Everyone present seemed to be taken high up into a harmonious spiritual sphere of an angelic nature.

I was surprised when suddenly I saw with my inner eyes a number of what I would describe as little grotesque beings, hairy, prickly, with long teeth and large pointed ears, and with claws instead of nails. They were running about wanting to enter and interfere with the sublime unity that was being experienced in the lounge.

The door handle, which happened to be touching my hip, slowly moved and the door opened slightly. There was not much room to move but I managed to move towards the gap and listen with one ear.

"You have been given the wrong VIP lounge, you must all come out! It's urgent," I heard a muffled feminine voice say through the tiny gap of the door. "Sorry, but it's not possible now," I murmured back and pushed the door until it closed.

Bapak was still singing; the incident had been apparently unnoticed. I closed my eyes and went back into my quiet inner state to enjoy Bapak's receiving.

Again I perceived the many angry little devilish beings, and this time I blocked the handle of the door with both hands. I found myself ordering them to go, moved by a kind of divine authority. It was effective. I heard the faint sounds of footsteps dissipating in the distance down the corridor.

Relieved, I relaxed in to Bapak's melodious voice. Some time later, the little material gremlins came back in to my inner vision and were at it again, coming to create a disturbance. Then, a few moments later, someone was knocking at the door. In my inner quiet, I saw the little beings angry and menacing, rushing about in all directions wanting to create confusion. As before, I reached the level inside myself were there was a peaceful yet powerful authority. And from there, I ordered each one of them to go and leave us alone. It took some time as they were many, but finally the knocking stopped. This story, I understand, must sound weird to the reader. I can only explain that, at that time, it was my way to inwardly perceive the manifestation of a material disturbance created by the irritated staff of the airport.

Bapak eventually came to the end of his receiving; it seemed that everyone present was floating in heavenly waters and wanted to prolong it as much as possible. He looked at his watch, stood up and said, "It's time to go to the plane now, thank you and au revoir."

Everyone rose to their feet and made room to clear the way for Bapak to leave the VIP lounge. I quickly opened the door wide and, as he passed by, he discreetly looked into my eyes, giving me a smile, which made me feel that he had been aware of my struggle with the little material devilish beings.

As I followed the party down the long corridors of the airport, I reflected on what had just happened. Was that unusual experience the result of my imagination? Not really, as it was so real and unexpected; also, the annoying and aggressive gremlins seemed to appear on my inner screen each time moments before they actually materialised by voice and sound at the door. I did not look for a conclusion, and left the experience as it was. But after the party had gone, I went to the information desk and asked why we had been disturbed while we were in the VIP lounge. An official came to reply that there had been a mistake: the VIP lounge, which happened to be the most luxurious in the airport, had been reserved for the King of Saudi Arabia and his party. The airport authorities had been obliged to place his Majesty in another, ordinary VIP lounge.

The clown of God

Early in October 1983 on a visit to England, Bapak was to give a talk to Subud helpers and committee at the Tara Hotel in London. Keen to attend the meeting, Mélinda and I arranged for a babysitter to look after the children for the day.

At the time, I was part of the team of UK national helpers and we had prepared a short list of questions we hoped to ask Bapak. It happened that the person who was to be our spokesman could not attend that day, and I had been asked to replace him for the morning. I knew all the questions, as we had discussed them together previously, but still felt unprepared and slightly uncomfortable at the thought of going up on stage in front of Bapak and the large audience.

There were three main questions I was asked to put before Bapak; they went something like this:

- Testing about members who are not physically present during the session, can Bapak elaborate?
- How can we improve our receiving and ourselves?
- Can Bapak elaborate on the subject of open-ended testing?

As was his custom, Bapak opened the meeting by welcoming us all and then announced that he wished to talk this morning to committee members and helpers only; adding that he would give his attention to the members at another meeting in due course. Then I was asked to come up on stage to put the national helpers' questions forward. I had been doing latihan for over 25 years and was not nervous any more in the close presence of Bapak. In fact, I found myself deeply happy to have been given this opportunity to replace my friend.

Bapak responded to the question about testing. He always saw the whole picture, explaining that testing enabled you to become aware of how another person felt. But it could have a disharmonious effect because the person might feel that they are being criticised or singled out, and that would not bring a good outcome. He then explained that, if we ask Bapak questions, we're not really experiencing the answer, only hearing his reply and therefore not putting into practice the reality behind the question. He went on to describe the life forces – material, vegetable, animal and human – emphasising that the material life force is the one that has the strongest influence in man's life. He gave us the example of Adam, who had only to wish to have what he needed, but when God ordered him to go and live on Earth, he questioned it:

"But how will I feed myself there?"

"You will have to use your mind to transform the minerals and plants I have put there for you and feed yourself from your own work and effort."

Bapak pointed out how man, by the use of his mind, had been able to make a car from a lump of iron ore, and had been able to refine it to end up with a Rolls-Royce. "Talking about the spiritual without the experience behind it is hot air; it means nothing."

He had decided that to explain further about the material forces we would do some testing. He asked for two men to come up and stand quite relaxed in front of him. I went up together with a friend called Mansur. We stood there quietly, waiting.

First, Bapak said to Mansur, "Receive what is the character of

Léonard."

Mansur expressed through his receiving, his eyes closed, movements and sounds that had to do with my character.

Then Bapak asked what the receiving meant. Mansur explained that he felt an artist who likes making things, somebody who has good feelings towards others and who likes to bring people together. Then Bapak asked him, "According to your heart and mind, does it fit?" Then he added, "Yes, Leonard's work already shows the qualities that you have received."

Then he asked us to relax again. "The material life force, where does it dwell in your being?" For quite some time, Bapak let us follow our individual receiving. My hands slowly lifted up and enveloped my head, and inside my mind I felt great clarity. During the receiving I remembered an experience that I had had in Indonesia, about 10 years previously (story in Chapter 5), where blue flames were cleaning the inside of my skull.

Bapak asked me how it was, and I replied that I strongly felt the material forces in my head. "Yes! This is not a bad thing. It means that you're full of ideas in regard to this world. Léonard has clear and good ideas in relation to business, is that so?"

"Yes, Bapak, it is so," I answered.

He then turned to Mansur and said, "But Mansur is different – the material forces reside in your heart, so the ideas are still in your feelings and do not come out, cannot come to completion. Is that true?"

"Yes!" Replied Mansur.

Bapak stressed the importance of doing such testing and continued, turning to me. "Now Léonard, receive your nature."

As I let go and relaxed, I became my own nature. Feeling extremely centered and well in my being, close to lightness and laughter, I was probably smiling. I was moving about lightly, feeling that I had paintbrushes in my hands, and was talking to customers. Having observed my movements and expressions during the test, Bapak described my nature: "In the way you work you are like a clown. When you act in that way you are successful. But if you are serious, it does not work."

He then turned to the audience and said: "This kind of thing you can find out for yourself, how you really function, finding your hidden secrets."

He turned to me again: "Receive through your movement, Léonard. Whether your work is in accordance with the will of God." I received feeling close to my origin and living fully who I was. "That's good! That is why your wife has recovered from a very bad illness called leukaemia. You are her medicine."

He went on, "You are a clown of God. Bapak prays that your wife will be completely cured. You are her witch doctor!"

Everyone in the audience was now laughing.

"So, however ordinary you feel, you are still a good healer ... You're a clever clown!" And then he concluded, saying, "That's enough now. This is a demonstration of reality. Why did you bring all the questions? Who chose you to do this?"

"The other national helpers asked me as Muchtar, our representative, could not be with us this morning," I explained.

Bapak then remembered, "I saw Léonard at Coombe Springs more than 20 years ago and had thought at the time that he was an amusing person and that he would always stand on his own feet."

This had been a powerful experience. Bapak through the open testing had led me to experience how my inside corresponded to my outside behaviour, making me feel more confident in myself. That same morning, I had acknowledged to Bapak that when our children were ill or suffered from one pain or another, I would sit quietly by them, sometimes putting my hand where the pain was, until it had completely dissipated.

Chapter 3

On the subject of names, conception, sex, life and death

Becoming parents

Our first child announced itself by inducing Jean (later renamed Mélinda) into a series of mild contractions. She felt the first ones in the morning; by the late afternoon, when they became more frequent, we felt it was time to go to the Montsouris clinic, near the University of Paris, where Jean had been seeing the gynaecologist.

A nun registered our arrival in a leather-bound notebook and led us to the lift. On the third floor, we were shown to a small room. We had been preparing ourselves for the birth and Jean had lovingly put together all kinds of newborn baby clothes that were neatly packed in our straw basket. After having arranged Jean's few belongings in the temporary bedroom, I decided to pop out before the shops closed to get her some fruit and water to drink; also I had decided to book a cheap hotel room nearby, in case the birth came late into the night.

It must have been around 9pm when I came back to the clinic; I rang the bell and waited for what seemed ages. Finally I heard short fast steps coming to the door. Slowly the door opened just two inches, and a long nose appeared followed by a pale blue eye that looked at me with suspicion, "We are closed; come back tomorrow!"

"But my wife is having a baby," I replied with some consternation, "it's probably happening now!" I pushed the door with gentle force, then jammed my foot between the frame and the heavy glass to stop it from closing.

"Go away or I'll call the police," said the nun menacingly.

Using what I felt was legitimate force, I pushed my way into the entrance hall. The Mother Superior was red with anger, trembling all over, and stood there speechless as I headed straight for the lift. Before she could catch me, I pressed the button and the doors closed automatically in front of the exasperated nun.

Jean was not in the bedroom where I had left her. I went down the long corridor and found the operating room. I knocked three times timidly, opened it and looked inside.

"Hello, are you the father? Come in. The contractions are more frequent now; the gyneacologist has been told; he shouldn't be long," said a happy young nurse, reassuringly.

Jean was lying on a childbearing table covered by a white sheet. Her knees were up; she looked slightly anxious and said in English, "I'm so relieved you are here at last, wherever have you been? They tied my ankles up, I feel like a prisoner, I don't like it!"

I held her hand and stood by, quietly smiling, "Have you been doing your special breathing?" I asked.

"Yes, I'm trying to, but it's awfully hard when the contractions come, it hurts so much!" she replied, grimacing, wanting to share her suffering with me.

The contractions were now coming at quicker intervals, and each time they started I did the breathing exercises with her, my mouth close to her left ear to encourage her to keep up the rhythm while the contraction lasted.

It must have been around 11pm when the door to the operating room was flung open. The gynaecologist entered the room full of himself; he reminded me of the actor Errol Flynn with his little thin moustache and empty, worried-looking large blue eyes. I was very surprised to see him dressed in the most bizarre way: long tight boots made of white shiny oilcloth came up to his bare knees. He wore a pair of shorts of the same material, had no shirt on, but a large white glossy apron covered the front of his chest and reached down to just above his knee caps. His arms and back were completely bare.

When she noticed the strange outfit, Jean gave me a questioning look and a slightly amused smile before it was stolen away by a new wave of contracting pains. The doctor looked at me and said in a slightly teasing but warning voice, "You know Mr Lassalle, it rarely fails that young fathers like you faint during the birth of their first child; I would advise you to leave the room now, as it won't be long before the baby is born. We don't want you unconscious on the floor while it's happening, do we?"

I was feeling drowsy, that was true, and probably looked rather white, but it was due to the repetitive, accelerated breathing I was doing with my wife; I was certainly not going to leave the room at such an important moment of our lives!

"Thank you for warning me; I feel that I will not be a problem during the childbirth," I answered him with a big smile. Jean gave a last enormous push; the nurse and the doctor exclaimed their appreciation in the form of an extended admiring, "Ooh! Ooh!" A crumpled, wet, frowning, serious- looking and wrinkled black-haired little head appeared. I suddenly felt a sharp pain in my right hand – Jean's nails had entered right into my skin as she gave the final delivery push.

Now, the doctor, holding the baby's head in one hand, was carefully guiding its body out with the other. The tiny, wet slimy body followed without resistance and was soon held upside-down by its feet, while the umbilical cord remained linked to the placenta, which was still in the womb.

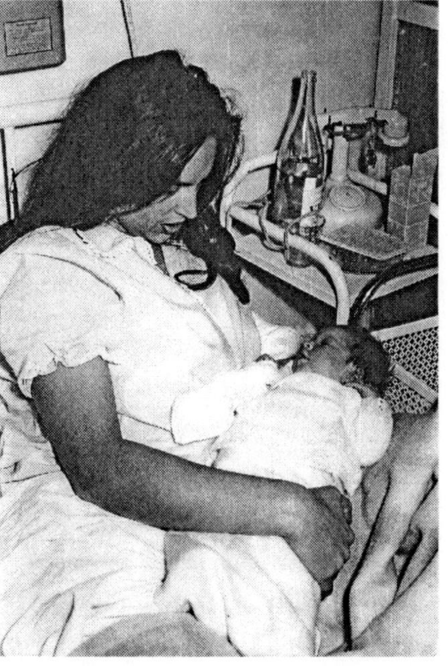

1st hours of Joanna Melia

"It's a girl!" they exclaimed in unison. Jean lifted her head as she rested the upper part of her body on her elbow. She was looking amazed and completely charmed and delighted by the new arrival. Then, she looked at me, her smile radiant, every part of her face covered in little pearl droplets of sweat, expressing joy. Full of compassionate mother's love, she turned her head back to her baby that was still hanging upside down in the firm hand of the doctor.

After two or three sturdy shakes, the newborn suddenly screamed furiously. The strident sound froze my spine, creating instantly in me a deep instinctive and powerful need to hug her, to reassure her that everything was okay, but I resisted the impulse. I noticed Jean's face looking worried: we both at that moment independently had become aware of a new reality: that of being parents.

The doctor laughed and said loudly to override the child's protestation, "Now, now, there is a healthy looking girl expressing a strong and lively character!" Her still-bent forearms and tight little fists over her chest showed much anger, as if she disapproved thoroughly of being treated in such a disrespectful manner at such an important moment as her arrival into her new world.

Now appeased, lying on her mother's tummy, her umbilical chord was folded tightly, clipped and severed from her original source of nourishment and security, her tiny body was relaxing, breathing regularly, and her well-shaped purple lips came together to froth up a little bubble of saliva.

The doctor pulled gently the other section of the deep purple twisted cord, while pressing down firmly on Jean's tummy to extract the nine-month-old magic bag that had been the shelter in which our child had been formed ...

Now that we had become a trio, I was aware of our new situation: we formed a family. Jean, delicately holding her daughter, was admiring her with great tenderness. Then she looked up at me and asked, "What shall we call her?"

We had no idea what to call our new child. We had decided that upon seeing her after the birth, it would be easier to find a name, but now we were at a loss ... Some names came up in our minds, but they felt somehow artificial. So we decided to sleep on it.

Baby was showing signs of hunger. She was opening and closing her mouth and turning her head from one side to the other as if searching for something. I found myself becoming the spectator of the unfolding process of motherhood.

Jean, while holding our wriggling daughter in her left arm, freed her milk-swollen left bosom, then gracefully held between her index and middle finger the chocolate-coloured protruding nipple that she guided gently towards the demanding mouth. The first contact was passionate; the little lips were now holding tight the generous tap and were sucking noisily and avidly what I imagined to be a delicious drink.

I was in awe of the beauty of the maternal scene, it was as if the baby had reconnected back to the mother, both of them experiencing oneness and expressing deep satisfaction. I suddenly felt out of the picture. I was watching, observing, but knew that in no way could I share the amazing experience of being a woman.

"And that's how the world has been created," I thought, "the female part completely different from the male part, each with its particular role, both living their different fields of awareness."

I have to say that I felt rather alone at that moment, standing there, observing beauty but somehow being out of it. Baby was now asleep, having loosened her grip, hanging off the nipple as if she had gone elsewhere. Jean looked suddenly tired, and it was time for me to leave them to rest. I lifted our child into my arms, brought my nose close to her peaceful little face and smelt her delicate baby odour as I rubbed my nose gently on to hers. I then laid her with great care in the waiting cot.

I kissed Jean on the forehead, looked into her eyes and said, "Brilliant, darling, for having made such a beautiful baby."

She smiled and then said as I walked to the door, "By the way, you see the thick brown paper bag over there on the floor? It's the placenta. Apparently the father has to get rid of it somehow?"

I lifted the precious and heavy bag, waved goodbye and left the room. As I exited into the street I breathed in the cool night air deeply, looked at my watch and was surprised to see that it was past 1am. Walking rapidly towards the hotel, I observed a difference in myself.

Something had changed in my awareness; I could not quite put my finger on it at the time. But now, as I write, I understand that my consciousness, following the evening of the birth, had broadened to include into my being what we call 'family'.

The newborn was now nestled cosily in my inner feelings, giving me more strength: actually it was as if some of her strength was contracted to me in exchange for loving and caring for her.

Approaching the hotel I noticed a row of dustbins. I stopped, lifted the lid of one of them and hesitated, thinking, “How could I throw away this amazing natural bag that has contributed to giving us such a beautiful daughter? Should I keep it and bury it somewhere under a tree? Yes, that would be ideal. But when, where and how? It won't keep and I can't put it into a fridge now!”

I heard steps and laughter some distance away; a couple was walking towards me. Rapidly I dropped the wet placenta bag into the bin and quietly replace the metal lid. I walked on with a heavy feeling of guilt for my lack of reverence and respect to the incredible magic bag. My cheap hotel bedroom was pretty bleak, the bed hard and narrow, the whole ceiling was like a veranda letting in a constant dim yellow colour from the Paris night lights. I could not sleep; my mind was full of names and pictures. I could not separate names from faces of people I had heard, seen or known. After a long time of agitation I decided to get up and see if the latihan could help me. I stood on the small carpet beside the bed, and let the latihan flow into my being. After some time, maybe 15 or 20 minutes, when I felt I had reached a peaceful inner state, I asked, "What is the correct name for our newborn baby?"

I saw the Pacific Ocean, an island with coconut trees, also a piece of large printed red and white cotton fabric that I recognised; it had been brought back from Tahiti and given to us by close friends of my mother's on the Ile du Levant some years before. The fabric was flapping in the sea breeze and I saw that it was also wrapped around a very pretty dark-haired girl who gave me a broad smile.

"Joanna" resonated loudly in my heart and mind. "That's it! It's got to be her name – Joanna, yes, that sounds super," I thought. I had not realised, at the time, that I was very much still in the passionate subjective world of reaction. It was only much later in my life that I understood that the name had come not from an objective source in my inner self, but from a reaction to imagery and probably an association with a Joanna I had once seen on a movie and liked. The next morning I went back to the clinic feeling light and happy, carrying in my head the name Joanna.

"So, what name have you found for our little girl?" asked Jean, as I entered the room. Not being sure of myself, I would have preferred for her to tell me first what name she had found ...

"Yes, but you tell me first ... What's yours?" I begged.

"Melia?" she said slowly.

I wasn't sure about 'Melia'; it felt a little short, but it was unusual. I wondered where Jean had found it.

"Joanna," I pronounced my choice clearly. "What do you think?" I asked, longing to know her reaction ...

We both leaned over the white painted metal cot to observe our peacefully sleeping daughter.

"Melia?" I murmured. The child went on sleeping undisturbed.

"Joanna?" said Jean with her soft voice. The child did not react either. We both laughed.

Once we decided to call our daughter Joanna Melia, I hurriedly left the clinic to go to the local town hall to register her birth and name. I do not know if this is still the case today, but at that time in France, if you did not register your child's name within three days, the employees of the registrar's office were allowed to register the baby under any name they chose.

On my way back, much to the disapproval of the nuns, I arranged for an ambulance to take Jean and Joanna back to our seventh floor flat in the rue Cardinet; Jean did not like the clinic and we were longing to be by ourselves in our home.

Having experienced the extremely positive metamorphosis in myself when Bapak gave me the name Léonard, and the feeling of oneness I felt each time someone called me by that name, I soon realised that Joanna was not reflecting correctly our first-born daughter's nature. Jean agreed with me and we decided to ask Bapak for a new name for our child. The name Laura was given and suited her well. We were both satisfied and realised how important it was to have a name that corresponds to one's inner nature, yet we realised how we did not have, at the time, the capacity to choose a name objectively for our child.

Usually, Bapak would send parents two initials, one for a boy, one for a girl, and a request that the parents would give him five names for each that they liked. Once he had received the 10 suggestions, he would then choose the one for each sex that sounded closest to his perception for the correct vibration. It is interesting to note that before the birth of each of our other six children, something unexpected and out of the blue arose to make us feel more agreeable to one name on the list, compared to the four others. It was as if the children's inner natures were already trying to give us indications about their name.

It would take too long to tell you about the story behind each birth, which were in themselves unique experiences but I will, later on, cite one or two of them, just to give you other examples of the unexpected events that took place in relation to the naming of our children.

Findings about my blood father

Myrette Dewèvre, the lady who kindly rented us her flat, decided in the new year 1961 that she would like to renovate it, as she needed it for herself. This was sudden and unexpected, we had no idea where to go next. My mother had come up from Cannes to Paris to see Joanna soon after her birth and gave Jean and myself many useful recommendations on how to look after a newborn baby. It was a wonderful help to have her with us and she was thrilled to have become a grandmother.

It was important for Jean to show Joanna to her mother, so we decided to go to England for Christmas, not knowing quite where we would lodge on our return to Paris. We tidied up the flat, put away all our belongings into a corner and left for England.

Jean's parents, the Ortons, were delighted to have us in their home in Kent and to meet their newly born granddaughter. We also visited our close friends, Jennifer and Peter Gibbs, in their oast house near Crowborough. The spiritual training practice of the latihan had become an integrated part of our lives and of course when we were with friends who also practised the latihan, we would usually do one together.

On one such occasion, when Peter and I had just finished a latihan in the large, carpeted, round upper room of the oast house, I said to him: "I have a question that has been bothering me for some time. You know about my true father, whom I have only met twice, called Henry Valensi. I keep feeling about him and wondering why I have not been able to see him since we moved to Paris. I have telephoned his atelier many times with no result. I cannot understand why it is so difficult. Could you help me, through the latihan, to find out from the inner aspect what it is all about?"

Peter agreed, and we stood in front of each other, relaxed with our eyes closed, quietly being in our own receptive inner state. After a time of silence, I heard my friend say slowly in a low voice, "Léonard, receive through your surrender, where at this moment is your blood father?"

We both understood that when he used the word 'surrender', he meant a state of non-resistance and total acceptance. Rapidly my consciousness went down into my inner depth, and I felt propelled into a different universe, which I did not recognise as my own. As if my legs were not to be part of this experience, I felt the need to lie on my back and I followed. My consciousness was now travelling through nebulous spaces, where there was no colour, but different tones of grey. I suddenly felt my father's strong presence surrounding me; his feelings seemed to be very disturbed by my arrival. I found myself not welcome; I was his son, but rather I was like another being who had violated his space without having been announced first. Ill at ease, but not wanting to go, I stayed in that unpleasant place. Suddenly it was not like a dream any more. It had become real and my consciousness was sharp and attentive.

Unexpectedly, an angry, large, hissing tomcat came into my field of awareness, all claws out, demanding I get out of his presence or else ... I had become a little kitten, crouching down with my ears back, obstinately refusing to go even at the risk of being hurt. The blowing and hissing animal force was powerful. I distinguished an acceleration of my heartbeat; my throat was tight, and I felt rejected, unwanted by the man I wanted so much to love.

"Léonard? Léonard, are you okay?" I faintly heard Peter's distant voice calling me.

"Yes, I probably have had enough of this," I thought, but how would I get back into my own space? It took a while before I found a way to reconnect to my earthly self. Then it came to me how to go about it: once again to let go of my awareness of my father's universe completely and find peace and stillness within my inner self. Finally, I opened my eyes ...

My dear friend was standing next to me looking down with his kind blue eyes and generous warm smile. "Glad you're back," he said, and I sprang up and began to tell him of my experience. "It was as if my father did not want to see me, just like most tomcats who reject their own kittens ... It was powerful. I felt the action of a strong animal force and experienced a similar force within myself as I was refusing to go, not wanting to accept his rough behaviour. Strangely enough, I felt that his presence was not in this world."

A few days later, at Jean's family house, we were all having breakfast. The sun was pouring generously through the diamond-shaped pane glass windows on to the breakfast dining table, and although it was winter, it gave the morning a feeling of spring. The postman had arrived and Winifred, my mother-in-law, handed me a letter that came from my mother in the south of France. I asked them if they would forgive me if I read it at the table.

"Yes, of course, by all means, please do," immediately replied Jean's father.

It read: "My darling François, I have to tell you of some sad news: Your father, Henry Valensi, died of a heart attack while sitting in a friend's rose garden in Paris. He was 75 ... "

Henry Valensi

I did not want to hold back the flood of tears that instantly flowed down my cheeks. Although a few days before I had been sort of prepared by the test experience with Peter, when I felt that my father had probably left this world, the blunt reality was terribly painful. Head down, the salty tears now dripping on to the white tablecloth, I was feeling confused, sad and angry at the same time. Angry with him, for never responding to my calls or trying to see us while we lived in Paris. And now he had gone without saying goodbye. How could he have done this?

I heard my mother-in-law ask, "What's the matter with François? Why is he crying?" She refused to call me by my new name and had probably never seen a man cry before.

"His father died," Jean, who had just read the short letter, rapidly answered.

"But I thought his father had died in the war, in 1942?"

I realised that Jean's parents had not been told of my complicated childhood. I was not in a state to explain the gritty details of my youth at that moment and, excusing myself, I got up and left the table to go outside for a walk into the cool, witch-hazel scented air of the garden.

I will now jump forward 25 years, just to give you an illustration of how I came to understand that in my spiritual world, what I called 'time' was only a measure of my mind, and in truth there is no time in spiritual awareness – just beingness.

We were now living with our seven children in what we called the Oast House, near Wadhurst in Kent. I had been running a very stimulating and quite successful business in 17th-century antiques and interior design in the old part of Tunbridge Wells called The Pantiles. The Subud latihan was very much part of our living and I was regularly following the spiritual training; it meant a lot to me as it brought such a stimulating and broad dimension into my everyday life.

However, there was a situation in my inner self that bothered me greatly. I could not let go of the feeling deep in my heart that Henry Valensi had greatly let me down by being so distant and unloving towards me. Although I knew that it wasn't healthy for me to have a grudge against my genetic father, I simply couldn't help it and did not know, in my ordinary self, how to cope with it. As so often with unpleasant things I found difficult to deal with, I had pushed it down deep into myself, somewhere where I could not feel the unresolved pain.

One evening, during one of my latihans, I strongly felt my father's presence. Opening my eyes to check, I saw absolutely clearly, but with some amazement, Henry Valensi walking towards me. He had his arms out, was looking straight at me and I noticed that he was in tears. As he came closer, I heard his voice as if coming from inside my chest saying, "In truth, I've always loved you. I was frightened of what people would say. I've come to ask you for forgiveness. I had not realised the harm I had been doing to you by ignoring the reality of your presence."

By now I was crying too and our tears mixed as we hugged lovingly with our arms tight round each other. I put my right hand at the nape of his head and noticed how it felt as if it was my own, the form of the curve to the neck was identical.

We stood like this for some time then, as I pressed him against my chest, I noticed that he was merging slowly into my being and, as this was happening, I heard a very delicate high-pitched sound that vibrated upwards through my whole being, up into my skull and out through the top of my head.

I understood, at that instant, that his soul had been liberated and was now free to continue on its spiritual journey. I waited quietly until all my brothers finished latihan and left the room. I did not feel like disturbing the deep tranquillity I was in, the profound, satisfying feeling of reconciliation I had just experienced.

Driving back to our house in Wadhurst, I noticed how different I felt. The change was subtle but extraordinary. My heart was now filled with love for my father. I knew that all the grudge feelings had completely vanished and we had become so close that he was now part of me, and that he too had been freed from the tension of resistance.

Mélinda was already asleep when I got into bed, as usual leaving the small bed light on. As was my custom, I undressed completely and popped into bed. Before I put the light out I twisted over to kiss my wife good night. As I turned I felt something rolling between the upper part of my arm and my chest. Immediately I moved my arm away to see a brown nobbly thing lying on the white sheet, a little ball the size of a small olive.

I have to explain first that, for the past three or four years, a kind of soft large growth had grown out of a dark brown beauty spot near my right nipple. The vanity of my ego, irritated by this ugly growth, had tried, by tightly tying round its neck a piece of strong cotton, to make it drop off. It had worked, but had been such a painful process that I had decided not to bother doing it again, and it had grown and grown into a fleshy ball.

I picked up this strange thing, rolling it slowly between my index finger and thumb, turned round to Mélinda and said triumphantly, "Look darling! Amazing! My grudge with my father has dropped off, I have just reconciled with him during the latihan."

I threw the dark ball of skin across the room into the bin, and told her all about the liberating experience.

The next morning in the bathroom, my bristly beard covered in white shaving foam, I was singing lightly while pulling the razor down my cheek. As was often the case, our youngest daughter Marianna had popped into the bathroom to sit on the loo. From there she enjoyed observing her dad shaving.

"Dad? It's funny, what have you done with your little brown olive on your breast? Did you pull it off? Where is it?" she asked, intrigued.

"I threw it in the bin. It dropped off last night in bed as I kissed your Mum good night." I then explained, with much amusement, about the previous night's unusual latihan experience with my genetic father.

More about names

Back in 1964, Jean, recently called Mélinda by Bapak, was pregnant with our third child. We wrote to Indonesia weeks before the birth, and the letter R came back for a boy and D for a girl. We chose five names for each, and the letter was prepared, ready to be posted. We had decided that Mélinda would be the one to put the letter in the post box. Each time I came back from work, I would say, "Darling, have you remembered to post the letter to Indonesia?"

The reply would come back, "Oh dear! Sorry, I forgot."

About two weeks later as we were having supper, Mélinda said, "I am terribly sorry, but I just can't post that letter to Bapak as it stands. I feel we should alter the list of Rs by adding Richard to it." So we followed Mélinda's feelings and to our great satisfaction, the name Richard came back from Bapak with its meaning, 'the ruler, or the one who leads'.

Another name experience

I hope that you will not mind me sharing with you once again a name story. Once, in 1968, during a cold early winter's night at around 4am, I woke up feeling powerfully physically attracted to Mélinda. We came together, and our bodies went into a harmonious rhythm that brought our consciousness far up into a sphere where neither our hearts nor our minds were present. The energy was intense but at the same time blissfully serene; as the crucial moment that carries the vessel of life heightened and delivered, the name 'Dahlan' came out from the depth of my chest and rolled off my tongue clearly, giving me at the same time a feeling of completion.

Not feeling absolutely sure about giving our son with a Muslim name, we wrote to Bapak. His reply had been a D for a boy, so of course we had put the name Dahlan on the list. A few weeks later when the letter from Indonesia arrived, we found that Bapak had chosen the name Dahlan. It was good to receive his confirmation, as the experience during conception had been so unique, we felt that Bapak's choice would clarify it for us.

The circumcision

While I am on the subject of names, sex, and conception, I hope you will not mind if I carry on with a few more related stories.

At the end of 1966 and beginning of 1967, we moved to London from Bridport, Dorset. It was a time in our lives when we found it difficult to find a home to rent. Estate agents would say to us, 'Sorry! No children, no pets, no coloureds." Close friends kindly lent us a room in their large house in Hampstead.

During this time, I noticed that in the course of the day, when I fantasised about women, I would often experience a burning, prickly feeling under the foreskin of my penis. It was the kind of problem one doesn't especially want to divulge, so I kept quiet about it, but it became a real bother as it became quite painful. Furthermore, our lovemaking had become painful for me, instead of being pleasurable. Mélinda and I decided that I should go see a doctor for advice. He prescribed a special cream, but after 10 days careful application, the condition had not improved.

At that time, my close friend Varindra Vitachi had just returned from Jakarta where he had been to see Pak Subuh. Varindra was the chair of the World Subud Association and often travelled to Indonesia. After a latihan in Highgate, we went to a café to have a cup of coffee together and I mentioned my problem. He listened with attention and said, "It's interesting you mention this, Léonard. I have just come back from Jakarta where I received a light surgical intervention. I am now circumcised."

I remember thinking, "Well, he has just become a Muslim and all Muslims are circumcised; that makes sense for believers who follow a religion. But I do not feel the need specially to join Islam nor am I keen to interfere with what nature has given me whole."

Varindra must have read my thoughts because he went on to explain: "Let me tell you, Léonard. Bapak explained to me before my circumcision that the true reason for this small operation was to allow for the evaporation of a strong acid and abrasive fluid that secretes out around the bulb when passionate sexual thoughts weave through our sexual feelings. In fact, it is a way for the body to evacuate this acid, and by cutting away the foreskin, it allows it to evaporate more rapidly instead of collecting under it, where it can create problems."

How strange that my friend was describing exactly what I was experiencing. It took me several days of debate, with my many selves and exchanges with Mélinda, to decide whether or not to be circumcised. There was much resistance within me to interfere with what nature had given me. The day after we made the decision to go ahead with the operation, a friend called Hanafi rang to tell me that he had decided to be circumcised and to ask if I had any idea where he could go to have the operation done. In the meantime I had found a small clinic in Notting Hill Gate run by a Jewish doctor who specialised in circumcisions. We decided to have it done at the same time together and booked a double bedroom for the following week.

We were required to come with only a toothbrush, pair of pyjamas and a cheque book. The operation would be performed in the morning and we would only be kept one night in the clinic.

We arrived on Monday morning, and to our great amusement realised that the clinic was run solely by nuns. The head nurse led us to our first-floor bedroom, asked us to put on our pyjamas, and wait in our respective beds for the visit of the surgeon at 10 o'clock.

An African nurse entered the room with a tray of syringes. "I've come to give you the anaesthetic injections ... But tell me something.

How is it that such handsome guys like you would want to do such a thing? Why aren't you satisfied with what God has given you?"

Hanafi and I were by now in such fits of giggles that we could not answer. The nun came to me first, I presented her with my forearm, and with great expertise, she injected the powerful liquid into my protruding vein.

The last thing I remember was seeing a tall, ginger-haired figure in a white gown, freckle-faced with a moustache, whom I vaguely understood to be the surgeon.

Hanafi and I left the Notting Hill clinic the next day at lunchtime, our respective precious organs well-bandaged with strong recommendations from the head nun not to use them for at least 10 to 12 weeks to allow time for healing! This is not the kind of story I have told many people but it does lead to another unusual experience that I wanted to share with you. Mélinda and I were going through a difficult financial patch. The six of us lived in one bedroom, sharing a kitchen, toilets and bathroom with an office, which happened to be the Subud Britain office at the time. However hard I worked, I was never able to make enough money for our daily needs. Peter Gibbs, who was later called Lambert, offered us his croft up in north Wales. "It's a beautiful place, you'll see, not far from a beach called the Whistling Sands, it's not being used at the moment; I know it's a bit far out but at least it's a house."

We gladly took up his kind offer and, in our Citroen 2CV, were off to Wales in the early winter months of 1967. Six weeks after our arrival at the croft, I had an unusual feeling as if someone was hovering very close around me. Today I would name it a soul, but at the time I described it to myself as a presence.

The master bedroom of the croft was under the pitch of the attic roof and its only access was by a very narrow, creaky, wooden spiral staircase. One cold and dark windy night, we put the children to bed and, after giving the necessary attention to housework, it was our turn to prepare ourselves for the night.

I had not told Mélinda about the presence I felt, but as we were going up the narrow staircase, I felt it more clearly and strongly than before, so I mentioned to her softly, "You know what? Darling ... "

As if she too was in expectation of some 'annunciation', she immediately replied, "No, what?" We both stopped in the middle of our spiral climb: "Well, it is strange, but I feel the presence of a child who wants to incarnate; I have been feeling this for some time now, but the feeling has become more constant lately."

I shared this in a whispering voice. Melinda acknowledged it by saying, "That's funny, me too. I have been aware of a boy child, but I did not mention anything about it because your thing is still healing."

We finished our climb to the attic room in silence, the atmosphere heightened by the creaks of the old oak floorboards; now both aware of the boy child waiting to be conceived.

The coming together was profound and intense; indeed at each conception our consciousness of the experience has been different. With this child, we were both taken into a quality of gentleness as if its incarnated soul had enveloped us in a loving blanket of feelings.

Laura, Miriam, Marianna, Hermas, Dahlan, Laurence, Richard & Fly at 19 Frant road

Some months later we received from Bapak the initials L for a girl, H for a boy and we found it difficult to find five names that we liked beginning with H. GG, my beloved grandmother, had some years before given me a magnificent French Bible edited by the biblical school of Jerusalem. Looking for a boy's name beginning with H, I opened the book haphazardly and immediately my eyes fell upon the name 'Hermas'.

"Here it is! I've got it!" I shouted to Melinda, who was in the kitchen with the children preparing lunch. I rushed to her with the Bible open on the page where the name had appeared. We looked at it together to discover that St Hermas had lived in the south of France in the Middle Ages. We both felt positive for the name of our coming child and it was put on the list with the others.

Some weeks later, a letter from Bapak's secretariat arrived and we read: "If a boy the name will be Hermas."

On the 4th of December 1967, a most tender and delicate healthy boy was born in the home we had recently moved to in Tunbridge Wells. He was named Hermas.

Mélinda, dealing with illness

In the mid-70s Mélinda's health started deteriorating rapidly. At first we noticed that she was getting very tired and felt constantly weak. Then there seemed to be an acceleration in the degradation of her general health, and she became extremely anaemic. When having her blood analysed at Dr Sharma's clinic in London, we discovered that she was at an advanced stage of leukaemia. The white blood cells had completely overtaken the reds.

Her blood cells had been analysed by a lady from Finland who was an expert in blood cancer. Based on her long experience analysing blood, she said, "This person, for sure, has been exposed to atomic radiation."

At that time, the UK was not very strict about where its source of blood came from. There had been complications during the birth of our number seven in the spring of 1971, when Mélinda had to receive a complete blood transfusion. We presumed that radioactive contaminated blood was probably the source of the problem.

At that time leukaemia was not curable. Treatment using cobalt rays was just being developed, but it was far from effective. Had we the funds, it would have meant sending Mélinda to New York, where the latest technology on cancer research was available. A close friend of ours, Dr Mitchell, explained that she had an extremely thin chance of survival.

Dr Sharma, who had just opened a private clinic near Liphook in Sussex, said he was prepared to try and save Mélinda but that he would need to keep her in the clinic for at least eight weeks. She had become extremely pale, her voice was faint and she seemed distant, as if something in her head had already gone somewhere unknown. She seemed to be disconnecting herself from everyday life, from the children and me. She did not seem to be behind her eyes and looked at us with obvious detachment.

We decided to follow Dr Sharma's offer and after preparing her a small suitcase, the children and I took her to Liphook. I knew from inside how important it was in these difficult moments not to dramatise or bring fear into the situation, but to accept fully what was happening and the possibility of losing my loving wife, our wonderful Mum.

As we left her in the brand-new clinic, I noticed that when she kissed the children goodbye her usual loving presence was absent, though she went through the family ritual of kisses and hugs. I cradled her in my arms gently, lovingly, and kissed her rapidly on her dry lips and cold forehead. When we left her in the great hall of the clinic, the children, full of life, as if they did not want to be trapped by sadness, were already running outside towards the car. I turned round to give her a final smile and she waved back timidly.

To be honest, I was pushing back sad negative feelings and constantly re-adjusting myself close to my soul where I could find positive energy. I was soon taken and carried along by the liveliness of our children who were much better at living in the present than I was. We sang during most of the journey home; at other times there were long silences where each of us went into his or her own world, where thoughts and reveries would carry us away from earthly realities.

Our Norwegian au pair girl had gone out for the evening and I took the opportunity at supper to exchange with the children how I felt about the situation and share with them what I knew of the health condition of their Mum. I explained quietly about the illness of leukaemia, about the fight between the white and red blood corpuscles that modern medicine had not yet found a way to cure. Also to help Mum the most, we should not be worried about her but trust that nature would follow its course in the best way.

The children were all listening attentively and when I finished they said spontaneously in harmony together: "Don't worry Dad! We will be all right and we will look after you if Mummy has to go."

This positive affirmation coming from my children gave me tremendous strength, and a wave of love and gratitude swelled inside me. Yes, we would be all right and so would Mélinda whatever way life would take us.

Olivia, my mother, together with our au pair, helped us to keep the daily work in the house running smoothly; we rapidly fell into a rhythm that became quite manageable. I stopped taking the children to see their mother, as she had become so absent from worldly doings that she could not give them the loving attention they were used to when she had her full health.

I managed to visit her twice a week, but not on weekends when I would stay with the children. Mélinda had been put on a very strict diet, which seemed to consist mostly of lemon juice and raw vegetables including raw beetroot. She received homeopathic treatment, massage, hot and cold baths and went for short walks in the beautiful gardens of the property. Every time I went she was a little further into her invisible world. She talked very little and mostly about the activities that happened in the clinic.

The eight weeks went by rapidly for me, between the family, the shop with its demanding clients and going to see my wife. So, one sunny Monday morning in early spring after a lovely drive through the southern England countryside, I felt light and happy to be going once again to see my Mélinda.

I walked into her bedroom and saw her sitting in bed brushing her attractive long black hair. As soon as I saw her smile I realised that something miraculous had happened. She looked radiant and I rushed up to hug her. As I held her in my arms I felt that life vibrations were flowing back into her body. She had lost a lot of weight and looked very thin, but the pale green eyes were sparkling with excitement at the recapture of her earthly energies. She proceeded to tell me what had happened.

Two days previously, after the daily massage session, she stayed resting on the massage table as had become her habit. Lying there quietly, her eyes closed, she heard crackling noises. She slowly opened her eyes to find that her whole body was surrounded with yellow flames that turned orange and red; they were dancing all around her. She looked up and saw a deep blue sky high above. A very ancient voice resonated in the room, “May the disease in Mélinda’s blood be cleansed.”

She had thought she was dying and completely surrendered to the situation, then started singing loudly and finally must have fallen asleep.

Sometime later she woke up, not knowing on which side of life or afterlife she was. Wrapped up in her dressing gown, she walked back to her bedroom and crept into bed thinking, "If I'm going to die, I’d better be in my own bed."

The next morning when she opened her eyes she noticed that everything was in colour again, as during the eight weeks in the clinic, everything had seemed to her a monochrome of greys. She rushed to the windows, opened them wide and breathed in the spring morning air. She was startled by the beautiful colours she could see everywhere in the plants and trees, and also by the poetic whistle of a blackbird that was announcing the yearly rebirth of nature.

Mélinda dressed quickly and rushed downstairs where she passed the masseur of the previous day. "My, my, who have we here?" he exclaimed.

She answered with a joyous smile.

It was 9am and she knocked discreetly at the doctor’s office door. She did not wait for an answer but went straight in. Dr Sharma was at his desk. He looked up at her and said positively, "Well! Now that it has been decided you will live, I can heal your body."

The next day I joyfully brought her home to the delight of the children and my mother. She was cured, the leukaemia had gone and her blood was back to normal. For the next two years Dr Sharma gave her a strict diet with white fish once a week and mostly raw vegetables.

Mélinda had greatly changed and would not carry in herself all the tragedies of the world any more. Before, she had carried other people's problems and worried about them as if they were her own. After this experience, she became more centred and closer to her own inner feelings. This experience was valuable for all of us. It showed us how important it is not to cultivate negative emotions, but to keep one's consciousness fully in the present.

The sound of the Earth

Once, as was often the case, we came together in the early hours of the morning, and our lovemaking had taken our awareness a long way up into a sphere where there is no mind nor heart, just beingness, with all our senses heightened, in complete receptivity.

I distinctly remember hearing the busy, crispy and full sounds of a swarm of bees. It was so real that I opened my eyes thinking that maybe some bees had come in through the open window of our bedroom. What I experienced was breathtaking: my consciousness was in space; although it was in darkness, the light came from the colourful Earth that looked as if it was floating in the universe. It was turning around and the orchestrated sounds of a swarm of bees emanated from it. I remember reflecting that there are many sound vibrations in space.

Soon after that experience, I was in London listening to a talk that Bapak was giving. He was speaking about the universe and saying that everything reflected a sound and that the sound of the Earth was like a swarm of bees. On hearing this, tears flooded my eyes.

He would often say to us, "I don't tell you to eat sugar, but when I see that you have had the experience of its taste, I say, 'that's called sweet'."

Edgar and the mystery of the bad odour

From the observations I gained through living with my darling life partner, I could say that sexual union and birth are very similar to a holy gateway, the passage from one world to another. The imagery of this can be seen when one experiences the conception of the seed of a child and then how, nine months later, this child is born. But in my experience, it is also a gateway to the far beyond of this world, as we know it in the ordinary sense of the word. It is the gateway to the immaterial world where consciousness can travel and evolve back towards its source of existence.

The story I am going to tell you now is a strange story, because it bridges this real physical world to what most people would call an imaginary world. I call it the world beyond, that one only sees with spiritual eyes.

Our close friend, Lambert Gibbs, visited my shop one day to share with me something that was really bothering him. Lambert and his family had recently sold the beautiful house that he built in the middle of the forest near Forest Row, not far from Crowborough in East Sussex. He had then bought an impressive property built by the Regency English architect Decimus Burton on the Calverley Park Crescent estate, right in the centre of Tunbridge Wells.

Sometime in the 50s, the large stone property had been turned into three flats. Lambert's aim was to bring it back to its original grandeur, and modernise the toilets, bathrooms and kitchens with the latest technology. He had decided to move his family into the basement flat while the transformations took place. The steep incline on which the house was built allowed the lower flat to receive much daylight, making it a most pleasant space in which to live.

Lambert was an excellent storyteller and described a strange situation that he and his wife Maria had found themselves in. Since they moved into the flat, they could not help but notice an awful smell as they walked down the wooden staircase that rested against the outer wall of their bedroom. Further, he went on to explain, since they had moved into the bedroom, and although they pulled the thick curtains over the single window, his wife would not undress with the light on, even though in the past she would have done. Lambert had questioned her about it and she had replied that she did not quite know why but felt most uncomfortable. He added too that, for the same reasons, they had not had sex together since they moved into the bedroom.

He then asked me if I would join him in doing a 'clearing' latihan in the bedroom and I agreed. It was decided that I would come after closing my shop at 6pm that day.

I entered their flat, shouted a loud hello and started slowly to walk down the creaky wooden staircase. Halfway down I noticed a most unbearable stench. Was it a dead rat or cat? To make such a stink it must be something pretty big and pretty rotten, I thought.

"Can you smell it, Léonard?" Lambert asked, and I nodded in confirmation. I asked about a dead rat, but Lambert said he had looked everywhere under the stairs and had found no dead animal. We entered their bedroom and I recognised the same unpleasant odour.

I went in first. To my immediate left was the large double bed, then a space with a table and chair. On the centre of the wall to the left was a window with a thick velvet curtain. The wall opposite was entirely covered by a built-in wardrobe with rather nice period doors. To the right was a small door that led to the bathroom. We both took off our shoes as is customary before latihan and stood quietly, preparing ourselves inwardly for the training. I was standing at the foot of their bed while Lambert was in the corner near the bathroom.

We started the latihan and both immediately had a strong receiving. Lambert was singing loudly, almost rowdily; I was making strange sounds and singing some rather sombre melodies that came spontaneously. I moved to the left part of the room near the corner where there was a pair of cupboard doors, and after some time became conscious that there was a presence in the cupboard. I opened my inner eye and to my amazement saw a crippled old man sitting in a Victorian wheelchair.

His untidy thin white hair had probably at one time been fair. The unshaven skin of his face was stretched over its bony structure, showing prominent cheekbones; his blue eyes were sunken and his toothless mouth gave me a faint smile. His clothes were very dirty and hanging off his thin body. His knobbly hands gripped the arms of the wheelchair; he looked up at me and our eyes met. I inwardly heard his shaky voice say, "I have been waiting for you to come. I need to start this spiritual thing you're doing."

"What's your Christian name?" I asked him.

"Edgar!" he replied, giving me a large grin.

While this short, silent conversation was going on, my friend's consciousness was completely absorbed by his loud latihan. I went up close to him and said quietly, "Lambert, sorry to disturb you like this, but is it okay if we do an opening now?"

"What? An opening? But who?" answered Lambert as, startled, he opened his gentle blue eyes to look at me.

"Edgar. He is in the cupboard at the bottom of your bed," I said as seriously as I could manage, holding back my amusement at this most unusual situation. I smiled and explained what I had just witnessed and Lambert agreed that we should proceed with Edgar's request.

We stood by the cupboard, I closed my eyes and said the words we usually say before a person starts their first spiritual training. Then we started our latihan together with Edgar. Agreeably, I found that my inner eyes had reconnected to the old Victorian man in the cupboard who was now receiving his own latihan. There was something extremely funny about the situation and I started laughing. The laughter was not mocking but rather came from an extremely happy state, and it seemed to become contagious as I heard Lambert's loud voice exploding into laughter as well.

So the latihan had become a mix of laughing and singing with terrific joy and lightness. I looked at Edgar and realised that he was laughing too, and as his waves of laughter came and went, he rose a little higher and it seemed that the chair rose with him, which made the whole thing even funnier.

After some time, both Lambert's and my latihan stopped. Edgar had risen and disappeared in lightness and happiness. We looked at each other and noticed that the unpleasant smell had completely gone. We exchanged thoughts about what had just happened and came to the conclusion that the smell was Edgar's way of bringing his presence to our attention. The bad odour around the staircase had disappeared as well and later on Lambert told me that Maria was again able to undress in the bedroom with the light on, and that they were now able to come together intimately as they had always done before.

The departure of my grandmother GG

Our children's great-grandmother GG came to visit us, staying in a private nursing home in Tunbridge Wells. She wanted to be close to her great-grandchildren and had also asked Mélinda if she could share the latihan experience with her. My mother had come from the south of France especially to be with us and to see her Mum on the same occasion. I felt deep gratitude that my mother, grandmother and wife could do latihan together, as it weaved between us a common awareness of the closeness of our souls. I felt gratitude also that my brother, sister, two uncles and a cousin had been able to have the latihan experience too. After two weeks of pleasant family gatherings held at our home, my mother returned to Cannes to attend to her small lampshade business.

GG, Laura and Jean in 1962

One Saturday night in late June, we were having a party

with some friends at our house in Frant Road. At around midnight, my feelings became filled with the presence of my grandmother. It was so clear and strong that I said to Mélinda: "It may sound completely crazy at this time of the night, but I feel I must go and see GG right away."

I left the party, cigarette smoke and loud music to enter the silent darkness of the early summer's moonless night. Pushed by a feeling of urgency, I rapidly walked towards London Road where the nursing home was situated.

The white-painted Regency building showed no light, except a faint one from behind the curtains of the basement kitchen. A flight of five stone steps led up to the columned porch of the main entrance door. I found it closed and decided not to ring the bell, in view of the time, but to try and climb into my grandmother's room through her sash window. I saw that the top of her window was slightly open and climbed across the short distance from the porch. Then I slowly pushed the window down enough for me to climb over it and land silently in my grandmother's bedroom.

There was enough light, coming from the town's orange street lights, for me to see around the bedroom. GG's bed was against the right wall, she had her back turned away from the window. I came up close to her and said in a very soft low voice, "GG, it's me, Léonard. I felt that you were not well, so I came to see you."

I knelt on the floor close to the head of the bed, kissed her forehead, and found her hand, which I held cosily between my own. "It's good you are here. How did you know? Just stay by me."

I snuggled closer to her. "Yes, like that ..." she said. "I don't mind that I am going to die; in fact I have been waiting for this moment since Edward left me, over 15 years ago now ... But I don't want to become a cripple and have to depend on others to look after me," she muttered in a long breath.

"Would you like me to fetch a doctor, GG? Or a priest?" I suggested wrongly, thinking it was what she might have needed.

"No! Neither of them, just you stay next to me," she ordered in a whisper.

I was aware that she was inwardly agitated. Although her body lay motionless, her mind was active and her feelings disturbed. I had been next to people dying on two occasions before and had found that the way to be was completely to let go and stay close to the latihan. While still holding her hand, I went into a deep peaceful receptive state and allowed the latihan to flow.

In my field of awareness, I felt the universe surrounding us and heard melodic sounds that seemed to come from somewhere in its immensity. The musical vibrations reached my vocal chords and we listened together to the soothing and reassuring music that my throat was offering. As the singing went on, my grandmother's breathing became quieter and more regular; we were now together in a space of complete peace where anxiety had no place.

It must have been an hour or more when she suddenly said: "I want to pee, can you help me? I have to turn round; the chamber pot is on the other side under the bed, thank you."

It was painful and difficult for her to move, as her intestines had not been functioning properly for many days and her tummy was enormously blown out, so with much effort I lifted her on to the chamber pot. We managed, and after a while, she made a slight affirmative grunt which I understood as meaning: "I've finished!"

I then settled her back carefully into her bed, this time on her right side facing the window. I pulled round the narrow mahogany armchair that stood next to the bedside table and sat in it. She stretched out her tiny, frail, shaky hand and rested her cool, dry palm against mine. I reconnected to my peaceful inner state from where flowed harmonious melodic sounds. GG seemed to be listening, her eyes closed, her wrinkled lips showing a slight smile. We stayed like this for quite some time until suddenly she flickered her eyes open and murmured, "Léonard?"

"Yes GG, I'm here next to you," I responded.

"Could you put some make-up on my cheeks and lips? Tidy my

hair? Make me look pretty, and don't forget a sprinkle of my perfume. You'll find everything just there, on the bedside table."

I did as she asked: on her dry flaky lips I delicately painted the pale pink lipstick, brushed her long hair and tidied it up as best I could, carefully powdered her still-taut, round cheeks and her well-shaped chin.

"Voilà, Madame, tu es très, très belle à présent."

She liked hearing me talk French to her. Her face showed signs of effort and pain as she wriggled herself back into a comfortable position. With her right hand she took mine again, then looked at me absently. After some time, she gave my hand three gentle squeezes in rapid succession as if to say, "I am going now."

I looked into her watery, shrunken eyes suddenly lit by a light that seem to come from inside. All my attention was now directed to the pale pinky-blue irises. There I witnessed projecting out the film of her life unravelling rapidly in reverse, all the feeling parts of her existence on Earth right up to her birth. I observed, through the intensity of their expressions, a rapid succession of the distinct emotions that she had experienced during her long life: amazement, fear, tenderness, anger, disapproval, joy, love, ecstasy, questioning, stillness, sorrow, hope, approval, pain, acceptance. Then descended, like a delicate sweet scent, a peaceful stillness, which invaded gracefully the room. My hand detected imperceptibly two slight squeezes as if she was saying now, "Au revoir."

I experienced a very, very fine musical vibration, starting near my feet and rising through my body ... As it reached my chest, throat and head I uttered loudly to my great surprise the equivalent in Arabic of "God is great!"

The ethereal musical vibration rose, taking my awareness with her, leaving my body behind. I went into an immaterial space, wide and peaceful. I understood at that moment that her soul had left her body and was now free to rise on its way to another reality.

I opened my eyes, which had been closed during these last few minutes, to see my grandmother's body cooling and stiffening in spasmodic jerks. The delicate hand that I had been holding was already going cold and I noticed large violet plaques developing under her paper thin skin. Her eyes were now static, staring expressionless.

I rose up slowly, crossed her hands on to the crest of her chest and drew down her parchment eyelids with the palm of my hand as if I was closing the shutters of her windows, bringing privacy into the space that only belonged to her.

My nostrils detected a heavenly smell in the room, and I felt serene peace in my being as I rearranged GG's appearance, knowing how important it was for her always to leave a good impression of herself. I told the night nurse who was rather surprised by my presence in the building that my grandmother had died peacefully, and walked briskly back to our house in the cool morning air.

All the lights were off at home, the party was well over and my family was in the depths of sleep. It did not feel right for me to go straight up to bed, so I walked into our sitting room to do a latihan. It was a good-sized room, faintly lit by the yellowish street lights that filtered through the bay windows where stood a well-worn, comfortable sofa strewn with soft flowery cushions.

Facing the large windows, I stood in the middle of the room, abandoned my heart and mind, thoughts and feelings and placed my awareness in my inner space where neither plus nor minus exist, where there is just consciousness in stillness.

After a short time, I strongly felt an imposing presence to my left. I turned towards the sofa and to my complete surprise, saw my grandfather Edward, who had died 15 years before, sitting there looking at me angrily. Although I had I feared my granddad as a child, I liked him very much and was pleased to see him in our house. But I could see he was disturbed by finding himself in my sitting room! The scene was so ludicrous that I burst into laughter, and the more I laughed, the funnier I found it, as I started to walk round the sofa. Soon grandpa was laughing too. His enormous moustache and heavy thick eyebrows were shaking up and down, moved by the waves of his relaxed laughter.

We were now both in fits, the whole thing was so strange yet amusing. I was facing him, still laughing, and noticed that in his sitting position he was slowly rising up out of the sofa in the direction of the sky. My grandfather laughed until he came out of my inner sight and disappeared into his own space. I felt that he had come to find the spiritual connection, which freed him so he could continue on his journey. I felt tremendously light and happy and prepared for bed.

As I slipped quietly to snuggle under the weightless duvet, Mélinda, coming out of her sleep, mumbled, hardly pronouncing the words: "She hasn't died, has she?"

"Yes, she has, an hour and a half ago."

And before I could share with her what I had just experienced, a powerful sobbing shook her whole being. I embraced her and held her close to me while she allowed her sorrow to flow out. Inwardly I was not sad, and although Mélinda was still heavy in her tears, I felt detached and light.

After some time, I was quite bewildered when I felt an erection developing slowly, vigorously and irrevocably. And I thought to myself, "Come on Léonard! You are a strange fellow, now is not the time for this. Your grandmother has just died and there you are with a flaming erection!"

I didn't know what to do with it as it was bringing down my awareness to its lively need. I went quiet inside and tentatively asked my soul, "Should I follow this impulse?"

The reply was immediate: "Yes, it is important, do follow it."

Close against each other, our cheeks united in the wet of the salty tears that were still flowing, I whispered into Mélinda's ear, "Darling? You're going to think that I am completely crazy, but I feel we must come together."

"What ... now?" she exclaimed almost indignantly, a pinch of desperation in her voice. Then, she abandoned herself for the natural process to take place, there was no resistance, no questioning, we just followed the fulfilment of this unusual journey.

Soon we were taken over by a serene life rhythm that unified us into one feeling. Away from imagination, earthly passions and desires, my awareness grew all around me in a three-dimensional expansion. Consciousness had grown now beyond the house, out and up; I felt the Earth below and directed my attention up towards the Milky Way. As the height of the physical moment came in a burst of powerful energy, I became aware that the spirits of my grandfather and grandmother were being boosted up, through the Milky Way, of which the star-illuminated shape resembled that of a vagina. Mélinda was now blissfully sleeping, so I turned around and let myself float away into the currents of my reverie. Reflecting some time later on this experience, the thought came to my mind: "We come into this world through the gate of the material/physical vagina, we also go back out of this world into the other, through the spiritual vagina."

Now, of course, when it comes to sharing these spiritual experiences, I am obliged to use ordinary language and analogies that are only an attempt to give an idea of the spiritual reality I am trying to share.

A few days later the funeral reception was held in our house. The whole family was present and a feeling of lightness and joy pervaded throughout the day. As had been her wish, GG was cremated at Tunbridge Wells crematorium, just a few minutes up the road from Number 19; her ashes were later scattered on the Derbyshire moors as Edward's had been before.

Connecting to the source of existence

Now I am taking you to the Pacific coast of California some 45 years later. Mélinda and I had gone there to attend the openings of two exhibitions of my paintings: one at the University of the CIIS centre in San Francisco, the other in a large private house of a friend and art collector.

One day, Mélinda and I went to the house of Emmanuel Williams, a friend who lived in the delightful small town of Pacifica. Emmanuel and I had decided to do the latihan together when the telephone rang. My friend picked up the phone and handed it to me.

"It's for you, Léonard ... from England."

It was Sebastian, the partner of our youngest daughter Pamela (previously named Marianna) who had recently given birth to their third child; he had named the newborn Lucas.

"Léonard, our baby is not well. Pamela feels that the reason is that the name Lucas is not appropriate for the child. Could you possibly do a test to find the correct one?"

I accepted and asked Emmanuel if he would join me in the testing, but first suggested we did a short latihan. He agreed, we both stood up, relaxed completely and let the latihan flow ...

When I reached the place within myself where there is emptiness yet full consciousness, I felt I was being carried into outer space where my attention was drawn by sounds that came from far away on a delicate, sweet-scented breeze – they seemed to come from a distant galaxy. I turned my face into the current, breathed in fully the delicate scent, while listening to the melodious high-notes of trumpets and bells, making a harmonious mix of sounds. Then I opened my inner eyes.

My attention was drawn by a presence that came from the depth of the universe where I could distinguish a nebula that was slowly swirling round as I came towards it. I was captivated by the unusual tumbling of colours, mostly from pale yellows and soft orange cloudy shapes, which stood out on a dark grey and violet background. I felt the content and qualities of a soul that expressed extreme loving gentleness together with an ancient maturity.

"Melvin!"

I heard distinctly the name that resonated in my chest as it enrobed the presence of the gentle soul of our grandchild. Emmanuel and I concluded our latihan at that moment.

I told him what I had just experienced and that I had heard clearly the name Melvin. So I suggested to him that we should test together whether my receiving of the name was correct. We both felt that it was.

Sebastian and Pamela accepted the new name. They called their son 'Melvin' and he soon stopped crying, found his appetite, slept better and regained his health.

To conclude this story about our grandson, I will share this moving anecdote. Each year it's a family tradition to send self-made Christmas cards to each other and, this year, our daughter Pamela had sent us two printed cards beautifully designed by her boys Ciaran and Melvin. Ciaran's card represented the holy family cut out in black, set on a deep blue sky background. I looked at it for some time, admiring the composition.

When I came to look at Melvin's card a shiver went down my spine and my feelings were projected back eight years to when I'd had the powerful experience about Melvin's name.

Just off centre on the card, a yellow bell shape was floating on a deep blue starry sky. Bands of bright colours – green, deep blue, vermillion, pale blue, and brilliant red –vibrated out like an aura. A thin line of sparkly diamonds surrounded the bell shape, separating it from an evolving nebulous cloud made up of a gentle warm grey moving into violet, then black, then to an orange that finalised the cloud back on to the starry blue sky.

The bright colours surrounding the yellow bell were, to me, expressing Melvin in action on Earth. The unusual colours of the nebulous cloud were the same ones I had seen when I did the latihan in Pacifica. I mentioned the sounds ... the high tingling of bells mixed with distant trumpets that were symbolised by the colourful shapes echoing out of the yellow bell, like ripples on a lake.

I was suddenly moved deeply by an immense feeling of gratitude towards the Creator, that I had been able to experience and be shown a fraction of a spiritual perspective that related to my grandson.

Chapter 4

The effects of the latihan on the family's daily life

An accident helps us move north

I will now take you back to the spring of 1960, when Jean and I were enjoying our new married life in Vallauris. I was painting and feeling greatly inspired. I also worked in a local pottery, decorating, pots to earn money to pay for our daily food and the rent of the charming, tiny stone house we lived in. It was set in terraced orange groves and from its windows we could see the mimosa hills in the distance set against the blue sea beyond.

Jean had become pregnant and it completely changed the dynamics of our relationship. My love for her swelled forward; I became aware constantly of a new spiritual dimension within our cosy world. The presence of the forming embryo, its being-ness, made us feel that we had become a family unit and we were both filled with joy at anticipation of the birth. I noticed a metamorphosis in Jean; she was now pulled irresistibly by the presence of a baby in a pram, or a shop displaying babies' clothes, or by other pregnant women. There was a faint smile of satisfaction on her face when we came into close contact with children. The natural process of motherhood had taken place in her and I could not help but be in great admiration before this incredible, magical phenomenon.

In some way, life on the Côte d'Azur was almost too easy. Jean's pregnancy, my painting, the latihan sessions in Nice, and the very little money we needed to survive, made me feel that something in us was going to sleep. The wish to make a place for creative success in the world was numbed by this seemingly heavenly life. I felt I needed more stimulus for my heart and mind, and we both agreed that if the

Jean and Léonard in Cannes

occasion presented itself, we would move to Paris. Now, in retrospect, I understand that the desire to move, although completely irrational on the material plane as we had just enough to live on and certainly not enough to pay for the train journey or the move, came from a deeper place than our hearts and minds.

Strangely enough, soon after experiencing the feeling of wanting to move north, something completely unexpected happened ...

Jean was now three months pregnant, and did not feel like making the long journeys on the scooter to Nice twice a week any more. I too found that I had some difficulty in separating myself from our new romantic nest for any length of time. But, on a latihan day one late afternoon, I pulled myself away. Moved by the obligation to be present at the spiritual training in Nice, I jumped on to my scooter and went off hurriedly for the long drive to the Salle Marie Christine. Some five minutes later, I looked for my watch to realise that I had not put it on. Annoyed at myself, I turned around and drove back to the house.

"Back already?" Jean said, surprised by my unexpected return.

"Yes, I've forgotten my watch," I answered in one breath as I rushed to grab the watch and head out again on the Lambretta.

Now it was dusk; I was going down the hill as fast as my scooter would take me, and my head was busy with thoughts of being late to the latihan. The road was flanked by high stone walls where there was no pavement; as I came round a sharp blind bend, a car with no lights or indicators was reversing from the inside of the curve directly cutting into my path.

There was no time to break, and as I tried to slip through the space between the back of the car and the high wall, my right handlebar hit the backlight cover of the car violently, breaking my little finger and sending me flying over the boot and down the road for some 30 metres. The Lambretta followed, gliding on its side a few metres behind me. I was shaken and trembling all over as I got up to assess the damage.

After sorting out the insurance details with the Swiss owner of the car, he kindly ran to the nearest café to call for an ambulance. I was taken to Antibes Hospital where the doctors insisted that I should stay the night in case I had brain damage. From the hospital I managed to ring up somebody in Vallauris to go and tell Jean and my mother of the accident and that I would be back the next day.

The doctors did the necessary examination, placed my little finger in a splint and immobilised my forearm in a sling. I remember feeling how strange life was: first forgetting my watch, then going back to fetch it, then the accident and now in a hospital bed with bruises and a broken finger. At the time I did not know the meaning of this nor the reasons for it ... Was it just an accident? But why?

I arrived back home at noon the next day, limping and feeling sore all over especially inside my tightly bandaged little finger. The Swiss insurance company that covered the car responsible for the accident wrote to me some weeks later. They explained that the little finger was one of the most painful parts of the body and as I was right-handed it would prevent me from working. We received maximum compensation, which I promptly accepted and with the money we were able to prepare for our move to Paris.

Moving to Paris

In September 1960 we left for the big city. The journey was smooth and we moved into the same flat that I had rented as a student at Paul Colin's art school some years before (see my previous book *Chestnuts, Walnuts and Goat Cheese* for more details about my student days). The small apartment was on the seventh floor on rue Cardinet; a long climb that wasn't so easy for Jean now that she was seven months pregnant.

There was much to do, as we had to create a source of income to survive. Paris certainly was more money-demanding than the simple life we had enjoyed on the Côte d'Azur. Rapidly we organised our batik scarf and clothing business from the tiny kitchen of the miniscule flat. We made a whole pile of attractive large silk scarves that I took round to the chic shops of the city to sell. We had some positive feedback and started a small business.

Unfortunately, another visit to the military was necessary. Now it was to be in Vincennes, near Paris, and I was feeling quite nervous about having to fast again so as to avoid going to the Algerian war to fight. The thought of leaving my pregnant wife behind gave me the incentive and determination to do my best to make myself as unsoldier like as possible. I decided to start the fast 10 days before actually receiving the official military call.

Fasting in the big city was not as easy as on the warm Côte d'Azur. Somehow the city seemed to demand more determination, power and money simply to survive in its turbulence. Through selling our silk scarves, I had befriended the owner of a fashion shop on the Champs Elysées. He was called Mr Ray and he gave me the go-ahead to redesign and redecorate his whole shop window that gave on to the famous wide avenue. This was an enormous project for a man who was fasting and who had never done this kind of work before. But, pushed by a survival instinct, a wind of inspiration blew into my creativity; I crystallised it into a few sketches and presented my design to Mr Ray. On seeing my proposition he exploded with enthusiasm: "Brilliant! Start as soon as you can; I agree, my shop needs a complete revamp."

He kindly suggested that I turn the cellar of his shop into a small workshop. I chose to use 4cm thick rough planks of burr sycamore wood. Keeping the apparent irregularities of the bark on the edges of the sycamore planks, I planed smooth the rough surfaces by hand, then sandpapered to give them a silky smooth finish that I finally waxed and polished. It was a tremendously hard physical work with the primitive tools that I possessed, and twice I fainted in the overheated cellar.

It was paradoxical how Mr Ray expressed his appreciation of my work each day by offering me a large expensive box of handmade chocolates. I would take the precious tempting present back to Jean in the evening, and we would laugh together about it while she ate the chocolates.

"You know, Mr Lassalle? You really intrigue me," Mr Ray once said in a suspicious voice. "I have never seen you eat any of the chocolates I have been offering you. Furthermore, every time I have invited you to lunch you have found a valid excuse not to come. You are truly an extraordinarily unusual young man," he exclaimed, expressing his perplexity by raising high his eyebrows.

Certainly I would have not told him the reason for my strange behaviour, as nobody except Jean and my mother knew why I was fasting. As well, Mr Ray was trying to arrange a meeting to introduce me to a close friend of his – a famous French general who was greatly interested in the arts, especially painting. "I will arrange a supper with him so that we can talk about the wonderful subject of art; you know, he is a keen promoter of the arts and delights in helping young artists," Mr Ray suggested. However attractive the proposition, I was not in the right frame of mind or body to be sitting at a banquet next to a general, even if he was a promoter of the arts.

It took me a month to finish the shop window and it was a success. In 1960 the windows of Paris fashion shops had a certain classicism, so the contrast between the silky wood, rough bark and fine clothes made its impression. Sales of Mr Ray's clothing business took off, and he was most satisfied.

Finally getting free of the military

During this time of fasting I had to stop going to the latihan, as I had become too hypersensitive and acutely receptive to how others felt and thought. I noticed many states of awareness in my being that, due to the fast, were different from when I had been eating three regular meals a day. As the fast extended from days into weeks, I became aware of the hidden powers of the vegetable world that normally we take in daily through eating, smoking and drinking.

How necessary they are to give us the energy we need, yet how harmful they can be when taken in an unreasonable amount. These forces seem always to want more, as if our passions become involved with them and open the way for them to become the rulers of the decisions made inside our being.

I remember one early morning lying in bed awake, the half-open window of our seventh floor bedroom letting in a wonderful odour ... of a crusty French baguette, which through my sensitive nostrils rowdily invaded the quiet inner state I was in, like a marching army would invade a peaceful country. I shot out of bed and went to the window, put both hands on the wooden handrail and breathed in deeply. It was magnificent, the appetising smell transforming itself into a wide field of wheat slowly swaying in a light breeze under a deep blue sky ... And now the marching army had penetrated into my wants and desires, the cup of coffee with milk, butter and marmalade joined in.

The pull to go downstairs became tremendously powerful and I visualised myself flying down the staircase, entering the baker's shop and even hearing the bell of the door ringing as I rushed in. My breathing was now faster, and imperceptible shaking took over my body as a hot burning feeling spread through my chest. Horrified, I looked at Jean who was still fast asleep in our small double bed and I suddenly remembered why I had been fasting: the baby to come, the war in Algeria, getting out of the army ... Abandoning the dining room of my inner castle that the invading vegetable force had overtaken, I breathed in deeply to let go completely of my starving ego, and slowly crept back into my awake neutral inner state.

The day before the recruiting appointment with the army doctors, which would decide whether or not I would be healthy enough to become a soldier, I decided to lose a few more grams to be on the safe side by having a steam bath in the sauna in the rue de Courcelles.

The sauna was run by two charming effeminate guys, dressed in white towelling gowns. I explained that I wanted to lose a little weight. Looking surprised after rapidly weighing me on the old-fashioned scales, the smaller of the two men said in a high-pitched voice, "Would you come this way please? " The pitch-pine panelled room smelt of aromatic herbs and oils; it was hot and humid and I chose to sit on the higher slatted bank to obtain maximum effect. I don't know how long I was there, maybe half an hour, when suddenly I became aware that my heart was doing unusual things and that it was beating extremely slowly and irregularly. I heard a voice coming from far inside, "Time is up, time to go back into the world of duality, go back into your body and go back to the flat where Jean and the baby are waiting for you."

As I opened my eyes, they fell on the little window in the door. The man was waving his hand asking me to come out. It took me a few instants to inhabit my fragile body again and, wrapping the wet sweaty towel around, I struggled to the door. The cooler air of the dressing room helped me reintegrate myself into my worldly responsibilities.

Before I paid for the session I went back on the scales: a further 600 grams had melted away.

The next morning I woke up early, as I had to be at Vincennes military camp by 9am. Once there, we went through the process that I now knew well. Standing in just our underwear in front of the doctors who were examining our military medical papers, I had a strong feeling that this time they would decide to let me go for good.

I overheard the army doctor saying in the ear of the general who was sitting next to him: "This Buchenwald character will never get fatter. He has lost even more weight since last year. He is like a walking ghost!" A ray of sunshine invaded my chest, however awful these words might have been, they soothed me, and I felt that the loss of that 600g had given the final push. When I was handed my military book sometime later, I was delighted to read across the front page in two large, red letters: RD, meaning 'declared unfit for service in the army'.

Although it was well into autumn, walking down the street and looking for a place to break my long fast I felt as if spring had come. I came to a café and sat on the terrace where I ordered a large milky coffee and a Gruyère baguette sandwich. The waiter arrived with the order which he put down with reverence in front of me saying, "Here we are sir, bon appétit," not being aware, of course, of the explosive dormant powers that he was delivering me in this simple cup of coffee and sandwich.

After some time, I decided to wet my lips on the edge of the cup of the frothy milky coffee... The gates were now unlocking themselves and I saw in myself a crowd of little snickering devils all chatting excitedly to each other, while moving in with all their belongings to inhabit me again; they looked happy enough to return home after three weeks forced hibernation.

During the fast, my state of consciousness had become deep and wide. Now as I chewed the sandwich with great physical difficulty – nevertheless enjoying immensely the mix of different tastes – it had the effect of bringing me back into a narrower state of consciousness; more local, more in my body sitting on my chair by the tripod table. It was as if I had walked down an invisible ladder joining one higher, fine ethereal world to another somehow coarser, where the life forces were highly active, interplaying each other at great speed in their relative realities.

My jaw bones, muscles and teeth were beginning to hurt from the chewing, the animal and vegetable energies I was swallowing were beginning to reactivate themselves in my body and I felt my physical strength slowly coming back. I also noticed how different my looking was now that I had taken in some food. When I first sat down at the table, I had been distantly aware of a young lady absorbed in a book a few tables away. Now, in my regained earthliness, irresistibly I had turned my head in her direction and my earthly eyes had taken in the beauty of her delicate features. She must have felt disturbed by the energy of my intense stare as she lifted her head slowly and looked at me without a smile, as if to say,

"Stop looking at me like that!"

I realised that I had trespassed into her space and rapidly turn my head away.

"Hey, what am I doing in this place sipping coffee and looking at girls, I must be crazy," I thought. Jean appeared in my feelings; I saw that she was waiting impatiently for me, longing to know the result of my visit to the military. I rode back on my Lambretta as if I was flying like a bird through the streets of Paris, feeling high and happy to have put the military situation behind me now; knowing I would not have to go to war but would stay constantly close to my wife and child to be.

In search of an income and a place to live

After our 1960 Christmas and New Year visit to the UK, we went back to Paris. We had lost our flat in rue Cardinet and our close friends, Richard and Arifah Togonal, kindly offered us a dark small room in a corner of their ground floor flat. At the time I had no work and found myself desperately short of money, so I decided to go see Toby and my sister Sylvette who had just moved into a small attic flat in the rue Notre Dame de Lorette.

The walk took an hour and a half along the boulevard. I climbed the five flights of stairs to the flat only to find that they were not there. I waited for an hour but to no avail, so decided to walk back, feeling a little sorry for myself. As I passed the Place Clichy, I saw a large five franc coin some distance away on the pavement. I was about to pick it up when a young man with his girlfriend coming from the opposite direction rapidly bent down before me, grabbed the coin which he tossed up in the air and asked, while turning around to his companion, "Heads or tails?"

"How could I miss such an occasion when I could have brought back some bread to my family?" I wondered as I walked on, hearing the young couple's laughter in the background.

A little later, as I walked round the corner into our street, I saw an elderly tramp sitting on some newspapers. He looked at me with sparkling but sunken blue eyes; his face was weathered, a greyish beard surrounded his kind looks. I went up to him and as I was about to show him that I had no money by pulling both empty pockets out of my trousers, he drew out his arm, opened his hand in which was a glittering five franc coin. "Here, take it!" he uttered in a raucous voice.

Surprised, I asked as I took the coin, "Oh thank you, but how on earth did you know that I am desperately broke?"

"It's easy," he replied, beaming with a practically toothless smile, "when looking at your face, it is so apparent!"

It was no easy matter to be living in Paris with a young child and no money whatsoever; I took on different odd jobs, including selling newspapers door-to-door. We could no longer stay at the Togonals, we had already been there three weeks. A couple of friends, Mr and Mrs Jacques Fournot, whom I had met at the latihan one evening, had kindly offered: "If you'd like, Léonard, we have a property in Champigny sur Marne where my parents live; there is there an old coach house with two maids' rooms above. You can have it free of rent and maybe you could keep an eye on my aged parents. But I warn you! There is no water, no kitchen and the toilets are primitive and downstairs in the garden."

We took the offer and moved into the coach house. We got on very well with Jacques' parents. His father had been a sailor, his mother a meticulous housewife and very good cook. A high flint wall surrounded the property which included an extensive vegetable garden perfectly kept by Maurice who, although 80 years of age, was still a very enthusiastic gardener. Jean would take Joanna, now called Laura, for walks along the Marne River or to shop at the vast Champigny market. I rapidly installed water into a tiny adjacent room that we called 'the kitchen' and fixed a sink with a drain. Installing butane gas enabled us to cook and have hot water. The coach house rapidly became our cosy little nest. I felt that my family was safe and could go off to Paris on my Lambretta in search of work.

Challenging myself

It wasn't long before a close friend of ours from England, called Dorothy, came to visit us in our new lodgings. It was on a Friday, I remember she had said to me as we were discussing how difficult it was to earn a living: "But Léonard, you speak English and French fluently, don't you?"

I agreed.

"Well, why don't you do simultaneous translating for international congresses? It's well paid, you know." She went on speaking positively: "It just happens that last night, a very close friend of mine called Philip, who is a professional simultaneous translator, told me that he had a big problem: for family reasons he is obliged to go back urgently to England tomorrow and cannot honour an important job next week. He gave me the number of the agency in case I knew someone who could help him out."

She went on as she felt my hesitation, "You might feel nervous about the thought of doing it, but why don't you give it a try?" She looked through her handbag and pulled out a squashed packet of Benson & Hedges cigarettes on which was scribbled a telephone number.

Feeling ill at ease at the thought of taking on such a job, I complained, "But I've never done this kind of work before! I have no idea how to go about it."

"Never mind," she replied, "you could give it a try. Here is the number of his agency, go and see them tomorrow morning."

At 10am next day I walked into the Paris office. The secretary welcomed me and rapidly told me what the job entailed: it was to do simultaneous translating in French English/English French for one week at the Palais des Congrés; the subjects would be of a scientific nature. After asking me if I had done it before and being satisfied by my lies, she read in French one of the texts that was going to be dealt with at the Congress, while simultaneously I translated it into English.

I have to say that I had never before in my life sold myself on lies and had obviously managed to hide my great embarrassment. Surprised to see her apparent satisfaction at having found a replacement translator for the coming Monday, she said, "Very good, this is fine, you'll start at 8.30am on Monday. Do not be late as the boss wants to meet you before."

I left the translating agency with a thick wad of scientific papers that were to be discussed during that week and a chest full of very mixed feelings. Happy at the prospect of having a job earning £60 per day, which in those days was an extremely good income. Yet nervous at the thought of having to translate subjects about which I knew nothing. How was I going to cope with this new situation? How was I going to translate all these scientific terms? I remember thinking as I drove home on my Lambretta, "Léonard, what on earth have you got yourself into? You are crazy, and all this on lies too... It is completely irrational."

I spent Saturday afternoon and all Sunday studying the new scientific language, taking notes, looking up unknown words in a dictionary and trying to memorise them. Jean felt my stress building up; she had not seen me like this before and she was good at reassuring me that everything would work out all right.

I woke up early on that crucial Monday and arrived in good time at the Palais des Congrés. The English, German and Italian translators each had a cabin of their own overlooking an immense conference hall. Each attendee down below would wear earphones and could manipulate a dial on a small black receiver to find the wavelength that corresponded to their native tongues. The boss of the agency was a Frenchman and he rapidly presented me to a tall, lanky, agitated American called Andy. "You will work together as a team, half an hour each in relays. This will be your cabin." Then he left. Looking at my watch, I saw we had five minutes before starting and, having no idea how to kick off, I offered a Gauloise cigarette to Andy and suggested hesitantly, "Would you like to start first, Andy?" I thought that, as he was a professional, he could teach me a lot if I could watch him for the first half hour.

"That's funny, I was just going to suggest the same thing to you, Léonard, why don't you start first?" replied Andy with a pronounced Californian accent. I had not planned for such a strange situation to develop just before the start of the conference!

"Actually, Andy, I'm dying to go to the loo and they're about to start... Please take over, I won't be long." I felt justified, as my nervousness created by the anticipation of starting first had induced in me an urgent need to urinate. Coming out of the toilets, I noticed that the lights of the Congress Hall had been dimmed, the stage lit and a French-speaking scientist was talking standing by a microphone. Intrigued to see how Andy was doing, I crept silently into the English translator's cabin and sat down.

Was it my sudden presence that disturbed him? Or was this his usual way of working? When I put on the earphones, I realised that his translation was not really coherent. He seemed to have lost track; the words he was sending down the microphone did not link up together properly. And suddenly, to my amazement, he started to make noises similar to a radio crackling, then making a very loud and high-pitched continuous sound, then crackling sounds again ...

I looked down at the audience to see all the English-speaking scientists looking at the dials on their receivers in search of a better wavelength. It was highly comical and I could not keep my laughter in. My hand covered my mouth to dampen my giggles but the tension was so immense that my whole body was shaking, the situation was ludicrously funny.

Andy looked at me in absolute fury as if I was the cause of this trouble. Not being able to stop my laughter, which had now become extremely painful, I got up and left the cabin. Once outside, to recover some sanity, I breathed in deeply several times to quiet myself. When I felt completely relaxed, a voice that I recognised from the rare occasions it had come when I was in extreme circumstances, said clearly, "Go to the place within your inner self where there is stillness and follow what comes."

Immediately on hearing this reassuring voice, I felt as if I had been dressed in a garment of peace, my being quietened, all my fears vanished and I was now looking forward to starting the simultaneous translating. I walked into the cabin and sat next to Andy, who sustained a long icy stare at me as he handed over the microphone. He was obviously still furious with me for having laughed when doing his funny tricks. Now, looking at me arrogantly, he put a Camel cigarette in his mouth and without lighting it, walked out.

Still connected closely to my inner feelings, I waited attentively for the voice of the next speaker from the floor. This time, it was an English scientist who was talking about the latest discoveries made on how to store memory in cold cathode tubes; the budding birth of what was to become the now indispensable computer. As he talked with much conviction and keenness on a subject he had worked on for the past year, I found myself very interested in what he was saying and realised that, as he talked, words were pouring out of my mouth in French. I did not have time to check whether what I was saying made sense or not; I just let a kind of automation take place as I knew that if I, my ego, interfered together with my mind, I would have gone into complete chaos and lost the thread, like my unfortunate translator partner Andy.

At 11am it was time for a coffee break. I went down to the basement gents to relieve myself. As I stood there, neck and head stretched towards the ceiling, feeling oneness with the creator, I noticed to my immediate right a tall man with a big belly in a striped dark blue and grey suit. It was evident that he was English. I asked him, "Well? How is it going? What do think of the translating?"

"Bloody awful, I have to say. But never mind, actually we get it all in print later anyhow. Tell me... why do you ask?" I noticed his Oxford University accent.

"Because I am one of your translators!" I replied laughingly.

"Oh, I am awfully sorry, I didn't mean to offend you or anything like that... Actually it wasn't so bad," he kindly retorted. The polite and gentle Englishman had comforted me when he explained that all the talks would come out translated and in print at the end of the Congress.

The work was very tiring as it needed constant attention and concentration so as not to give room for doubt and ego; every time while translating when I felt tension building up in myself, I would immediately use this awareness as a reminder to completely let go of those negative feelings and reconnect to a peaceful receiving state.

Listening to the other professionals I was surprised to hear how much they missed, or rather they dropped certain words or phrases which they felt were not important; it had the effect of breaking up the flow of speech. I could hear that there was a definite technique, which they had no doubt trained in for many years.

Halfway through the week the boss of our translating agency paid us a visit. When he met me in the corridor he shook my hand profusely while giving me a wide smile. "Good morning, Mr Lassalle, I have to tell you how happy I am to have you working with us." He then looked round to make sure no one could hear what he was going to say and lowered his voice: "You're the only one among my translators who speaks into the microphone constantly, with regularity and calm."

I replied, feeling slightly embarrassed, "Thank you very much. Yes, I realise that I work differently; what is important for me is that the listener understands as much as possible what is being expressed."

These words made my boss even happier and he enthusiastically added, "If you agree to it, we have decided to keep you on our team. We have another Congress next week, this time on marketing." He then proceeded to tell me where and when to be for the next job. As we separated and walked away from each other, I turned around and asked, "By the way, do you speak English?"

"No, not a word, that's why I've got you guys here!" And he walked off, chuckling to himself, thinking that my question was funny.

To illustrate how much the spiritual training helped me in my daily life I will share with you another short story about my translating experiences. It was in the conference room of a large renowned hotel near the opera house. The meeting was to last a week, between English and French scientists and engineers, the subject was the latest developments in high furnaces and kilns for melting iron ore.

On the last day, I was faced with a completely unexpected situation: my boss came to me and said, "Léonard, they like your voice and would like you to take the chair today on stage and read aloud their conclusion document."

In my book *Chestnut, Walnuts and Goat Cheese*, I tell the story of when I was first taught to read and how difficult it had been for me having a most acute dyslexia problem. In those days, the teachers did not know about this handicap and my teacher had greatly tortured and publicly embarrassed me by twisting my ears until they bled... Reading aloud had become for me a real nightmare.

It took me some time to reply, as my throat and mouth had become suddenly so dry that I could not set my lips or tongue into motion. "But Monsieur Lemaire, it's not my job, I'm sure that among all the people present there is a better reader than me," I answered hurriedly.

"Don't be so humble, Mr Lassalle. We all know that you are perfectly capable of doing this simple job, now, come on." I was trapped, and as it was the last day of Congress, I accepted reluctantly, saying to myself with amusement: "Well, this might be your grand finale!"

I felt like an actor having stage fright appearing in front of an audience. A small, round Englishman with large thick glasses handed me the final document to be read as I walked by him on my way to the lectern, which stood on a low, carpeted platform. The only light in the high dark hall came from the spotlight that illuminated the lectern. The audience was now silent, waiting ...

My feeling of nervousness was heightened by having seen, in the document, equations and numbers, which had always been a problem for me to decipher correctly due to my dyslexia. The document was on the lectern in front of me, my hands resting either side of it. My heart was thumping heavily, and I felt for a moment as if I was back at school at the age of seven, the firm hand of Nelly, my teacher, grabbing my bright red ear menacingly.

"That's not the way to go," I said to myself, desperately trying to find the space in which to be, so as to be free of my fears and anxieties. It is difficult to judge time in such moments of confusion, but it must have been a matter of minutes as some people in the audience began to shift on their chairs and clear their throats, showing signs of impatience.

I decided to close my eyes, knowing that this would help me to isolate myself enough to reconnect to my inner finer feelings. I breathed in deeply and managed to let go totally of the frightened little boy that I had just been. At last my awareness found presence in a neutral space, and a feeling of peace took over, enveloping me lovingly.

As I started reading, I became aware of the slow regular vibration of my voice. Actually it was quite pleasant hearing myself, I noticed how clearly and well pronounced the words seemed to be flowing out of my mouth. It took 45 minutes to read through the text. At the end, I heard applause from the audience and noticed that the serene feeling I experienced while reading was still there. The lights of the conference hall came back on and my boss, together with the conference organiser, came up to thank me for what they said was an excellent reading.

A feeling of thankfulness invaded me deep inside. The spiritual training I had been following was showing me how to include it in my daily living.

Although I managed to cope with this new work situation, I have to say that my nights were highly agitated. Nightmares would wake me up drenched with sweat and in the mornings I felt as if I had emerged from a battlefield. The translating job had taken over 95% of my days and nights; I bought myself a technical dictionary and, at any spare moment, I would study and prepare the next simultaneous translating session.

Jean was getting worried, she had never seen her beloved so intense, and although money was flowing in more regularly than ever before, the family was suffering. Several months later, my boss suggested to me, "Mr Lassalle, we need you in Brussels as there is a lot of work there for you. If absolutely necessary, you could take your family with you ..."

When I came home, I told Jean what Mr Lemaire had offered. But it was clear that neither of us wanted to move to Belgium, and we both knew that the translating work was too stressful for the family; also, I did not feel that I was fulfilling my artistic talents. As soon as I gave in my resignation, my whole being felt instantly lighter and clearer, my nights became restful again and the sun's rays came back into the heart of our family.

Finding a profession that became a source of income for many years to come

Now I will tell you the circumstances which helped me become an antiques dealer and later an interior decorator and mural painter. Toby Jellinek, my brother-in-law, introduced me to a master printer called Maurice Darantiere. He lived in rue le Sec des Tournelles behind the Place des Vosges, in a magnificent building called hôtel Mansart, which had belonged to Louis XIV's famous architect. Toby, who was most inventive and gifted with his hands, repaired all kinds of antique objects, statues and even furniture for the old collector. M Darantiere had been collecting antiques all his life and had filled the apartments of his hôtel with works of art dating back from high antiquity to the early 19th century. He was a high-quality traditional printer specialising in editing luxurious art and poetry books; he also did printing for top fashion designers, restaurants, famous actors, and so on. He now needed someone to represent him and to become his go-between in the luxury world of Paris. The old printer entrusted me to be his representative salesman and I accepted as I had no other income at the time.

One day, he called me into his office and said hurriedly in a shaky voice that revealed that he was under high pressure, "Léonard, I need you to help me, it's urgent. If I gave you, on a sale or return basis, some antique objects and told you what I wanted for them, could you possibly go out and sell them for me? For instance, at the flea market in Clignancourt?"

"Yes," I replied instantly, always keen to help but not realising that, from that moment, I was starting a new career that would become my main profession for the next 30 years. I took the challenge and prepared myself to become a street salesman...

Toby kindly offered me a handsome old worn Persian carpet on which to present the precious objects. He also, together with my brother, lent me a few interesting pieces on a sale or return basis. I acquired the complicated paperwork that any French person needs to obtain the license to have the legal right to sell in the street.

Once in line with the law, my brother kindly lent me his Fiat 500 and for several months I went in and out of the hôtel Mansart and started to become familiar with the high-quality antiques that filled M Darantiere's museum-like property. He took pride in describing with much eloquence the history of each piece and how he had come to acquire it, completely forgetting the clock but teaching me a great deal about the objects in the process. I was now unconsciously becoming trained and accustomed to recognising artistic quality in works of art and finely crafted objects. Also my training as an artist had probably given me an eye to spot the originals from the fakes.

It was cold and wet when I first started early one Saturday morning in late November. I installed myself on the pavement of rue Paul Bert at Clignancourt, the vast secondhand and antiques market, called the flea market. On the damp, glossy pavement, I laid down a thin sheet of plastic beneath the beautiful old Persian carpet, taking care to put a heavy paving stone at each corner so that the erratic gusts of wind would not send everything flying. Then, with great care, I displayed the precious objects as if I was composing a painting, making sure that the eye could circulate freely and no one object would hide another. Once satisfied by the dis-

Léonard selling Mr Darentière antiques, 1962

play, I sat behind it on the wooden crate I used for packing up the goods and lit a cigarette, feeling happy with my efforts. I had not been there five minutes when a jovial council officer, who collected the small rent for the spaces, came and asked me for my selling licence papers. All was in order and he told me that in future I should move three spaces down rue Paul Bert, where a place had just become vacant. I paid him the very reasonable fee, in return he handed me a brightly coloured receipt that looked more like a lottery ticket.

It was now 6.45am and already the flea market had begun. Antiques dealers, their eyes riveted on the pavements that had become temporary display cabinets, would rapidly scan the stalls to find the rare object that would end up in their shop windows. The large Paris flea market was composed of five fair-sized markets, each with lock-up stalls that were more like small shops. In total, apparently, there were about 2,500 merchants including the poorer ones like myself who dealt straight from the street pavements.

I soon picked up the vocabulary of this strange world: the early morning visitors were called dealers, at least by those of us working from ground level. It must have been very unusual to find high-quality antiques directly in contact with the pavement as, very soon, the early morning stressed-looking dealers were piling up around my carpet, picking up my objects and asking me, all at once, for prices. They were very tough at bargaining, but little did they know that I could see by the light in their eyes their keenness to possess the objects they were holding in their hands. Soon I learned to put up my prices slightly to give me the correct margin I needed to make a profit.

By 7.30am three-quarters of my precious objects had been sold. I felt a reassuring comfort when I sensed the many banknotes in the pockets of my black wool raglan coat. I rapidly rearranged what remained of the unsold objects on the carpet, then covered the whole with a thin transparent plastic secured by the heavy paving stones. Fine rain had started to come down as I walked across the road to the yellow and burgundy painted Café Paul Bert.

Entering it was like coming into a completely new world. The air was dense with heat and humidity mixed with the smells of croissants, hot coffee and cigarette smoke, which emanated from the noisy crowd. The cacophony was extreme; it was as if everybody knew everybody, and they laughed and talked with each other regardless of whether they could hear what anyone was saying. The atmosphere was certainly jolly and it was apparent that everybody enjoyed being there. As I squeezed a passage to the bar, I noticed that the floor was covered in sawdust and scattered cigarette butts.

While I sipped the welcome black coffee and ate my croissant, every time the front door opened, I would quickly glance up through the opening in the direction of my carpet to check that no client was waiting for me. My mind and feelings were full of new impressions; I found that I liked this crazy, lively atmosphere where everyone was lost in his own world of self-interest without seemingly being aware of the other. I suppose I was in my own world too.

I noticed something that was completely new to me: I really was enjoying the selling part of my new job. This was probably due to the fact that, in my heredity, on my father's side, there had been excellent salesmen and sharp businessmen; and amusingly I thought, "My dear Mum could not sell anything without losing something on the deal! Surely, the happy salesman in me must come from my blood father's family!"

And so I rapidly became involved in the world of antiques dealers and art collectors. Once I paid back my brother Rainier, Toby and M Darantiere, I was able to invest some of the profits into more articles for sale.

The flea market was open three days a week, from Saturday to Monday. This gave me time to be with my young family in Champigny sur Marne, leaving one or two days to find the antiques I needed for the weekend market and to visit M Darantiere to collect more of his antiques. I would pay him for the articles previously sold and choose new ones to sell. It was very difficult for me to know which ones to choose. He would sometimes shout from his bedroom so as to be heard in the vast flat, "Just take whatever you like, I trust you, don't take only the tiny insignificant pieces, but take more important ones, don't be afraid!"

I did all I could to choose the antiques that would not obviously make holes in his wonderful and unique collection. I settled more on fine master drawings or sepias, 17th to 18th-century pottery, books, metalwork such as locks and keys, small polychrome wood carvings, antique cloth fragments of tapestry, damasks and silks.

Soon, Toby and my brother ran out of objects to dispose of but the old man was still in desperate need of cash. He was obviously living beyond his means, and although I was now bringing in some cash to him weekly, it was not enough for what seemed an ever-increasing need for funds. Six months later, he became weak, sick and finally bedridden with a fast developing cancer. A few months later, M Darantiere died and his whole collection was put up discreetly in a saleroom somewhere in north France.

I became known for being the first antiques dealer in the flea market to sell high-quality goods straight from the pavement. Every Saturday morning, seven or eight dealers would be there already waiting for me, and as soon as I parked my 2CV at the back of the wide pavement, they would focus with intense curiosity on the articles I was slowly unwrapping from their protective newspaper wrappings.

"How much for this?" the dealers would ask hurriedly.

"Well, actually, this one is truly a very fine piece and in perfect condition ... I want so much for it!" I would reply knowing that it would be the beginning of a lengthy negotiation. My strength in these deals was that I knew the margin between what I had paid for it and what the dealers could sell it for. I soon found out that the art of selling was in the buying: a well-bought quality article would always sell.

An unusual incident occurred a few weeks after I started, which greatly helped spread my name amongst the flea market dealers as an expert in the pottery and porcelain fields. One early spring morning, a dealer called John who specialised in French, Spanish and Delft

17th and 18th-century pottery came up to my stall with a pottery plate under his arm.

"Léonard, I would be interested if you would be kind enough to give me your opinion on where this plate was made?" he said with a questioning frown on his brows, as he unwrapped the newspaper from an early 18th-century polychrome soup plate. I was very new in the trade, yet obviously this expert dealer in European pottery thought I might be the one to help him to solve the mystery article.

I held the delicate object in both hands and looked at the intricate design that decorated the shaped border which had been hand-painted in yellow ochre, ferrous red and pale green with scrolls and leaf motifs. In the centre was a small medallion showing a country scene. My mind was blank, inactive and in the silence I heard my voice slowly pronouncing clearly every syllable: "St Jean du Desert."

The dealer's reaction was immediate and he said dryly, as he snapped the plate out of my hands, "No, no, no! If you have no idea, why not keep quiet!" And he stormed off.

I thought, reproaching myself, "Why on earth did I say that? I must be more careful and not give an answer if I don't really know. After all, he's the expert in European ceramics, isn't he?"

Strangely enough, two Saturdays later John reappeared at my stall with a full smile and came straight up to me, pulling out his hand for me to shake, his small pale blue eyes expressing respect and admiration. "You know, Léonard, I have to give you my apologies, as you are much more of an expert than I thought!"

"Oh yes?" I exclaimed truly surprised by the remark.

"What you said the other day about the plate irritated me greatly at the time, but on reflection I thought I'd better go to the museum and check. You know that you were bang on? It is from St Jean du Desert; they have one which is practically the same as mine!"

From then on the word spread throughout the antiques dealers' markets that I was the expert to consult on 17th and 18th-century European ceramics.

What was interesting was how the specialised merchants and collectors, not only in ceramics, but also in furniture, wrought iron, glass, tapestry, fabrics and rugs, through their keenness to display their knowledge would unconsciously share it with me by hurriedly telling me first what they reckoned an item was. When I agreed with their historical evaluation of the object, they felt most satisfied, which reinforced the esteem they might have for me. So little by little my clients, through their specialised knowledge, instructed and informed me into becoming quite an astute antiques dealer.

I liked my new profession, as I was discovering parts of myself that I did not previously know had existed. The latihan was continuously present within, guiding me in all kinds of unexpected ways and bringing a wider dimension to my living. For instance, the spiritual practice trained my consciousness to move beyond my ego and self-interest. This would make it possible, in my work, to see the objects, the client or the dealer with a detachment that gave me an overall view of the situation. My priority, as a merchant was to be absolutely fair in the deal so that the client would benefit and feel happy with his purchase. I felt satisfied when a client walked away from my stall confident that, not only was the object they had purchased not a fake, but also that its price had been completely fair.

Finding genuine stock was no easy matter; the goods I was looking for were rare in those days as they are today, and as I developed into an antiques dealer, I found that using my flair was a good way to find the articles I was dealing in, mostly from the 17th-century. At first I asked: which salerooms to view? Which direction to go? Which road to take? In which town would I find the rare Caucasian rug or the unusual Delft plate? But I soon stopped thinking that way, instead letting myself be guided by scanning, in my feelings, the countryside and following the impulses as I drove along. Of course, many people who do not practise the latihan will also recognize in themselves in what I have been describing above. The huntsman greatly relies on his instinct to find the hiding place of the desired animal; hunting for antiques is not dissimilar, the object taking the place of the hidden prey. I try to put into practice listening, and then trusting the voice that comes from deep within me, instead of the voices that pop up from my many egos and wants.

Finding it difficult to find 17th-century furniture in France in the early 60s, I would sometimes drive to England in my 2CV and come back, a few days later, with the car loaded with the desired goods. I soon became used to the English roads that led to the shops and traders where I could find what I was looking for.

Although my new trade was giving us a reasonable income, Mélinda and I, now with three children, decided to move to England in order to educate the children; we found the French school system a little too restrictive and archaic, lacking in the creative arts and sports.

Moving to the UK

In spring 1965, six months after we had made the decision to move, out of the blue we received a letter from a friend called Judith, whom we knew when Mélinda lived in Coombe Springs. She offered to rent us the upper floor of her house in Kingston upon Thames. We accepted and within two weeks I had sold and cleared my stall and small stock of antiques at the flea market, and the five of us, with all that we possessed plus 300 francs in our pockets, set off in our 2CV on the road to Calais. Our 14-month-old youngest son, Richard, was hanging in a hammock across the width of the car with his two sisters sitting on blankets behind, amongst our few belongings.

First days in UK in Richmond Park, 1965

We installed ourselves in the first floor two-bedroom flat in Manorgate Road, Kingston-on-Thames. Early next day, I was on the hunt for a rare article in which I could invest the £30 that was all of our capital …

I drove south of Kingston to find an enormous traffic jam

along the River Thames. In those days my vision was extremely sharp and while waiting for the traffic to move forward, I entertained myself looking at the large double window of a shop that sold faked antique mahogany furniture.

Was I mistaken? It seemed to me that the large barley twist gate-leg table, displayed in the window, was a late 17th-century period piece. I concentrated my focus more and deduced that the wood appeared to be walnut. I had to go investigate, and as soon as the traffic unblocked a little, I drove my 2CV a few metres and parked in a side road.

I had already learned that when I walked into a secondhand or antiques shop, it was better to ignore the piece that attracted me the most and give the impression that I was looking more closely at other insignificant pieces. As I pushed open the glass door, which set off a loud buzzer, I glanced at the gate-leg table to my left, and a warm feeling invaded my heart. Yes, this was an eight-seater, late 17th-century walnut double gate-leg table in perfect condition! I had never seen one so fine before.

A short wiry elderly man appeared from the back of the shop through a heavy, burgundy-coloured velvet curtain. He was wearing a dark ochre overall covered, as well as his large hands, in what seemed to be a mix of French polish and a deep reddish mahogany wood dye.

"Good morning, may I look around please?" I said positively.

"Please do," he answered as he pulled out of his pocket a worn tin box of Old Holborn tobacco and set himself to rolling a skinny cigarette.

I walked round the shop, stopped at one or two pieces as if they interested me, then on my way out I said nonchalantly pointing at the double gate-leg in the window, "By the way, what are you asking for this old table?"

"£30 sir, it's a good reproduction and in good nick, as you can see for yourself."

Although I could have bought it for that awfully reasonable price, I needed £5 to pay for the rent of the flat that same evening, so I boldly offered: "Will £25 do? That's all I can afford, I am afraid!"

Feeling satisfied that my offer was at last going to get rid of his old table, without hesitation the dealer accepted.

The wiry old man could not hide his delight with the cash and enthusiastically helped me carry the table outside and put it into the boot of my 2CV.

I was feeling tremendously thankful, light and happy in my heart; to find such a rare article on my first hunting day since the move, felt like a confirmation that my family was being looked after by the great life force.

There used to be a dealer in England called Robin Thompson, who dealt from his private house on the outskirts of Alton. I thought he would be just the right client for this walnut barley twist double gateleg table. As I drove along the attractive lanes of south England, I was thinking about the price I would ask for it.

"I reckon that he could sell such a piece at between £600-£800 and therefore I should ask him for around £450. His profit would be excellent and so would mine."

I drove through the open gates and on to the gravel parking area of Robin's house, making sure that the boot of my car faced his front door. I walked into the large showroom that had previously been a sitting room with an imposing 16th-century inglenook fireplace.

"Anybody in?" I shouted, knowing that Robin was probably at the back of the house as he was a keen gardener. He finally appeared with a pair of leather gloves and pruning shears and said welcomingly, "Oh, Léonard, how nice to see you, I was just in the garden about to cut some roses to make a bouquet for the shop. How are you?" Then he added, as he knew what I was usually on the hunt for, "Unfortunately, at the moment I have no oak joint stools for you, but I have some rare iron work that you might find interesting ..."

I felt it was not fair to make him think I might be buying from him, so I rapidly told him that I was in truth selling today. "Actually Robin, I have just recently moved to England with my family, and I'm hoping to continue dealing in the same sort of goods. Would you, by any chance, be interested in purchasing a barley twist double gateleg walnut table ... an eight to 10-seater?"

I noticed that a spark of interest lit his eyes as he answered, "I've just sold a large oak refectory table, it's true that I've got the space, it doesn’t hurt to see it, does it?"

We went outside and as I lifted the boot lid, I looked at his face to read his reaction. He could not contain his excitement and asked avidly as we were lifting the table out of the car on to the gravel courtyard to inspect it, "How much...?"

I couldn't help make this exciting moment last a little longer.

"Have a good look first, make absolutely sure you're happy with it." We settled at £425. He knew that I was aware of how much he could sell it for and therefore did not try to bargain, but promptly wrote out a cheque. The next day I was able to go to the local Lloyds Bank to open an account where I took the opportunity to ask the bank manager how to obtain a licence to sell goods from my car or at secondhand markets.

He looked surprised at my question and answered, "A licence? What on earth for? Here in England you deal as you wish providing that, at the end of the year, you declare your income to the local tax inspector." I realised then that English government policies were to facilitate trade by making it accessible to anyone who wished to start a business.

And so I became what was then called a 'runner' and started to deal from my car. I also rented a garage opposite the small flat from which I started to restore 17th-century oak and walnut furniture, which was entrusted to me by the owners of specialised antiques shops I knew in London.

Adapting myself to demand

One day, I found myself walking into an antiques and interior decorating shop in Welbeck Street. I looked around the room and did not see anything I felt I could make a profit on, so asked the dealer if he had any old carved pictures or mirror frames he might want to part with.

He didn't, but then he asked me, "Talking about old carved frames, you wouldn't by any chance know anyone who could do some gilding for me?"

He disappeared into a back room and brought back an elegant French Charles Xth armchair which had lost most of its gilding. The chair was made of beech wood, probably dating from around 1830, with upholstered back, seat and crest on the armrests. I examined it carefully and heard myself say, "Yes, I could do it for you, if you like."

The very nice man instantly accepted my proposition. I had once watched Toby doing gilding to repair one of M Darantiere's 17 century leather caskets, and knew roughly what the job entailed. With the challenging chair in the back of my car, I drove to Charlotte Street where I had noticed, once before, one or two gilding materials suppliers.

Six weeks later the chair was sparkling and glowing, ready to be taken back to the dealer. It took me a long time because I could only work at nights as during the day with the children around it was not possible to handle the volatile gold leaf as the tiniest movement or draught would pick it up and carry it into the air.

The Welbeck Street dealer was delighted with my gilding work, paid without a squeak and asked me if I would repair and gild a carved wooden frame for him. I had added another string to my bow.

Our first property

Here is an experience that contributed to ripen a new understanding within myself about these two realities: the material reality and the immaterial reality what is in truth the spiritual reality.

After months searching for a home to rent in the south of England, I finally found myself in Tunbridge Wells. At that time there were three conditions on people wanting to rent a dwelling: no pets, no coloureds, no children. I remember walking by several estate agents in the high street without being able to enter any of them. Was it that I could not face again the humiliating feeling of admitting that I had children, as if it was a bad thing to have descendants?

I carried in my chest a heavy feeling of desperation as I walked up the steep hill. Suddenly, as I reached the top, that feeling completely lifted and I unexpectedly found myself entering the office of the director of Parris & Quirk, the poshest estate agent in town. The kind man offered us a large old house with a fair-sized garden on the hill at the back of Royal Tunbridge Wells' famous Pantiles. The Pantiles was a large stone-slabbed pedestrian area, planted with lime trees. The older, upper part was built in the mid-17th century, the lower buildings were built during the English Regency period. It was a nice part of town where one would enjoy browsing through the many clothing, hat and antiques shops, as well as stopping for tea and cakes in the old-fashioned teahouses. There was even a small spa of ferruginous waters that was apparently good for curing stomach problems.

Although the monthly rent was high for us at that time, knowing of the difficulty of finding a home I did not hesitate to sign the contract. We moved in with much joy and a feeling of great relief: at last we had secured a roof over our heads! The front garden of this elegant Georgian-style house gave on to Frant Road, at number 19. Having searched for a place to settle for over a year and a half, this attractive property was a complete godsend.

19 Frant Road, Tunbridge Wells

What had made me walk into the most expensive-looking estate agent in town? I would never normally have done so. What had freed this property from any restricting conditions, so that the whole family could move at once?

With its four rooms up and four rooms down, the house seemed vast to our children who had so far been accustomed to only small spaces. It had a good-sized garage, an enclosed front garden and a large back garden with a greenhouse, a tall Bramley apple tree, and a square lawn surrounded by mature rose bushes. The children were running about delightedly, investigating every corner of the house. Although at the back of my mind I did wonder how I would manage to pay the rent, somehow I felt that it would be okay. My little family was now happy and secure in this beautiful home; I could now concentrate on how to make money while Mélinda organised the schooling.

What had made the old, gentlemanly, upper-class estate agent accept a young artist without obvious employment and a father of four children, as a lodger to one of his better properties? It was only much later that I understood the positive thread of events that unfolded steadily from our initial move. From then on, situations concerning finding a home for the family always came about in the most unusual ways, but whatever our financial situation, we would always have a roof over our heads.

The experience showed me that fear and anxiety residing in my ego had been invading my search for a home, even if my wants came from an apparently noble reason of a father needing a home for his family. I discovered that with my heart and mind tied to an ego filled with fears and doubts, my vision was extremely limited. This finally brought me to realise that the field of possibilities becomes much wider when the ego and wants are put aside, to give place to the real need. Not the need that the wants and desires make you believe they have to have, but the need that comes from an understanding of the soul.

This is when the spiritual actually guides the material, where the immaterial consciousness can ease the way through this complicated and often confused network of the gross material world.

The family had now established itself in Tunbridge Wells; the children went to school, my new enterprise, an antiques shop in The Pantiles, was settling into a more regular business, and our life at last had a harmonious rhythm.

Two years later, again something unexpected presented itself. As I was walking up the High Street in Tunbridge Wells I felt an extremely powerful pull to walk into the office of the estate agent Paris & Quirk that had rented us the house. I asked to see the boss, and while I was waiting I prepared what I was going to ask him. It was clear in my mind now, we liked the house we lived in, it was convenient being close to the shop and maybe we could let the proprietor know that we might be interested in purchasing it.

"Yes, of course, I can write to the proprietor, but what is your offer?" asked the kind director.

Although my shop was beginning to pick up with its sales of antiques, my finances were pretty low and I had no reserve whatsoever, so I said, "As you know, I am a man who buys and sells antiques. And how do I know how much to sell my antiques? It is because I know how much I have paid for them. Mr Johnson surely knows how much he paid for 19 Frant Road and how much he will want for it." The estate agent agreed to write to Mr Johnson, who lived in Singapore, and ask him if he wished to sell his house, and at what price. Two weeks later, I received a letter from the estate agent saying that yes, indeed, Mr Johnson had been thinking of selling Number 19 as he would shortly be returning to England with his family. The price he wanted for his house was £5,500. Would we let him know rapidly if we were interested?

At that time, the price of houses along that side of Frant Road were fetching between £12,000 and £14,000. I became very excited by the offer and decided to go back at once and offer £5,250 to the estate agent who immediately wrote back to the owner with my offer.

In the meantime, I had gone to my bank and explained to the manager about this wonderful opportunity. He agreed that the price was reasonable for the quality and position of the house, and added that the bank would put up 95% of the total provided I found the remaining 5%.

The big day of the signature arrived and Mr Johnson came especially from Singapore the day before to sign the sale documents. Together we signed the agreement and exchanged a few words as he was in a hurry to catch his flight back to Singapore that same evening. He was softly-spoken, gentle and seemed a kind man. He told me that he was married with two children and was hoping to move back to England shortly.

I came home that lunchtime feeling completely elated and as I walked into what was now our house, I affectionately squeezed the thick front door and shouted: "This is our home! We've bought it!"

Mélinda came running towards me from the kitchen and we swirled round dancing in happiness. It was our first house.

Two months went by when one evening I received a phone call from Mr Johnson. His voice was cold and carried anger. He explained that he had come back to England to live with his family in the vicinity of Aldershot and had found that property prices in that part of Hampshire were roughly twice what he had sold his house to us for. And he put the phone down abruptly. I felt devastated by this news, what could we do? The poor man, he had been out of the country for 12 years and had not kept up with the price of property in UK.

It happened that the same evening there was to be a latihan in our Subud hall in Pembury Church. With a heavy heart, I started my latihan and quickly was on the floor sobbing. I asked inside, "My God, why have you privileged my family? It is not right that Mr Johnson and his family have no home. Please, show me the way." The prayer was heard, I immediately became deeply quiet, all the sorrow vanished together with ego and self-pity. After some time my inner voice echoed clearly in my head, "Fast for 10 days."

So I fasted. It had the effect of keeping me completely connected to my inner being, away from my ego, heart and mind. I used my mind, of course, for my work and everyday events, but did not connect it to any emotional problems. This does not mean that I was not aware of Mr Johnson and his family; on the contrary I felt my soul enrobing them with caring love every time the situation came up in my consciousness.

Exactly 10 days later the telephone rang and it was Mr Johnson. His voice was now warm and gentle, almost joyous and he explained that he had been driving in the country feeling desperate about looking for a house, when he saw an old man's head appear over the hedge he was cutting. He stopped his car, and asked him if he knew, by any chance, of a house for sale in the district.

That same morning the old gentleman had been talking with his wife and they had decided that the house and gardens were much too big for them now and that they should sell and retire to an old people's home they knew and liked. They had decided that £5,250 was the price they wanted for their property.

Mr Johnson then said, "Isn't that amazing! Exactly the same amount as the house you bought from me!"

Mr Johnson and his family had their house, we had ours, and I felt immense gratitude to the Source of Life for having once again shown us the way.

So, we purchased our first house and, instead of paying rent, I paid the bank the interest on the loan plus a percentage of repayment; I felt that I was paying the rent to myself. What a powerful feeling of security this brought the family. No more of the hidden pressures of perhaps having to move to some unknown place. Also, we now felt that we belonged in the town of Tunbridge Wells, and the children, although the schools were far from ideal, felt secure going to school from their home.

Altogether we stayed in 19 Frant Road for 12 years: 12 years in which I had time to develop the antiques business into a business of design, interior decorating, architecture and mural paintings.

Acquiring the shop

A few years previously, just after we moved into Number 19, an elderly lady called Mrs Spear who had a bric-a-brac antiques shop in the lower part of The Pantiles, told me she wanted to sell the lease of her shop. Always on the hunt for a rare article, an early piece of Delft ware, an antique rug, an unusual painting or whatever attracted me and where I saw a profit, I had dropped into the old lady's shop. During our chat, she mentioned that she wanted to move out and sell the lease of her premises, which actually belonged to the council.

The eastern part of the long Regency building gave on to a small dead end street. Mrs Spear's shop was on the corner and stood on four floors, plus a spacious cellar, which led on to a pocket handkerchief-sized garden at the back. She lived in a small flat on the third floor. The building was full of light: next to the shop display window were three steps that led up to the ground floor showroom. On the first floor were two other showrooms, one of which gave on to a balcony that overlooked The Pantiles. The place was attractive and I thought I could do something interesting with it.

"I am afraid that I want £4,000 for the lease!" she said defensively, while flickering her pale Persian blue-painted wrinkled eyelids.

I had not a penny to rub together at the time, our move into 19 Frant Road was absorbing most of my very meagre income but, as if pushed by a wind of intuition, days later I walked into my solicitor's office and asked him to make Mrs Spear an offer of £3,000 for the lease of 21 The Pantiles.

I was beginning to listen and follow these unusual spontaneous feelings that did not come from my rational thinking. I was beginning to trust them and see how they would unfold. If they came from the source of my soul, they would turn out positively for the whole family. I suppose the latihan had taught me to recognise the difference between impulses that came from my passions, wants and desires and those that originated from a deeper place within myself which, at that time in my mind, did not seem rational.

Some months after my visit to the solicitor, my beloved grandmother GG unexpectedly died (as I describe in Chapter 3). My mother had come up from the south of France for the funeral; she told Mélinda and me how difficult her life had become in Vallauris and how she missed not being close to her grandchildren. So I showed her 21 The Pantiles and told her that I had put an offer for the lease of the property, explaining that, although I did not have the money, it felt the correct thing to do. If my dream materialised, then I would keep the top flat for her use.

Roughly three months later a letter came from my solicitor saying that Mrs Spear had accepted the offer and could I please call at his office on the following Wednesday to sign the lease. The morning of that amazing day, a letter had arrived from my mother in France containing a cheque for £3,000. Confidently, feeling full of gratitude, I walked down to my solicitor's office to sign all the necessary papers and obtained the lease. I rang up my mother and said with enthusiasm, "We've got it! Your cheque arrived just in time for the signing of the lease. I will prepare your flat above the shop and you can move in whenever you're ready."

What an exciting moment this was, to redecorate and furnish this most elegant building! But how would I find the money to buy stock? I knew from inside that my first obligation was to get the building ready and not worry unnecessarily how I would stock it up.

21 The Pantiles,
Léonard Lassalle Antiques

Two months later, quite unexpectedly, another cheque arrived from my mother through the post, this time for £1,500 which was the minimum I needed to find enough stock to furnish the ground floor of the shop and start dealing. She, along with her Provençal husband Marcel, moved into the flat in the late spring of 1967.

The shop was named Léonard Lassalle Antiques and became the cornerstone of our material stability and growth. I soon discovered that I couldn't be in the shop and do the buying at the same time, because the shop needed replenishing with 17th-century English and European furniture, and that kind of merchandise was, even in those days, difficult to find. I employed a permanent secretary who dealt with my post and telephone as well as looking after the shop in my absence.

The purchase of Bassett's Oast House

I hope, dear reader, that my continuous hopping about in time through the different stories will not be too confusing; you see, I'm trying to keep to some kind of sequence...

In early spring 1979, Mélinda had fully recovered from her illness and expressed her longing to move to a house in the country with a large garden. She felt that she needed more space and to get away from the noisy main road. From past experience, I knew of the benefits of fasting to help to me find my way through the material world, so I decided therefore to fast for a house. Normally, one would have gone round the estate agents of the town, of which there were many, and asked to see all the available houses in the country up to 10 miles south of Tunbridge Wells. But I did not do that, I just did my usual fast and went about my business without thinking or planning to bring to fruition my wife's need to move.

It seems that it takes roughly 10 days of fasting for the doors of the unforeseeable to open. Usually, I would go for a walk during the lunch hours to stretch my legs and breathe some fresh air. One day, I closed the shop at 1pm and walked out briskly in the cold air with a peaceful state of mind. My legs took me straight along a little street called Chapel Place and up into the High Street, when suddenly my feet turned sharp right and took me into an estate agent's called Bracketts.

"Sorry sir, we're closing now. Please come back this afternoon," said the young and efficient secretary."

I tried to explain what I was looking for and she answered that she knew all her files and was absolutely certain that she did not have such a property on her books. I insisted and, irritated by my insistence, she got up angrily, went to a file cabinet and proceeded to flick rapidly through the houses in the price bracket I had given her.

"Sorry! But you see? There is nothing in your price range," she exclaimed, hoping that this would settle the matter. But I insisted, while wondering within myself how I could be so rude.

She asked me to leave the agency, but I answered by asking if I could see the boss. She became exasperated by my stubbornness, knocked twice on the door opposite her desk, then without waiting for an answer, opened it and leaned into the boss's office.

"There is a man here who is rather insistent about some property he thinks we have. He says now that he wants to see you." She was obviously angry. She left the office door open and promptly left the agency.

I walked up to the threshold of his office. He rose up and came towards me, offering me his hand to shake. I told him exactly what we were looking for: a house large enough for a family of nine plus and, if possible, a small flat attached. I was looking for four to five hectares of land, within 15 minutes drive south of Tunbridge Wells.

Surprised by my description, he answered, "How strange. I was in the pub last night with an actor friend. He told me he wanted to sell his house near Wadhurst and it roughly fits what you're describing. If you like, I could arrange for you to see it tomorrow." I was delighted, and the next day we went to see the property.

It was called Bassett's Oast House. It was situated at the end of a long country lane and had obviously been part of a large farm complex. To our delight the property had three magnificent circular oast buildings, one of which still had its original wooden cowl that moved with the direction of the wind. We knocked at the white-painted entrance door that led into the first oast. A kind-looking man with a short beard opened the door. I immediately saw by the expression in his eyes that he rather liked Mélinda. He was called Mr Spice and led us into the hallway of his attractive property, in which a major feature was an alignment of three round oasts that gave it the look of a small castle.

Bassett's Oast House

To the left of the entrance hall was a large sitting room, to the right was a small room, bathroom and flat. Straight opposite, in the middle oast, was a dining room and kitchen; off that a small room led to a toilet and shower. Up the narrow wooden staircase a landing served five bedrooms and a bathroom. The gardens were spacious, including a large field surrounded by mature oak trees. Both Mélinda and I immediately fell for the property and agreed to buy it. Mr Spice was delighted at the thought of selling it to us and then told us that he had found a possible property in Lansdowne Park Road in Tunbridge Wells. Before we parted, I mentioned to Mr Spice that he would be welcome to take a look at our property, as he might be interested in it.

Mr Spice and his two daughters fell for our house, and they bought it for £10,000 less than we paid for Bassett's. The direct deal of the sale of our house saved us estate agent's fees. We moved into Bassett's Oast House and lived there happily for the next 12 years. On the strength of the property, we were able to borrow enough money to buy a small Provençal farm from which I am writing this book today.

A few years later, we invited my mother and her partner, Marcus Hamilton, to live permanently with us in the adjacent flat.

Getting established and discovering my many talents

One day I received a letter from the British Antique Dealers' Association asking me to call at their office in London. I made an appointment and went to meet them, intrigued and wondering why they wanted to see me. The secretary led me to the office of the chairman. "Hello, Mr Lassalle, how do you do?" And without giving me time to reply he continued, "Quite a few of our members have brought to our notice the excellence of your shop in Royal Tunbridge Wells, the quality of the goods you sell have given you a good reputation in the trade. Would you accept our invitation to become one of our members? You would then be the first foreigner to join our association."

I felt chuffed by his compliments but was not keen to join a club of antiques dealers, also I knew from experience that belonging to the British Antique Dealers' Association was no guarantee of honesty. I thanked the chair and told him that I would let him know in a few days.

Weighing up all the pros and cons, I finally decided to accept the offer and became a member, which added quite a few advantages to my trade. Sometime later I received the renowned round badge, which I promptly displayed in my shop window.

To attract interest and increase trade, I decided to have an exhibition of a pre-Charles II interior. I would use the upper showroom, the one with a fireplace with two French windows giving on to the balcony. I would need to find 17th-century oak wainscot panelling to cover the walls, an Elizabethan four-poster bed, 17th-century crewel-work curtains and all the objects that would furnish a bedroom of that period. I sent 500 invitation catalogues to clients and dealers and advertised in Country Life and other glossy magazines. Two weeks before the opening I had found everything I needed, except the wainscot panelling. Over a pint of bitter beer in the St George pub just across from my shop, I asked a young antiques dealer friend if he knew where I could find such panelling.

"But Léonard, did you not tell me that you were a painter once? Why not paint an Elizabethan mural on the walls? I have a friend who has a 16th-century Kent farmhouse in which there is a bedroom completely decorated with wonderful flowers and plants, all perfectly preserved." What my friend said resonated right in my chest and teased my sleeping artistic creativity.

The kind lady of the farm took me to see the Elizabethan bedroom, which had, by the way, a National Trust preservation order on it. I frantically started drawing on my A3 layout pad, inspired by the 16th-century travelling painters of the time; taking notes, page after page, of the beautiful details of the 16th-century mural inspired by the flowers of the English countryside.

Back at the shop, I looked up a painting formula in an old book that gave all the painting recipes of the past masters. I chose the dry fresco technique, which only needed the yoke of an egg, pure linseed oil and distilled water. I had now the binder, today we call it the medium; all I needed to add were the natural pigments which I found in Cornelissen's art shop in London.

The day before the opening I was still hurriedly finishing the last

Shop interior in upper showroom

touches of the mural. The effect was quite stunning. The heavy crewel-work curtains kept day-light out of the room, which was only lit by many candles fitted in period candlesticks, wrought-iron candle/rush holders and a Flemish bronze chandelier. A large basket of Norfolk rushes filled with oak logs supplied the glowing fire that was cradled in a wrought-iron basket that rested on a pair of 17th-century firedogs. A fitted plaited reed carpet that smelt of dry grass covered the floor. I had found a period embroidered silk bed cover and even a delightful petits points cushion showing Charles I walking in a wood with his Queen.

The exhibition was a great success and not only did I sell many of the articles on display, but I also acquired a new profession: I had become a fresco painter. Three or four clients, attracted by the Elizabethan murals, asked me whether I could do the interior decorating of their homes and also paint Elizabethan frescoes on their walls. All this was very exciting and satisfying as I was using my artistic talent in a new and completely unexpected way.

From East Anglia to south-west England, I was asked to paint murals and redesign the interiors of old country houses. In the process, I came to design furniture, garden furniture, landscape gardens and finally architecture, where I had to employ an architect to get planning permissions passed. Every time I was asked if I could do a certain job, I did not say "No" but "Yes, of course!" I found the latihan was giving me the necessary detachment, which made it possible for me to see the realm of my capacities.

Designing is to do with the distribution of space, harmony of lines, colour and form, not forgetting, of course, the importance of the practical and functional aspect of whatever is designed. I found that experts were always keen to share their expertise. If I needed to design a plan for electrics, drains and water, gas or whatever, the experts in these different fields would willingly give me the symbolic sign language needed to draw them into a readable architectural plan.

The office at 21 The Pantiles was buzzing with creativity and activity. I had acquired an old architect's drawing board on which I produced the numerous drawings needed for all the different jobs. Before I started drawing I would first of all feel the needs of the client, his/her nature and character, and the space that would have to be created to harmonise the surroundings. Then, holding a lead pencil in my hand, I would first go completely quiet inside and only when I had achieved that would I allow my hand to draw. Usually, only one proposition would appear and I would develop it until it was ready to show the customer. S/he seemed always to accept what I presented to them.

The next step was to bring the chosen designs into a material reality. I soon found myself instructing builders, cabinetmakers, carpenters, upholsterers, curtain makers, electricians and plumbers. For the painting of walls, whether frescoed or plain, I would do it myself or with the help of my teenage children. I had previously learned how to obtain the special paint effects, how to mix the natural pigments with old-fashioned binders, and how to obtain the desired colours.

Besides all this, I was continuously on the look out for antiques and works of art needed to supply the shop and furnish the interiors.

To illustrate how the material and spiritual can work in harmony with each other, here is another story of a job that took me to Norway. I will call this client Mr S, as I know he would not like his name mentioned for reasons of privacy and security. One Saturday morning in autumn, Mr S called me to ask if I was prepared to go to Norway and design for him the interior of a two-floor 13-room apartment, part of a luxurious building that had just been constructed in the hills behind Oslo, west of the famous Holmenkollen ski jump.

Feeling that I might accept the job, he added, "I'll ask the Swiss architect, who designed the building, to send you the plans as soon as today."

"But Mr S, I have to see and feel the property in situ before I can come up with the design. I would want it to harmonise with the surrounding landscapes."

I had worked with Mr S's character long enough to know that, when he had made a decision, everything became instantly urgent and had to be accomplished in the shortest possible time. Our conversation continued, "I am having a meeting with the builders, the architect, electricians and plumbers in Oslo at 10am next Wednesday. I want you to present your completed design project and explain it to these guys. Oh, by the way I will pay for your fare, expenses and time of course."

Fortunately, it happened that a very close Subud friend of mine, an architect, had built his own house not far from the site and I knew that, at that time, his wife Katarina, who was Norwegian herself, was living there. She kindly agreed to fetch me from the airport and to look after me during my short stay. My flight arrived in Oslo on Monday afternoon and, as we landed, I noticed that all the lights of the city were already twinkling in the snow even though it was only 4pm, reminding me that most of Norway laid north of the 60th parallel.

I set off early next morning to find this new block of luxury flats. Katarina had kindly prepared some hot tea and sandwiches for my lunch, which I carried in my leather briefcase together with my drawing pad, pencils, tape measure and camera.

At 8am it was still dark, and most of the light came from the white reflection of the frozen snow. The temperature was minus 15°C. When my eyes became accustomed to the environment I realised that the road I was walking on was following the curves of the steep side of a tall mountain. My heart sank when I saw what had been called 'a luxury building'. In the poor light, all I could see were tall rough blocks of concrete following, like a gigantic staircase of eight steps, the sharply falling angle of the land. The unfinished building stood on the lower edge of the mountain road. Two large metallic unpainted garage doors stood defiantly in front of me. Just to the right was a small dark green door with a coded buzzer. It led into a vast space, giving covered parking for at least 10 cars. On the back wall were four lifts, one for each apartment, though not yet in working order. To the right an unfinished concrete staircase led down. Mr S had bought the two lowest levels.

The electric wiring was temporary, giving the absolute minimum light, the ceiling of each room had in its centre a dim light bulb fitted into a socket hanging directly from dangling feeding wires. The damp, penetrating cold was intense and as I walked round, discovering the layout of the rooms, I kept warm by sipping Katarina's comforting hot tea.

My artistic creativity had never been so challenged. Room after room was dark, grey and uninspiring: neither the L-shaped entrance hall nor a small room round the corner had any windows to bring in natural light. "What on earth did the architect have in mind when he designed such a space? Maybe a dark room for a photographer?" I thought, trying to bring a little humour to combat the gripping gloom.

Opposite, a door gave on to an almost square space at the end of which was a large window, which allowed the dim light of the Norwegian winter to creep into the room. The view was strikingly beautiful, and I spent some time absorbing it. Down below, I could distinguish frozen lakes surrounded by dark pine forest; in the far distance, as far as the poor light allowed me to see, were rolling hills. The building was facing south-west.

"This room should be his office," I thought as I walked through another door to the left of the large window. It gave on to a vast space. I stood there for a moment scanning it without thoughts. The whole wall to my right was composed of glass sliding doors with a wide balcony running across the south-west of the building and under which I presumed was the other part of the flat.

Immediately to my left was a two-metre hole in the rough concrete floor. There was no staircase but a rickety ladder enticed me to go down. To the extreme left, along the north-east facing wall, was what I thought to be the kitchen area, as in its right corner was a small semi-circular knee-height fireplace. With great care I went down the creaking ladder, holding myself on the concrete circular edge until I finally had to let go to reach the floor at the bottom. To the extreme right was the master bedroom, with adjacent toilet and bathroom, and two very oddly shaped children's bedrooms with their own toilet and bathroom. Across the hall, a door led to a narrow room that I thought could be the playroom. On its right, the sliding glass doors gave on to a terrace which was dug out of the hillside.

I had now in my mind the concept of the whole flat and climbed back up to the upper floor where I crouched down and looked absently at the empty virgin space that surrounded me. With some anxiety, I found that I had no inspiration and after about 10 minutes in an unpleasant kind of no man's land, I decided to go further into my inner awareness by completely letting go of my anxiety and fears about the project. I closed my eyes and reached into a space that was peaceful and where the feelings were not plus nor minus but just in waiting ...

After a while, the most delightfully harmonious sounds arose from the depth of my being, which I let out freely into the grey, uninviting concrete space. Gradually, I felt as if I was enveloped by an angelic state of complete peace, together with a sharp awareness of the reason for my being there.

I slowly opened my eyes and looked around to observe the completed interior design of the space I was in, the colours, materials, shapes and forms of all the elements that would make the area harmonious. All I needed now was to turn this spiritual reality into a physical one.

With great care, almost like the hunter who does not want to disturb his immobile prey, my hands found the sketchbook and pencil, which I settled on the floor in front of my feet. I looked at the gaping circular hole in front of me and saw and understood in an instant the whole concept of the spiral staircase to be. My hand started to draw rapidly with precision, making notes of the practical details of construction and colour as I went along, bringing into a two-dimensional reality the basic information necessary for anyone to understand the concept.

I was now looking at the concrete floor and saw it laid with a parquet flooring made of 60 by 70cm panels. If you can visualise the 4cm thick natural pine floor panel, with a coloured centrepiece framed by 20cm wide planks in their original pine colour. Each centre part was to be dyed a different colour: dark walnut brown for the sitting room, ochre yellow for the kitchen and hallway, ochre red in other rooms. The repetitive patterns would give a chessboard effect. The frame and centre panel would be glued directly on to a thick plywood panel base put together at the factory, then cut and adjusted on site before sticking them directly on to the cement.

Mr S told me a year later that, when the flat had been completed, the factory owner who made the floor panels was so taken by the idea and concept, that he industrialised them to sell on the open market.

And so I went on drawing, putting down all the information including the measurements I needed to do the working drawings. By 4.30pm, I was completely frozen, tired but satisfied that I had enough information to now work on my friend's architect table and transform the sketches into clear A2-sized drawings. I left the grim concrete blocks and walked down, happy to be moving and to be bringing warmth back into my numbed stiff body. After a hot shower and a nice meal kindly prepared by Katarina, I was ready to prepare the drawings that I needed to present to Mr S the next morning. In the deep silence of the Norwegian night I drew, sheet after sheet, until the whole concept was laid out clearly on paper. The clock read 4am and, feeling satisfied that all the points were covered, I was glad to hand over my tired body and mind to the goddess of sleep.

Punctually at 9am the doorbell rang. "Good morning, you're ready, Léonard? We'll go have breakfast in town now," Mr S said in his direct abrupt manner. He rapidly glanced through my drawings and said, "Looks fine, now let's go and make 10 copies of each ... we haven't got much time, the meeting is at 10am." He was not a man for giving compliments, but I could feel that he approved of the scheme as he had not asked any questions but was smiling while looking through them.

Around the glossy oval conference table were already sitting eight serious-looking construction professionals. First they were to look at my drawings, then express their thoughts, opinions and suggestions. It was impressive. Mr S sat at one end of the long table, me at the other, while the experts devoured my propositions. The room fell into a profound silence while the architect, builders, carpenters, electricians and plumbers, some with their assistants, studied my drawings. Inwardly I felt quiet and serene, confident that what I was proposing was absolutely feasible.

All successfully accepted the scheme. To my satisfaction there were no changes to be made and I was able to establish a programme for the realisation of what I had seen during that angelic moment of creativity in the freezing, sombre building on the Holmenkollen Mountain.

Some nine months later, my secretary Hannah handed me the phone. "It's from Oslo, Mr S, actually."

"Hello, Léonard, I am sitting in my office here in Oslo, looking at the beautiful view. I wanted to tell you that when we are in this flat, my wife and I do not seem to argue any more. It's the same with the children. It's as if the place was being looked after by angels."

Oslo flat interior

During 24 years running Léonard Lassalle Antiques, I have experienced many instances when, through the latihan, things that seemed not possible to my mind and ordinary feelings actually became realisable, though always in unexpected ways.

Learning through a painful experience

Here is an incongruous, strange and somewhat painful story, which happened one day while I was dealing in antiques. It shows, as I say in the introduction, my struggle in recognising and separating the actions of self-interest based on my wants and desires, from actions initiated by the unselfishness wisdom of the soul.

It was by no means easy to find the pre-18th century furniture needed to feed my hungry shop. One day, late in the afternoon, I was driving home feeling tired and disappointed at not having found anything really interesting to furnish my showrooms. I had been combing the south of England's secondhand furniture and antiques shops all day, and had only found a late 17th-century Delft vase and an early 18th-century pair of wrought-iron firedogs.

Coming out of my floating thoughts, I suddenly found myself returning home on a different road than my mind would have chosen and I thought: "I wonder why I am going back this way? It's quite a bit longer." But I accepted and carried on ...

Going through a small hamlet, I passed by a tatty-looking junk shop. "Might as well have a look!" I said to myself while I reversed and parked in front of the old, somewhat dilapidated building.

As I pushed open the front door and stepped down into the tiny shop, a small bronze bell fixed on a wide serpentine spring rang loudly. The place was a chaos of bric-a-brac with objects that gave the depressing feeling of having been rejected and abandoned by their owners.

An elderly, dusty-looking man came out of a back door and looked at me silently over his half-moon spectacles. After a rapid glance round the room, I asked mechanically, "Would you have anything else, by any chance, any other old furniture?"

I was about to step out of the decrepit building when I heard his creaky voice saying, "Well, actually, I have a few more bits of furniture here in storage if you want to look."

The old man turned round and went through the same doorway from which he had appeared. I followed him to discover another much larger room piled up with all kinds of very dusty furniture. I stopped on the doorstep and went into the special state of acute attention I used when I searched for the rare possible piece. The 15-

watt light bulb that lit the room made it difficult to see, especially as its light was shadowed by the leg of an upside-down table, which was precariously resting on top of a chest of drawers. But just next to my left arm was what looked like an extremely rare oak mid-16th-century food cupboard. I could not believe it as my hand was already stroking its smooth, dusty, worn surface to extract the first information.

As I swivelled the upside-down table slightly to shift the shadow of its leg elsewhere, the cupboard began to reveal itself. About 5½ft high, 2ft deep and roughly 4½ft wide, the two-tier standing cupboard was made of a moulded frame and panel construction. The side panels and two centred doors were pierced carved in Gothic double arch motifs. The decorative piercing of the panels was designed to let the air circulate over the food. I noticed my heart accelerating, its beat taken by the excitement of the find. The wrought-iron butterfly hinges nailed into each left side of the doors seemed to be of the period, as I opened the upper one, it dropped slightly telling me of its understandable and evident wear. To reinforce its long elegant legs, a chamfered Gothic-type arch plank had been grooved into its underframe and sides, giving it a most noble appearance.

"How much for this old cupboard?" I said with a flat tone of voice that revealed no excitement.

"I want £90 for it, sir," answered the old man.

It would not have been fair to bargain and I bought it at the full price, to the delight of its owner. On the way home my whole being was filled with the kind of material joy that catching a valuable and rare specimen arouses. I was projecting that I would display it in my window, standing on a fine Caucasian rug beside an early Venetian copper pot holding three white lilies. The price? Well, I would have to think about that later. Better do some research first, I thought, wanting to enjoy the piece before thinking about its value and sale.

My shop was already closed when I arrived. It was 6.45pm. I parked my large Citroën safari car alongside the building and with great care, using protective blankets, I moved the precious heavy cupboard off the roof of the car and carried it into the shop where I left it on its back for a careful inspection. I had hardly knelt down to start my examination to make absolutely sure that the piece was an original one, when the doorbell shook me brutally out of my concentration and excitement.

A recognised dealer in early English furniture, I shall call Mr W, was already towering over me, his eyes riveted on the cupboard. "Léonard, how much? Tell me!" His cold voice came cutting like a sharp knife into my vulnerable state.

As I stood up, my feelings were confused; I felt a panic setting inside me. "Oh, Mr W, hello, I've just arrived with this cupboard; the shop is normally shut at this time ..." I answered, trying to give myself time to think.

"How much for the food cupboard?" he asked again, authoritatively. My mind was whizzing in all directions. I lost control and rapidly thought, "Well, I've paid £90 for it, £600 would give me a fair profit." And before I could find space to agree with myself on the amount, my mouth and tongue had already divulged my thoughts!

As if jumping on his prey, Mr W almost shouted, "I'll have it! Here is the cheque. Bring it to my shop with the receipt tomorrow morning first thing." And he left, as furtively and quickly as he had appeared. I felt as if the devil was in my shop as well as in myself, laughing cruelly.

I was upset. Why sell it so rapidly? I knew only too well that one must never give a price right away; always let a day or two for research before deciding. I thought that I had understood fully this reality. But no! There I had just not followed what I knew to be the right way. Now I did not continue to examine the cupboard any more. It lay on its back on the fitted carpet floor.

On reflection, I estimated the value of this cupboard more likely to be around £20,000, as it was so rare. My heart became heavy, disturbed and confused. I looked up through the tall sash window into the grey evening sky and directed my thought up to the universe, "Thank you for giving me such an opportunity finding this unique oak cupboard so that I could feed my large family, but look! Here I go, look at my stupidity! I give it away to Mr W for practically nothing when he has only himself and his wife to look after!"

I felt angry with myself for having been so weak in letting Mr W push me into selling it to him. I tried to let go of the disturbance and reach peace but could not find it in myself; I felt like a cork being tossed about by a gale force wind drifting without control on a wild ocean.

I decided to share my agony with Toby, who had an antiques shop in London and who dealt in similar articles. "If the cupboard is what you say it is, then yes, effectively it is stupid to sell it at that price," Toby commented and added, "As you have not cashed the cheque, why not try to get the cupboard back? Invent some kind of story. I'll come down to see it tomorrow afternoon."

Toby helped me decide to try and re-acquire the cupboard. I worked out a feasible story, which went like this:

"The lady of the manor from whom I bought the piece rang me the next morning to say that she had made a terrible mistake by selling me the cupboard as her husband and children were furious with her and totally against her selling it, it was part of the family's collection."

First thing the next morning, I loaded the heavy cupboard back on to the roof of my car and, after securing it carefully, drove down to Mr W's shop, which was only half an hour away. Trying to lessen the bad feelings that were consuming me, I kept reminding myself, "But Léonard, you're only trying to feed your family! You'll give him his cheque back, he will have lost nothing, will he?"

As far as I was aware I had never before acted dishonestly and it felt as if I had suddenly lost all respect for myself. I felt my own dirt.

I parked my large estate car outside his shop, left the cupboard on the roof rack of the car and walked into his shop.

"I am upstairs, come up," he shouted down. Inside my chest, I was trembling like a leaf in an autumn wind and felt nauseated as I walked heavily up the carpeted steps. Mr W greeted me with a slight smile that was unusual for him. "Look, we will place it right here, in the prime position, bang opposite the staircase."

It was unfair to both of us to let this situation go on any longer, so I said right away, "Mr W, I feel very embarrassed to tell you that the lady of the manor who sold me the oak cupboard rang this morning just before I left, to say that she had to have it back. She had made an awful mistake and her whole family was furious with her about the sale. Here, I have brought your cheque back."

I said all this in one quivering breath. A freezing silence descended, immobilising our feelings; I observed Mr W's face tense up and contort over the infernal news I had bought. He could not find his words that were locked up by his anger at the unbearable thought of having to separate himself from this rare article. Finally, his icy pale blue eyes slowly rolled round to focus and lock on to mine. After what seemed an eternity he pointed his index finger at my chest, his voice carried by a suppressed rage, and said, "From anybody else in the world, I would never have accepted this crazy story! But coming from you, Léonard, I have to accept it as you are the only dealer I feel I can trust and respect!"

I smiled timidly. The tsunami had come over and left me completely broken up, tired and limp with just enough energy to stay upright on my feet. I felt the cheque being pulled abruptly from my hand. I thanked him for his trust and said goodbye feebly as I walked out of his shop.

Well, you can imagine how I felt during the drive home. I had lied just for the sake of money. This was truly an example of being possessed by the material forces. Where were my human qualities? How could I have done such a thing? There I was now, still with the cupboard and a most awful situation which I would never have dreamt could be possible. How could I get rid of, wipe out and erase all that smelly blackness?

I hid the cupboard behind the pair of thick burgundy velvet curtains that separated the corridor from the showrooms. I rang Toby to let him know what had happened in the morning and in the late afternoon he arrived from London. We both, with our respective expertise, carefully examined the 'rare' piece of furniture. It was very beautiful, almost too good to be true, but there it was, and it seemed to our eyes to be an original and therefore worth a hefty sum of money. I felt I could not sell it from my premises now, also that Toby would have better contacts amongst his London clients/collectors; so we decided that he would take it up to his shop in Westbourne Grove, place it in his antechamber and only show it to a few chosen clients. We loaded the cupboard on to the roof of his car.

The feeling of shame persisted. I told Mélinda the story when I came home and she did not judge my actions, but left it entirely to me to sort myself out over it. She loved me just the same and did not feel dragged down by my heavy heart.

That same evening I drove to the Subud Hall in Pembury, a few miles out of Tunbridge Wells, to do a latihan and try to reconnect to my soul. Indeed, since I had accepted the decision to lie to Mr W, I had lost that transcendental connection which was so precious to me. I felt lost within myself. The suffering, my hurt pride was isolating me from my beloved family. How was it possible, after so many years doing the latihan, to act like this? But there it was, I had acted deviously just for the sake of money. The latihan started and as I let go in complete surrender to my creator, I collapsed on the floor and sobbed and sobbed, the flowing tears gradually washing my confused feelings until I became completely peaceful inside.

In the inner silence I addressed myself to the source of existence and wisdom: "My God, please forgive me for putting myself in this situation and please show me the way out of the darkness I find myself in. How can I repair the harm that I have done?" With attentive awareness and inner receptiveness, in complete sincerity, I resided in a space where there is just 'being'.

"You must fast for 10 days," I heard clearly the reassuring and loving voice coming from the depths of my soul.

For 10 days I fasted. As the fast developed, the heaviness in my heart, the confusion in my mind and feelings, gradually dissipated and by the ninth day I felt fully connected to my soul again. On the 10th day, Toby rang me from London. "Léonard, I have been looking and looking and looking at this cupboard and I now think that it's a fake! Come up as soon as you can!" I jumped in my car and drove to Notting Hill Gate, my heart feeling light.

We turned the cupboard upside down and inspected it again thoroughly point by point, and came to the same conclusion that the cupboard was an extremely clever fake, probably made out of old oak in the early 19th century. As we laughed about the situation, I felt a wave of love and gratitude towards Toby. Now that we both knew for certain that it was a fake, what should we do with it? Put it in the salerooms? No, that would not be wise, as Mr W would be bound to discover it. Finally, Toby felt that he might have a private collector who could never afford a real 16th-century cupboard, and might be happy to buy this one as a rare example of an extremely good 19th-century fake.

A few days later, Toby rang me to say that he had sold, as a reproduction, the oak cupboard for £1,800, to the collector he originally had in mind. I marvelled at the power of fasting and the workings out of this story that seemed at one time so completely unsolvable.

If the reputed dealer, Mr W, had discovered it was a fake or had sold it to one of his collectors as an original and the truth had been found out later, he would never have forgiven me. By taking back the cupboard, I had saved, unconsciously as you know, Mr W from possible embarrassment. What seemed at one time to be an impossible situation had now turned round into a positive outcome for all parties.

Of course, the fact remains like a scar: I lied to Mr W, pushed by my blind desire of passion to make money, but due to the cleansing process of the fast, I was able to forgive myself and regain my self-respect.

I learnt a lot from this experience about the different aspects of myself and how fallible I am. It is reassuring to know that it is possible to repair my faults. And that I was able, through the total letting go of my ego, to allow a negative action to turn into a positive situation. The 10-day fast starved my wants, passions, desires and confused ego, then my freer awareness was able to transcend to my deeper inner self, reconnecting with my soul. Harmony was re-established not only within myself but also repairing the harm that I might have caused by my self-centredness.

A new consciousness was beginning to emerge in my being. I seemed to be able to shift my awareness to different parts of my own universe. To find this freedom, it was necessary to abandon my ego-centric self and find the space within where there is total peace, then just to follow the movements of my soul. To give a more visual analogy, imagine an allegorical white bird, my soul, free from the gravity of the material influences, flying weightlessly to all parts of my inner space and taking me to parts I had not been aware of before.

I find Bapak's Indo/Javanese spiritual language to express the structural realities of life so accessible that I often use it as a way of communication not only to others, but especially to myself when I'm using language to understand what is going on within myself. To give a simplified version of this code of expression, Bapak used an easily recognisable way to differentiate the levels of life forces that constitute the whole of our existence. That is, the material life force, the vegetable life force, the animal life force, the human life force, the angelic life force and the archangelic life force. I will not go into the possible other levels as they are out of my field of direct experience and understanding at this moment of writing.

With the practice of the latihan, my awareness has been able to become free, so that it can transcend all the levels of consciousness of my inner world. It seems that each life force, at each level, contains the potential parts of all the others, but each time within the limitations of its original level. I understand that these life forces constitute the necessary energies that enable my soul to experience this earthly life and are necessary for its growth, which evolves through their interactions.

To give another analogy: the cursor that we can move at will on the desk of our computer will respond freely to our command to reach all the different parts of the virtual world which the computer offers. In a similar way, thanks to the practice of the latihan, I am now able to move the cursor, my consciousness, either to the most light and pleasant parts of my being or to the darkest places.

But I will not continue with this form of symbolic expression. Better to go on with the stories that illustrate the reality of how the action of the latihan has influenced our lives, the 'our' includes of course the family, as I cannot possibly separate my own spiritual development from those of my wife and children. Although it is evident that the interactions of our living together have had an impact on each one of us, our individual consciousnesses are completely free and independent from each other.

Witnessing the powers of the material world

In his book, *Susila Budhi Dharma,* Bapak describes and explains the role of the life forces that influence us in our daily lives. These life forces are easily recognisable in ourselves, in our environment, and their influence can be noticed through our behaviour. The material life force, the vegetable life force, the animal life force and the human life force are the ones with which I am most familiar. Besides these basic four, there are other life forces which are certainly active, but to have access to them one needs to go through one's finer inner feelings. These finer feelings are difficult to talk about because their reality lies beyond words and therefore I can only give a vague pictorial description of their truth.

My understanding of the powerful influences of the material forces in my life grew much at the time when we acquired the Anugraha Centre in Windsor Park, near London. In a few words, I will try to give the reader a simple historic description of how the international Subud brotherhood came to acquire what was then called Dell Park.

In the early 80s, at a meeting in Kenfield Hall, near Canterbury, Bapak had talked to us about the importance of doing a large enterprise that could finance and support a Subud world centre. Apart from the large enterprises that he had initiated in Indonesia, no other such project had been started anywhere else. Yes, some of us had started our own small individual enterprises, but what he meant was something really big that could receive thousands of people. Bapak had suggested that England would be a good place to start such a project. There were not many of us present on that interesting afternoon, yet he felt it was the moment to create a team to start the ball rolling. He proceeded to choose, from the people in the room, the first nucleus to start the ambitious project. I remember thinking at the time, how interesting it is that Bapak only chooses from the people who are present at the meeting.

"And we'll need an architect," he had concluded as he looked in the direction of my close friend Lambert Gibbs.

I will not go into all the ins and outs of this tremendous enterprise, as that would be a large book in itself. So forgive me for going straight to the point where its growth and development stretched my consciousness to experience, at times with great pain, the action of the material forces within myself and on the willing and hard-working members who had taken direct responsibility for the project.

It needed a name, and the young team chose temporarily Amanco to register the company. With much energy and enthusiasm, they started looking for a site to build our international centre. After a few months of intensive search they found, near Windsor, a large estate called Dell Park. It was an impressive property in beautiful parkland with lawns, mature trees and shrubs. It had been built in the 19th century by a family of German bankers, who were also art collectors. The quality of construction and decorative details gave the property an importance and stature.

We were all excited by the scheme and the board of directors soon put together a workable financial plan, while the architect worked night and day to deliver a wonderfully designed concept from which the primary building costs could be drawn.

The project was presented to Bapak and he gave his approval, renaming the Dell Park property 'Anugraha', which means, he explained, 'the unexpected gift of God'.

Anugraha Ltd was promptly registered so as to raise the necessary

Anugraha macquette

funds to start the building work. The five directors, together with the architect, gave a presentation of the project to the Subud members at large. I had attended such a meeting, in Egham, and was very interested and attracted by what was being proposed.

Anugraha was to be a 120-room three-star hotel and conference centre, including a gourmet restaurant. The attractive red brick structure and imposing square building would be kept intact; however, its core would be radically changed and turned into a circular conference centre. A transparent dome would totally cover the large space and its opacity could be controlled at the press of a button, so that in full daytime, if necessary for instance to project a film, the space could be made completely dark.

The directors were sitting at a long table covered by a green felt cloth. The architect was standing next to a display board showing the drawings and plans of the proposition, as the chairman explained the scheme. It was interesting, certainly; more than that, it was captivating. Sitting quietly in my chair all ears, I was absorbing the seductive information when suddenly, to my great surprise, I became aware that the directors were not alone and that there was much activity around them, on the green felt, as well as on their bodies, especially around the speaker. I recognised the little beings – I had met them before at different times, including at Heathrow, as a manifestation of the material forces in action, when they try to take command of our inspiration and creativity. Each creature was not much bigger than a large apple, and I could see that they were enjoying what the speaker was describing as much as I was. They were nodding their expressive hairy faces up and down as they approved and, at times, they would poke him with their tiny hands to egg him on if he hesitated in his flow of speech.

The chairman went on: "We shall have the choice of having one great hall or two smaller ones. The circular ground floor will be able to rise to form two independent spaces or to come down to form a very large area. Each seat of the conference hall will be wired with speakers and phones so that each attendant will be able to communicate with the audience. Further, the Congress held at Anugraha will be able, at the same time, to be seen in other cities of the world. A large screen will display the faces of the speakers ..."

By now the little beings were having a party and frantically dancing on the green felt, expressing much delight. Although I found the scene extremely amusing, it disturbed me profoundly. Had passion, ambition and the desire to be the first in the latest technology taken priority over the basic needs of our international centre? Was the project too ambitious? Was not the cost of all this experimental technology too enormous for our means? I felt so uneasy that, when the meeting was over, in my naivety I went to the chairman, who happened to be a close friend, to share what I had just become conscious of and the anxiety it had woken in me.

"Do not worry, Léonard, it's okay! We are quite in control of the material forces," he tried to reassure me as he exploded into a loud laugh. At the time, I remember wishing that I had kept quiet.

Some months later, I mentioned this experience and the questions that had come to my mind to Lambert Gibbs, the architect, and he replied, "Funny you say that. I have been wondering at times if we're not being a bit too ambitious on some aspects of the project."

The development of the Anugraha project was a long and difficult road, a lot of it due to the inexperience of the people involved. Through my own involvement, I learnt a lot about myself, and how the power of the material forces had a disturbing effect on my whole being. Many technical problems occurred during the construction and, compared to the initial forecast, the costs had risen considerably and therefore so had the borrowing.

Finally, the alterations on the beautiful building were complete and the hotel and conference centre became a reality. A hotel manager was chosen, he formed his team of workers, and the project launched successfully.

Although the hotel management was doing an excellent job running the conference centre, the board of directors soon found out that the revenue from the hotel and restaurant were far from enough to cover even the interest on the financing.

A nice-looking ogre had been born and more money had to be found to keep him fed. His hunger grew steadily. Directors resigned, and others were nominated, while the road was becoming rougher and rougher. A new executive chairman was chosen, then a few weeks later the board of directors was reshuffled to create yet another team.

At that time, my life was already full. I was 47 years old, and Mélinda and I had a large family of seven children and a busy antiques and interior decoration business to run. I was also a national helper in the UK, so all these commitments took most of my time. The new executive director approached me to join the board of directors. After some hesitation, I accepted and explained that I could not be full-time, but was willing to attend all the meetings and give them full support keeping in view my other commitments.

Over the next two years, from early 1984 to early 1986, I attended the frequent board meetings and rapidly understood that the situation we were in was extremely precarious. The interest on the loans far exceeded the income that could be extracted from the conference centre and hotel. The hotel management was indeed doing well and the rooms were occupied at around 85%, which is a splendid average for any hotel to achieve. But even at 100%, it would not have been sufficient to pay the increasing debt.

The pressure was high, and the devoted team was working round-the-clock to find ways of answering all the many problems that were rapidly developing. After having studied scrupulously the alternatives, and to stop the infernal spiral of increasing debt, we came to the unpleasant conclusion that we would have to part with the property. This realisation was extremely painful as so much hope from so many Subud members round the world had been put into this noble project.

A Scandinavian client of mine had suggested that we approached a Swedish investment company that was looking for similar projects in which to invest. The Anugraha board contacted them and after a few weeks of negotiations we came to what seemed to us an acceptable offer. They would buy the property from Anugraha Hotels Ltd., but would keep the working team to run the hotel and conference centre and allow Subud members to use it to hold their events. Then, and this was the interesting part of the proposed deal, they would give us the option to buy the property back within five to eight years. In other words, we could go on using it while it gave us time to get our act together and also have the possibility of re-acquiring it at a later date.

The board agreed unanimously that it was the best option and before the deal was to be finalised, we organised an extraordinary meeting of shareholders to explain our decision. The great majority of Subud members, not only in the UK but also around the world, carried Anugraha deep in their hearts. We all loved the place. The building and its interior decoration was so beautiful, and the surrounding park and centenary trees gave it a majestic presence. We felt it was our international centre although in truth, financially, it belonged to the banks and a few of the wealthier investors.

An opposition team formed rapidly when they heard that the board had made the decision to sell Anugraha. They felt that we had let the Subud members down and were determined not to let us follow through on our decision to sell.

The last few months were extremely trying; the material pressure on the board of directors increased and I came to realise one day that I had not laughed for the last three months! My children noticed that during that time my hair had turned grey, and that I was no longer the happy dad I used to be. I even found it difficult to let go completely in my latihan. I felt stuck, as if covered in thick sticky treacle. During one latihan I stood in front of a powerful negative force and asked myself, "What is the best attitude you can have so as not to be swallowed up by this ogre of the material forces?"

I saw myself standing completely naked, arms apart, tiny in the front of a Colossus that had stopped only a short distance away. Powerful singing was coming out of my throat and chest, my consciousness became wider and led me to a space of serene peace while I felt full of light. I realised at that moment that my involvement in Anugraha had been too much from my heart and that the material forces had rooted themselves there and had got the better of me. I started laughing, as the situation was somehow funny. There I was standing naked in the front of this horrific monster who, by its sheer weight and power, could have squashed me like a bad useless flea, yet it had ground to a halt and started to decompose as it became smaller and smaller while I felt lighter and lighter. The whole experience took some time and after the latihan, I found myself light, clear and detached from my responsibilities as a director of Anugraha.

I remember feeling so thankful to the Source of Life that Bapak had put us in contact with. I now felt this contact close to me. Not only had it cleared my fears and anxieties, but it had also connected me back to my soul. In the three months I was on the board, I had lost contact with my soul: my awareness was only in the material world with all its confused problems and difficulties.

Feeling refreshed, as if renewed, by this latihan, I could see that many Subud members were caught by a kind of cathedral syndrome. They saw Anugraha as their cathedral and were ready to give everything they possessed, including their homes, to try to save it. Their enthusiasm to 'save Anugraha' had blinded them to the material reality that their homes would be lost into the great black hole that had become the debt. I felt sadness when I witnessed the split that was emerging amongst us. It was painful that this once noble project was now creating so much antagonism between Subud members.

Late one evening, after a difficult board meeting where some of the organisers of the opposition group had come to try to convince us not to go forward, I had gone to do a latihan in the great hall. I was feeling heavy when I knelt on the floor, my forehead touching the woollen carpet; how could it be that the harmony among us had been so disturbed? How could they not see that the situation had got to such a point that they would lose their homes? They said it was our lack of faith that had created the problem, that if we had all thrown our homes in as collateral we would have had enough security to borrow more from the banks and see the project through. But I knew from my observations that this would only increase the suffering and confusion amongst us.

Tears were running down my cheeks on to the thick carpet; I was again feeling completely disconnected from my soul and alone in my pain, low and empty, hardly breathing as if floating in a small, dark and narrow place. After maybe 20 minutes, I became aware of a presence that was kneeling by me; imperceptibly at first, a feeling of gentle love started to envelope my being, especially around my head and heart. I slowly opened my inner eyes to see that an enormous light and luminous hand was gently stroking my head as if saying, "Do not feel so lost, my friend, you are not alone ..."

My consciousness was now reconnecting softly to my soul, and I gradually began to feel whole again. My innate curiosity led me to follow the large hand. It belonged to a very large luminous being that filled the latihan hall, and I felt an angelic vibration inside.

It was late when I left Anugraha to drive home that night, and the pain in my chest, the tension in my throat, and the sad feeling created by the discordance between the Subud members had completely left me. I felt centred and peaceful as I drove down the M25.

My whole being was alive, full of the reality of that wonderful moment of reconciliation within my outer and inner self. I suppose that it is true that each individual person, when hearing or reading a word, understands that word in relation to his own experience of it. So, if I try to put it into written words, I will say simply that the large hand that had lovingly reassured me belonged to a being that inhabits the angelic level of consciousness. This particular level of consciousness, I understand, can only be accessed through me, as it is a part of my whole inner spiritual palette.

Finally, the challenging day of the meeting between the two Anugraha groups arrived, and we held it in the great hall. It was a wonderful, sunny early spring day, and many shareholders and other Subud members attended. The managing director, also chairman of the board, opened the session by explaining why the board had come to the unpopular decision to take up the offer of the Swedish group. Many sounds of anger and disappointment were heard amongst the audience as the chair spoke. It was becoming evident that many members were not convinced by our decision.

The leader of the opposition took the microphone and with much eloquence, drama and determination, gave a final pitch to the still indecisive shareholders present, that their way to save Anugraha was the only possible solution. "Let us see this project as if we were building our own cathedral. By offering our homes as collateral we can raise enough cash to pull our international centre project through..." He was then overtaken by his emotions and there was loud applause.

In light of this, it became obvious that the current board had to resign, and that is what we did. A new board was formed from members of the opposition group. I felt that it was my responsibility to take the microphone to reaffirm that, in my understanding, the figures of the accounts absolutely showed us that using private homes as collateral to raise more funds would put these homes at high risk and not solve the problem. The 'cathedral' group was now shouting so loud that it was pointless for me to try to further explain my rationale, and I passed the microphone on to another speaker.

During the turbulence of the meeting, even while I spoke, I noticed how peaceful, detached and light I felt. Our board resigned, the new board was formed and approved, and a revived sense of hope was felt amongst the greater part of the audience. Our board had followed what it thought to be the best way in all sincerity and with much devotion. The new board had taken the driver's seat to bring Anugraha to what they hoped was the best solution with all their sincerity and with equal devotion. The managing director of our board stayed on for a period of time until the new board had all the ropes of the enterprise in hand, and learned how to use them to fulfil their hopes.

Some years later we lost Anugraha completely, leaving each one of us, who had been implicated emotionally and financially in the project, to deal with the problem within ourselves. I dearly hope that each one learned something from it for the good of our own individual inner and outer development.

This powerful experience taught me a lot about how to recognise and handle the action of this material force within myself, so as not to be affected by it in my feelings and vision.

After Bapak's departure, 1987

I sometimes wondered how the period after Bapak's death would be for the Subud members round the world, who had witnessed his inspiring presence for well over 30 years. Deep in myself, I felt subtly connected to him, and had always looked forward to his regular visits to England. To many of us, he was a true spiritual father, always ready kindly and clearly to explain things to us when confusion occurred. He would make all the important decisions concerning the structure of our organisation and also where to hold our future world congresses, choosing the world chairperson, approving the new helpers and the testing to select the new international helpers for the next four years. He also encouraged us to start large enterprises as well as individual ones by giving his example: he had initiated several large projects: a bank, a hotel, and a large commercial and business building in Jakarta. Strangely enough, when Bapak died I felt extremely light and happy inside, although my ego wanted me to be sad, as is usually the case when one loses someone loved greatly. Suddenly I felt as if I had grown up, grown into an adult who had become spiritually responsible. In a way, my awareness grew wider and to this day, when I venture into my inner space, I feel Bapak's presence close to me.

It was at Anugraha that we commemorated the 100th day of Bapak's death. Some of the organisers of the commemoration ceremony had come to visit me in my antiques shop, Léonard Lassalle Antiques Ltd, to ask if I would say something about Bapak's life at the end of the ceremony. An imam was to start, followed by a rabbi, then an Anglican priest, then probably Sharif Horthy, who had been Bapak's private secretary for many years, and then myself. I accepted the request, but later felt quite nervous thinking about what I would say.

So, during the following two weeks, every spare moment was spent preparing what I was going to say. I thought that the imam, rabbi and priest would do the religious and spiritual part with prayers and so on. As for Sharif, I had no idea what he would say, but I thought it would be related to his role as Bapak's secretary. So I prepared a kind of scheme with key points, starting in Coombe Springs in 1957, and then developing a story of the next 30 years of Bapak's active existence spreading the latihan around the world. I would also talk about the many projects that Bapak had started or inspired us to develop.

Finally the day of his commemoration arrived. The ground and first floors of the circular Anugraha conference hall were completely packed. I arrived purposely just on time, so as not to meet anyone who might distract me from my concentration. I was asked to sit behind the curtains that backed the stage to the right of the audience, and to wait for my turn to speak. There were only four chairs and I was asked to take the last one. Surprised, I asked, "Tell me, are we not five to address the audience? Where is Sharif?"

The answer was brief: "In Indonesia, Léonard."

So I sat down and waited calmly for my turn. All the lights of the great circular hall had been turned off; only a spotlight remained lighting the lectern. Each of the religious representatives was a Subud member, and I enjoyed listening to their ceremonious speeches. When the Anglican priest had finished talking I thought, well, now it's my turn and started to get up ... I felt a hand resting gently on my left shoulder and one of the organisers said, "No, Léonard, Sharif first; you come after."

And before I had made contact with my seat again, I heard Sharif's clear soft voice resonate through the entire space of the hall ... I did not know that Sharif had not returned from Indonesia, and what we were hearing was a recording of the speech he had given on the day of Bapak's funeral in Jakarta 100 days before. As he spoke, to my astonishment, what he was saying was covering point by point the speech I had prepared with such care. It was extraordinary. Probably because I am close to Sharif in my feelings, as if he is my own brother, what he was saying was so similar to what I had spent two weeks preparing. I liked what he said, and it fitted well with what I would have said ... But now? What could I talk about?

The recorded voice of Sharif came to an end and it was my turn to go up to the lectern. I felt nervous as I stood in front of an audience that I could not see, for the spotlight directed at the lectern was so bright. Holding the sides of the lectern tightly, looking down, struggling to lead myself into my inner silence, I suddenly felt appeased by Bapak's presence enrobing me completely. I looked up and was comforted to see an enormous Bapak that seemed to be filling the whole space of the hall. I looked at him and asked from inside, "Bapak, please what shall I talk about?"

He smiled and I heard his voice say, "Léonard, talk about your experiences with the latihan."

"But which one, Bapak?" I questioned.

"You know – the one about the Prophets," he said, smiling. And as surprisingly as he had appeared, he disappeared.

From there on there was no more hesitation and I told them the amazing story of the Prophets just as I told you, above. As the words rolled easily off my tongue, I could sense that the whole audience felt as one with me, attentive to what was being said and moved in their feelings by the story; it was the first time that I had shared my spiritual realities with an audience.

At times during the story some people were crying, as moved as I had been the first time; and near the end of the story, when Bapak's kretek gave the small explosion, the whole audience burst out into a release of loud laughter.

There was a long, deep silence after I finished the tale. We were all united in one deep, peaceful and reflective feeling.

A few people came up to me afterwards, wanting to thank me for having told the story, which brought light on to a hidden suspected reality for them. One of them, a Jesuit priest, told me that he had been questioning and wondering for a long time who Bapak really was, how to place him in perspective to the Prophets in the Bible. Now, after my story, it was clear to him that all the Prophets were, in truth, one spiritual being sent to help humanity at different times through human spiritual history. Bapak incarnated them and had brought to us the latihan to give us direct contact with our source and connect to our own individual spiritual reality, he concluded, thanking me.

Chapter 5

Latihan on international journeys

First visit to Java

The screech of the turbojet aircraft engines that took us into the high altitude clouds turned into a comforting purr. I breathed deeply as I closed my eyes, abandoning myself to drifting thoughts. It was the autumn of 1970 and I had decided to spend the month of Ramadan in Indonesia, actually in Cilandak, Jakarta, where Bapak, his family and many of our close friends lived.

For some years, Mélinda and I had been following the yearly fast. We both gained great benefit from its practice; it acted as a break to the endless, passionate and turbulent life flow which otherwise would have been in continuous movement and taken all our inner space. Although Muslims do not fast while they are travelling, not being a Muslim – I do not practise any religion – I had decided not to miss a day so as to do the complete 30 days.

This was my first time away from the family and my first long distance flight. Feeling in deep peace, my mind was gently going through the previous day's activities; so much had to be done before I left. Peter, a devoted young man who was interested in the antiques trade, together with my secretary, would keep the shop open during my absence. My mother, Olivia, Ellen, our wonderfully efficient Dutch au pair together with Mélinda, would keep house and look after the children.

When I closed my eyes, loving feelings flowed towards my wife, mother and, at the time, our six children. All so different in character and looks, they reminded me of a bouquet of wildflowers, each one beautiful in its particularities. I was now smiling when my awareness directed to Mélinda's tummy to embrace our gestating Number 7, who was to be born the following April.

However there was, in my heart, one unsettling question: would Marcel live until my return? Marcel Laroche had recently married my mother and had moved from Cannes to live with her in the flat over the shop. He was overweight (120kg plus) and had only one leg, which gave that leg and his heart much harder work to climb the floors. On two occasions during the previous month, I had had to bring him back to life from violent heart attacks. Each time I was in my office when I felt that two floors up, something drastic was happening. I raced up the stairs two by two, to find him in his armchair unable to breathe and looking disfigured by the pain of the attacks. First, I took him by the wrists and lifted him up and down regularly, then did a firm pump action on his heart with both fists. It worked. He did not remember losing consciousness and was surprised when I told him what had happened. Knowing that neither my mother nor Mélinda would be strong enough to do this physical revival, I wondered whether he would still be alive on my return.

Feeling confident that I had left my responsibilities as best I could have wished, I relaxed deeply into a semi-conscious sleep. Our plane stopped for refueling in Rimini, Dubai, Karachi and Calcutta, and finally landed in Kuala Lumpur from where I took another plane to Jakarta. From Luton airport, the flight had taken 36 hours and I felt pretty tired when we finally landed at the hot and humid Jakarta airport.

Cilandak was like a mini-village, where its inhabitants all practised the latihan, giving the place a very special atmosphere. Arriving in the compound was like entering a familiar space. I felt instantly at home and welcomed by the smiling faces I encountered. Before going to visit my numerous friends from Europe and the USA who lived there

With Mas Sudarto Cilandak 1970

permanently, I went first to the Subud International office to register my arrival and find out where I was to stay. A good 50 to 60 people had come from different parts of the world to follow Ramadan in Cilandak and the office was busy registering and directing the newcomers to their locations.

Life at Cilandak during the fast mostly took place at night, as after an early supper around 6.30pm, most of us would stay up until breakfast, which we had from 3.30am to 4.30am when dawn was breaking. When I had observed the fast before, I'd always had to attend to my daily work and the family. But here, away from home, all the time was my own.

After three or four hours sleep, I would get up and go for long walks in the countryside, taking my drawing pad and box of watercolours with me. Everything was new to me – the fauna, the buffaloes together with the animal life, the local inhabitants and their villages. To be finding myself in a country where I could not communicate with words but only with my hands, smiles and expressions was a new experience. Sometimes to make myself clearer I would use drawings that I would quickly sketch on my pad to the great delight of the numerous laughing children who seemed to be permanently around.

The following year the Subud World Congress was going to be held in Cilandak and the work had already started on building a great latihan hall. In the meantime we did our latihan in a largish building that had been cheaply built some years previously.

It was most unusual not to be under the pressure of time and of responsibilities, I must do this, or I must do that, as one normally is under the demanding commands of the material world. So, some time after supper, I would wonder into the latihan hall and completely let go, knowing that I did not have to be back anywhere for anything special. I could just let the latihan flow freely and evolve until it would quietly reach a deep feeling of peace to finally tell me that it had come to an end.

On the 19th day of the fast the latihan took me through an unusual experience during which my awareness reached a spiritual dimension, not just of my own physical space, but also into a cosmic reality. Sitting with my feet tucked under my body, my forearms and hands resting on my knee, I heard crackling sounds, as if there was something burning, stirred by a strong draught.

I opened my eyes to check that there was not a fire in the latihan hall, and, reassured, closed my eyes again and looked inside as I became aware that the fire was actually burning in my head. Blue flames were crackling in the circular deep red-coloured closed chamber; I was inside my skull and felt that the flames were actually cleansing my thinking mind. The upper part of my body was swaying gently, following the circular movement of the flames in my head. I felt much pain, yet I was not attached to its intensity. After some time, as if the fire had no more fuel to feed itself, it gradually died down, taking away with it the crackling sounds together with the pain.

I felt a great soothing feeling inside my skull, like a cooling freshness. My consciousness was now hovering outside my body and resided in the vessel of my soul. I could see, further down, my body still kneeling on the floor of the large room where a few others were still doing their latihan. Then I felt my soul expanding and, as it did, I was above the latihan hall, and I saw the whole Subud compound with its twinkling lights. As my consciousness grew bigger, I was seeing, as from an ascending air balloon, the whole of Jakarta and its surroundings. The expansion continued, and I followed the need to look up into the firmament.

I gradually became spiritualy aware that I was between the gigantic legs of Bapak, at the same time being conscious of life down below; my soul, filled by a powerful feeling of love that seemed to come from Bapak, reached a level of consciousness that it could hardly contain. I was now nearing the place where the legs joined the body, knowing that I was not capable of going any further, as my vessel was not developed enough to contain more consciousness. I became aware that upwards was the rest of Bapak's spiritual body disappearing beyond the Milky Way ...

It took some time to return to my physical self. My latihan ended quietly, I rose up and walked slowly out of the latihan hall. The experience had been very powerful and although I felt extremely well and awake, I did not feel like being with anyone, so I walked into the moonless night on the narrow paths of the gardens, which were dense with tropical fragrance. I was crying, not from sadness, but from a kind of joy mixed with a powerful feeling of reverence and thankfulness. I had become conscious of Bapak's spiritual dimension.

It was only years later that I understood the significance of this experience. The blue flames burning fiercely inside my skull were like a purification of my mind, which in time became a more obedient tool to my soul, rather than the employee of my passions, wants and desires, as it had been for most of my life until then.

Although I saw Bapak in his physical body when coming across him in the Subud compound or during the many talks he gave us, on the spiritual plane, I inwardly understood that his broad consciousness transcended well beyond the Milky Way into the wider parts of the universe.

After the 30 day fast, I stayed on another week in Cilandak before starting the long return journey to Luton airport. White snow covered England, and although it was night, we could see no twinkling lights. Our aircraft was asked to circle round over the unlit airport for over an hour before we were permitted to land. A double line of small flickering yellow lights appeared on the ground below, and we proceeded to land. It was due to a general electricity strike that the whole country was in total darkness.

They were many stories to tell the family and presents to distribute when I came home. The third heart attack had taken Marcel away. Mélinda and Olivia had had to deal with sending the body back to Cannes where the funeral took place.

Changes in my spiritual responsibilities

As the numbers of people doing the latihan round the world increased, Bapak felt it necessary to give Subud a simple form of organisation. Firstly to attend to our material needs; that is, rooms for doing latihan or money for when members with international functions travelled. Also we needed to organise our four-yearly congresses. Secondly, to balance the material with the spiritual, Bapak needed help from his more experienced members in the latihan, to assist him to bring the spiritual training to all the different parts of the world where there was a request.

He called them International Helpers and every four years, at our world congresses, new ones would be chosen through testing by the outgoing international helpers. The same was valid for selecting the chair of the International Committee. So all members with an international responsibility would be completely renewed at each cycle. This would avoid creating a hierarchy within the organisation.

I think I mentioned previously that the latihan is an experience that does not repeat itself, so each time I practise it, I go through something different. It is often the case that what one experiences in the latihan is like a training preparing one for what is to come.

In the mid-80s, during one spiritual exercise in Tunbridge Wells, I was doing my latihan with a few other men when I became aware that I was standing on the bottom of a gigantic ocean. My eyes at the water line were able to see over the water with the endless sky above, as well as under the water with its cool pale blue-green freshness. I felt a deep slow pulsating rhythm, as if the ocean was breathing, making the kelp and algae that stretched towards the light of its surface sway in unison majestically. I understood, some two years later, the meaning of this through another unusual and rather dramatic experience. At that time, I was part of the team of national helpers for the UK. I had taken this responsibility once before and knew that although it meant allocating some of my time to its function, it was well worth doing, for it stretched my field of experience in dealing with the human and spiritual aspect of life. Also I had the pleasure of working in a team with others who represented the different parts of England, Scotland and Wales. The team was an equal mix of men and women, whether national or international.

Our beloved Bapak had passed away in 1987, and the next World

Congress was to be in Sydney in early 1989; it was to be our first World Congress without the physical presence of Bapak and we all wondered how it would work out. It was not easy finding candidates willing to take the responsibility of becoming International Helpers; I had been approached several times, but had turned it down in view of my work at the shop and the little time I had already with my large family. Mélinda and I decided to attend this Ninth World Congress joined by four of our children, Lucianne, the eldest (who used to be Laura), Richard, Hermas and Dahlan, plus Lucianne's nine-month-old baby daughter Liora.

It was the first time that I had been in this part of the southern hemisphere, where the crispness of the air, the burning heat of the powerful sun, and the incredible diversity of the flora was exhilarating. Longing to taste the yet unknown to us Pacific Ocean, a few of us decided to go to the beach in the late morning of the day following our arrival.

Driving down into the small green-lawned creek, strewn with gigantic pine trees that led to a brilliant white sandy beach, the majestic beauty was most impressive. The deep musical sounds of the large waves rolling in and drawing out inhabited all the audible space. A tall copper-coloured lifeguard, his feet caressed by the waves, with a red rubber bonnet over his blond hair, kept a sharp eye on the bathers. Hermas and I left the women with our belongings and innocently walked to the far right where the beach was less populated. With our impatience to meet up with these attractive-looking pale green waters, we both dived into an oncoming roller just before it crashed on to the sand. The immediate sensation of the cool water enveloping our overheated bodies was delightful. I instantly noticed that, although we were just by the beach, my feet could not touch the bottom and that a strong undercurrent was taking us out to the open sea. I heaved my head over the water wondering if I could see my son ... Yes, he was over there, further out, seemingly enjoying floating on his back. As I swam in his direction, I felt that I was being pulled down by my feet, I needed much more effort than usual to keep near the surface.

Hermas was now close and I asked, "Are you okay?"

He smiled and replied quietly, "Yes, but I don't know why I feel rather tired? I am going back."

When we turned our bodies towards the beach, we noticed how very far it seemed to be. I was feeling rather tired too, as resisting the incessant down drag was exhausting. I remember thinking about a story told by a friend from Indonesia that the Queen of the South Seas liked to pull men down by their feet and take them to her underwater kingdom. However beautiful the young Queen might have been, the thought of being dragged down was not at all pleasant and I pushed it out of my mind to concentrate on my return crawl.

I was now beginning to feel really weak and tired. My body did not seem to want to float. I was just able to catch my breath but not enough to feed my body properly with the oxygen it needed. I felt worried for my son and wondered where he was; also for my family on the beach, probably wondering where we were. Feeling that I might be losing my battle to survive, I turned to the creator inside my being and asked, "Is this your will? That I have come all the way to Australia to drown?"

The answer came back absolutely clearly, "Oh no! Just take on the responsibility to become an International Helper."

I felt as if I was being blackmailed. "Do you mean then, that if I don't accept it, I will go down straight to the blue kingdom of the Queen of the South Seas?"

"It's your choice; you must decide."

I had never felt my body so weak, it was as if all the energy in my neck, arms, legs and body had been removed and I thought, "How can I get back when I have no energy left?" Then I made a deal inwardly, "Okay then, I will agree, but then you must take my son and me safely back to the beach!" That was my bargain.

In a last struggle that came more from my brain than my body, I managed to pull my head out of the water and searched for Hermas ... Oh good, he was just there behind me, not too far, also just about managing to float. Coming from the open sea, three waves away, I saw a gigantic roller rushing towards us and shouted, "A huge swell is coming – look at it! Quick, we must use it to carry us back to the beach!"

As I felt the vibrant energy of the majestic wave take me in its stride, I found enough force left to paddle myself along with it and noticed, to my great relief that my darling boy was also benefiting from the miraculous ride. In a thundering splash, our exhausted bodies were safely delivered on to the wet sand like glittering lifeless seaweeds.

We both lay there, too tired to move. I opened my eyes to see that Hermas, a few feet away, was looking at me. He gave me a beaming smile, and said in a faint voice, "Okay, Dad? That was a close one, wasn't it?" I nodded in agreement and told him of my covenant with my creator: I would propose my name to be a candidate as an International Helper.

When we recuperated enough strength to go back to our beach camp, I told Mélinda and Lucianne of my decision. Mélinda's reaction was, "Oh, good. I always felt that you should put your name forward."

We drove back to the University of Sydney where the Congress was being held; we were a bit late for the 6pm men's latihan and as I approached the hall, I could already hear the latihan starting. I took off my sandals and walked into the huge gymnasium. It was completely full of men, each one with their eyes closed, independently letting go to the movements of their souls. There must have been at least 500 or 600 of them. I weaved myself to the far end where stood a small wooden stage on to which I climbed so as to find a little more space. I rested my sandals against the back wall and turned towards the great hall in a complete state of peace and attentiveness. I heard the cacophonic sounds of the men doing their latihan and it reminded me of the sound of the ocean. I let myself be cradled by it.

I remembered the experience I had had at the Tunbridge Wells hall, when I stood in front of the wide ocean. My eyes opened themselves slowly. From the platform on which I stood I could see the men who seemed to be moving, similar to the kelp and sea life that respond to the deep undercurrents. I felt love and at one with them, at the same time realising the oneness of humanity. All these men, each so individual, so different from each other, when surrendering to the movement of their soul, had become one in an harmonious whole. As if orchestrated by an invisible conductor, each individual in the room came to the end of their latihan, and a profound reverent silence took over.

I walked over to the group of International Helpers who were chatting together quietly and smiled to them, saying, "If you are still short of candidates, I am willing to have my name entered on the list." That same evening, after a short latihan, testing confirmed that it was good for me to take up International Helper duties for the next four years.

Janusz' first latihan in a Warsaw attic

We worked in teams of six – three women and three men – for each area of the world which was divided into three areas: Asia, south-east Asia and the Pacific including Australia and New Zealand; Europe and Africa including the Middle East; and the Americas. So in all, 18 International Helpers had the task of visiting the groups and isolated members of all the nine zones.

Int. Helpers 1989,
Kadariyah, Lusiyah, Rosalind

Int. Helpers 1989,
Reinbrant, Léonard,Hernando

Our area, Area Two, consisted of Western Europe and the Middle East, Eastern Europe including parts of the (old) Soviet Union, and the whole of Africa. The three women we were to work with were Lusiyah Bassi from Italy, and Rosalind Williams and Kadariyah Gardiner from the UK. The men, beside myself, were Reibrand Visman from the Netherlands and Dr Hernando Cacho from Spain.

Over the next four and a half years, the six of us would meet twice a year to organise ourselves for the next six months ahead. It was always a delightful moment to be together and share the stories of where we had been and whom we had met. Where which one of us would go was always decided through testing. From that place of quietness, each one of us would clearly receive whether it was right or not to visit a certain country. It was interesting to see how harmonious our receiving was, and how it generally agreed with what our three lady companions had received, as women and men did the testing in different rooms.

One of the first countries that the new team of International Helpers decided to visit was Poland. Kadariyah and I went for a two-week trip. We flew to Warsaw where Daniel Holt, a long-time member, met us and took us to stay with Anna Szeliska, who had been doing the latihan for many years. Subud members in Warsaw had been under the powerful domination of the USSR and under communism had learned, for their own individual security, not to communicate with each other. The result was that most members in the city were not aware of our presence. However, we managed to gather together a dozen members and do the latihan with them. Also, we told them of our plan to visit the cities and towns of Gdansk, Grudziadz, Olsztyn and Torun, where isolated members and interested people were expecting us.

Poland had just liberated herself from the Russian grip of oppression, and transport was difficult to organise, so we decided to hire a local taxi man who not only would drive us from place to place, but could also be our interpreter. We met Kasimir and his old Mercedes the next day. We instantly liked him and negotiated a price for our whole stay in Poland; he would drive us to all the places we needed to visit and translate for us when necessary. Kasimir was in his late 40s. His powerful body and low voice gave one a protective feeling, and we soon found out that he was a most gentle and understanding man. His English was good and enabled us to communicate freely. He rapidly understood about Subud, the latihan and the aim of our trip.

In Warsaw, it was difficult to find a place big enough to do a group latihan. A member named Natasha, who lived on the periphery of the large city, proposed that we use her attic flat. Ryszard, who was at the time chair of Subud Poland, joined our party. We parked the car on the side of a bypass and walked across to a tall dark reddish/grey brick building and gathered around the entrance while Natasha looked for her keys. A large bang, which sounded like a major car crash, was heard further up the road, and Kasimir departed to investigate while we went up to the fifth floor to have our meeting and latihan. The attic flat was rather smaller than we had anticipated. Ryszard and I were shown into a dusty attic storage place while the eight women would use the single room for their latihan.

The very steep pitch of the roof did not give us more than a metre of room before our heads hit the spider-webbed supporting beams. We removed a few old dusty cardboard boxes to give ourselves a little more space, and as I bent down my eyes were surprised to notice an old German army soldier's uniform and helmet that lay there forgotten, probably since World War II.

I looked at Ryszard and we both exchanged slightly wry smiles, then we stood until we had complete inner quiet, and the latihan started. The first thing I noticed was the sound of the street that seemed to echo under the slate tiles of the roof, and the strange musty smell of the place. I went deeper into my being and songs started to flow out of my chest. They sounded like Nordic ancient melodies that took me way up into a refined sphere of sensitivity. This lasted for some time, until I felt as if somebody was demanding my attention.

I slowly opened my inner eyes to see, as if I was looking down through the roof of our attic, a young fair-headed man, naked, his head down, looking completely lost. He was sitting on the railings of the dual carriageway, resting his elbows on his knees. Surprised, I looked further up the road and saw his young broken body lying across the road in a pool of blood; it was being covered up with a thick grey blanket by three paramedics. The remains of his dismantled motorbike lay unattended.

I was now standing next to the young man and asked softly for his name. "Janusz Petrovsky. What do I do now? My body is all broken, finished," he answered as he raised his handsome head and looked at me with large, pale blue eyes. As I saw his face, I grasped his whole background, what kind of person he was, his parents and their strong attachment to their only son, an architecture student at the University. Also his whole inner nature was revealed to me and I felt love towards him and his family.

"Would you like to start the latihan to help unleash your soul so that you can continue freely on your spiritual way?" I said encouragingly.

"Yes, I would," replied Janusz.

I was back in the attic; Ryszard's latihan had gone deep and quiet, and I called him gently by his name. He gave me a questioning look, slightly surprised as it is not usual to stop someone in their latihan.

"Would it be okay for you to join me in starting the latihan with a young man who just died in a car accident down below?" Ryszard gave me a smile and nodded in agreement. I said the usual few words of introduction before starting the latihan and we were off.

The latihan lasted a good 20 minutes. It was powerful, and at one time I felt a musical wave of fine vibrations rising through my body and up into the heavens: I knew that our young friend had started his new journey. Slowly, our spiritual practice quieted down to come to a finish. Close to my soul I looked down as if to confirm that Janusz had left the railings, and only his broken unanimated body still remained on the road with crowds of people who had gathered around it.

After this unusual latihan, Ryszard and I felt extremely light and happy and left the dark attic cupboard to join the women for tea and chocolate cake in the attic flat. When our taxi driver Kasimir reported back about the accident, he confirmed exactly what I had seen while doing the latihan.

An astral visit in latihan

I visited Poland on several occasions with, either Rosalind, Kadariyah or Lusiyah, each time with unexpected events. This story is a strange one, but nonetheless real. We were asked by Ryszard and his committee to visit the university town of Grudziadz, as there were a number of students there who were interested in Subud. We organised to meet them one evening in a university building to explain about the latihan. Many attended the meeting, mostly young students but also five or six older people as well. The meeting went smoothly, many questions were asked and answered, and finally we made a list of who wished to start latihan the next day.

I noticed a man with a thick moustache that curved upwards, who did not stop looking at me during the meeting. His laughing blue eyes and his smiling mouth carried a hint of cynicism; he obviously knew it all and gave me the feeling that he did not really listen to what we were talking about. I went up to him when the meeting ended, and presented myself. His name was Stanislas; he had served 18 years in the Polish army and was an officer. He told me that he was very interested in what he called spiritual matters to do with the astral. He asked if we could meet again and I asked him to organise it with our chair Ryszard.

Kasimir taking us to the park in Warsaw

The next morning, Kasimir drove Rosalind and me to a tall block of flats that stood on top of a windy hill. We took the lift to the sixth floor where a man named Roman and a lady friend of his met us. The flat was spacious, with large dining room windows that overlooked the city and river beyond.

Having been in so many private houses as an antiques dealer, always on the hunt for some rarity, my eyes mechanically scanned the room. I immediately noticed to my right a glass cabinet in which were many antiquities, mostly Egyptian. On the wall were the number of framed black-and-white prints of different hieroglyphic symbols, which I understood to represent life after death and the cosmos. A hefty Egyptian bronze cross of Osiris, known as the cross of life, was hanging majestically on the wall. From the general atmosphere of the room I could see that there was a very strong interest in white magic.

We heard the ring of the doorbell and Stanislas entered, all smiles. Ignoring everybody else, he came straight to me, his podgy hand stretched out. After a quick handshake we all sat down, Stanislas on my left, Kasimir and Rosalind opposite, and our host on my right. There was a strange feeling in the room as the Polish officer completely ignored my friends. Embarrassingly, his blue eyes were riveted on me, trying to catch all my attention. I avoided looking at him, went quiet inside myself and wondered, "What is all this about?"

Roman's lady friend served us tea and biscuits, while Stanislas who could not hold his tongue any longer, burst out in Polish with his heavy raucous voice. My eyes turned to Kasimir, who seemed completely surprised and stunned by what he was hearing. The speed at which the words were flying out, the intensity with which they were spoken, and the behaviour of Stanislas towards me gave me the indication that what he was saying was tremendously important to him, and that I was somebody very special. I looked at Kasimir again.

He had stretched his arm with his hand up in the direction of the officer as if to say "Stop! That's enough!" The raucous voice suddenly stopped. Kasimir, now looking angry and embarrassed, said to me, "This is all completely crazy! This guy is saying completely mad things. I don't even think that I should translate them!" I smiled broadly at my friend, saying, "It's okay. Just translate automatically, like a machine, and don't try to understand what he's saying. Just translate. Thank you, Kasimir."

My affectionate smile comforted him and he started to translate. It was true that for someone unprepared, what Stanislas said was completely bizarre but, taken in its context, seeing it from the officer's world, it made sense. I was a very high being in the hierarchy of the cosmos, and had come for a meeting that would be held the next day in Warsaw in a place that Stanislas had the honour and responsibility to take me to. There, I would meet another very high being who was, actually at this instant, travelling through the cosmos to be present for this very important meeting. Kasimir's warm expression shown through his orange/green eyes seemed to apologise for what he was communicating through his translation.

"Do you mean that I should be meeting White Feather tomorrow morning in Warsaw?" I said with a slight irony in my voice, knowing that the mention of the great Indian chief would throw Stanislas off his chair.

Now, I have to tell you that some years previously, my friend Lambert Gibbs had taken me to see an old Cockney healer in south London to help him with his kidney stones. I had seen on the wall a magnificent photo of an Indian chief and when I asked after the healing session who it was, the reply was "White Feather", the healer's guide.

Something in me had connected to Stanislas' sphere of understanding when hearing his message. Indeed he was stunned that I seemed to know about the Indian chief, but it confirmed to him the reasons for his admiration and reverence towards me. "This is a secret meeting of highest importance to the world ... Ah, you see Léonard, I knew that you were the right man. I've got the proof of it now," said Stanislas in a low voice.

I glanced at Rosalind. She was feeling uneasy and looked worried; I smiled at her before turning my head to Stanislas. "I hear what you are saying, that you are on an important mission, and of course you would like me to fit into the pattern of your conviction. But you do not realise that I am here with Rosalind to facilitate access to the latihan to the Polish people who wish to receive it. In no way do I want to be in Warsaw tomorrow, as we have other plans," I said.

Stanislas insisted, as if he hadn't heard me, by brusquely putting a small black book under my eyes. Rapidly his fingers found the page that he hoped would convince me to change my mind. The book had astrological calculations mixed with what I recognised as Templar symbols. The officer, tapping his finger on the page, hoped to uphold his request by showing me what he saw as the proof of the important meeting in Warsaw. All the signs pointed to it!

I gently took the book, closed it and pushing it back to him, saying quietly, "Stanislas, isn't it true that you are following what you feel is the most important mission in your life?" It was translated and he nodded in agreement, still full of hope.

"Well, actually, it is the same for me. My soul shows me a path and I am following it. I certainly do not want to deviate from it; it would not be right."

It was enough. We had other people to meet in the afternoon before the evening latihan at the University, and we left the flat.

Eight young male and six young female students were waiting for us when we arrived. It was refreshing and gave me a positive feeling seeing all these young people wishing to start the latihan. I followed the small crowd as we entered a long corridor. As we passed a small classroom close to the room where we would do the latihan, I saw Stanislas sitting in an old worn-out armchair through a window that gave on to the corridor. I immediately thought: "Oh, he must have come for latihan."

I open the door of the classroom and asked, "Coming in with us?" But he did not come into the room with us to start the latihan.

After saying the quieting words of Bapak, we flowed into our individual worlds and into the cradle of our souls. I was surprised to see how strong the latihan was. All the eight young men seemed to be receiving sincerely – some crying, some singing, one laughing; I felt carried by their youthful strength. Suddenly, I noticed I was being called and searched with my inner eyes to see, not without amazement, Stanislas going by across my field of vision, riding a metallic cigar-shaped vessel and looking at me smiling, waving his hand expressing a "Hello there."

I asked inside myself, "What is all this about?"

Then I saw Stanislas in deep concentration, sitting in the old armchair in the same classroom that I had passed. I understood that Stanislas was doing through his concentration what some people call astral travelling, and that he was travelling in the spiritual sphere of the material world. I felt immensely thankful at that moment, when I realised that surrendering in the latihan freed us from the material world, giving our consciousness access to other worlds through transcendence.

The next day, in the small flat that had been lent to us by friends of friends, I woke up early and was in the kitchen preparing breakfast. Kasimir, who was staying in a nearby hotel, walked in carrying his daily Warsaw newspaper. I saw him walk into the sitting room and bury himself in the latest news of the world. I was laying the breakfast table when I heard loud grunts coming from the sitting room. Kasimir, looking disturbed, burst into the kitchen pointing his index finger at his newspaper.

"It's incredible, listen to this small article! It's on the bottom right corner of the front page of Warsaw's largest newspaper." He expressed excitedly with much emotion and went on translating the revealing text. It said something to this effect: A crucially important meeting was to be held today, at a secret place in Warsaw, where internationally recognised wise beings were coming from different parts of the world and the cosmos to meet and exchange on cosmic matters of great significance for the planet, and so on.

It was very strange indeed. To me, what seemed weird was that such an article was on the front page of a national newspaper. I would have expected this kind of article to be found in a magazine about flying saucers or paranormal phenomena.

Kasimir, seemingly puzzled and feeling uncertain, said hesitantly, "Shall I run you to Warsaw, Léonard?"

Greatly amused by this situation, I laughed and replied, "Thank you, Kasimir. Our reason for being here is Subud and the latihan. Tomorrow we have a meeting in Torun which we must not miss!"

The archangel

Communication was still difficult in the USSR in the early 90s, as the rigid ruling of communism over the country had not yet loosened when we first arrived in Moscow. Letters were often opened by the authorities and one had to be very careful what one wrote in them. It had been difficult to organise visits and the first Russians to join Subud had managed to start their first latihan at the Amadeus Centre, in London. They included Sasha P, who was a translator of Russian and English working for the embassy, and Alexander R, a black market dealer in religious and esoteric books, which were officially not allowed at that time to be sold in Russia. Through this web, Alexander had come across a Russian translation of Mr Bennett's Concerning Subud, which had interested him. Sasha, Alexander and his wife Natasha were the first nucleus to take the latihan into the Russian bloc.

Léonard visiting Moscow

Officially no groups could be formed, so we organised our visit very much on the quiet. Rosalind, Lusiyah and I were to stay discreetly in a hotel in Moscow where only tourists were allowed. We had to conform by signing a register when we went out and again when we got back to the hotel, always before 9pm. The receptionist at the hotel was sympathetic and understanding, and I managed to convince her to let us secretly not stay at the hotel, but with our friends. The Russian people were longing for freedom and were pleased to be of service to foreigners, even when it meant breaking the regulations.

I was pleasantly surprised by the warmth and welcoming kindness of the Russian people who looked after and cared for us. Although the material conditions were hard, with a tiny living space and very little food, it did not take away their jovial humour.

Olga, who recently married Sasha, came from a family of diplomats, and had spent many years outside Russia. She mentioned Subud to her young brother Igor, a painter, and he was interested in starting the latihan.

Our guest flat was on the sixth floor of a poorly constructed concrete slab building. It consisted of a tiny kitchen, toilets, and a metre-square entrance hall that opened out on to the sitting room. The only bedroom was separated from the living space by a thin plywood door; a double bed and a large wardrobe took up most of its space.

Twelve or 13 of us crowded into the small sitting room and talked, laughed and drank black tea mixed with plum jam. Now had come the time for Igor to start his first latihan. Alexander and I rose to our feet and disappeared behind the thin plywood door to do a short 10-minute latihan so that we could approach the opening in a state of complete inner quiet.

As you already know, the manifestation of the latihan is usually perceived by an expression of sound and movement, at least for most people who practise it. But for Alexander, although he had been doing it for some time, his latihan was all inside with no outer signs of movement or sound. He seemed happy that way, and said that he felt good inside while practising it.

We had hardly been doing the latihan five minutes when something made me open my eyes to see that my friend was as white as a sheet and as straight as a wooden plank, toppling over sideways towards a shelf carrying an old-fashioned heavy Olivetti typewriter, under which stood a bedside table. I instantly dived forward catching the heavy machine just in time to save my companion's face.

He lay there on the floor, seemingly lifeless, his half-open eyelids only showing the whites of his eyes, his mouth tightly closed. I noticed some blood running from the side of his hand which must have hit the sharp corner of the bedside table. I knelt down beside his body; there was just enough room between the wall and double bed. I noticed he wasn't breathing, so anxiously I put my ear on his chest to discover that his heart made no sound. His whole body was rigid and lifeless. I now pressed my other ear to his chest. There was no sound, no movement; he was dead.

My legs and feet folded under my buttocks, I sat alongside my inert friend completely stunned, not knowing what to do. I could hear jokes and laughter coming from the tea drinkers across the thin plywood door from the sitting room. A turbulent river of anxious thoughts flooded my mind. "Should we call for an ambulance? What's the use if he's dead? Yes, but are you sure?"

I looked at him again. There was no sign of life. I listened to his heart once more, hoping that as if by some miracle it would have restarted, just by itself. But no beat could be heard, the whites of his eyes were still showing, his mouth and jaw still stayed tightly closed.

Sombre thoughts invaded my feelings: our presence in this flat was truly illegal, as we had clearly been told that we were not allowed to stay in the homes of Russian citizens. Surely we would be arrested, and how would I justify him being dead and the blood on his hand? Could there have been a fight? The KGB would investigate our presence in the flat, and our Russian friends would probably be arrested, too. Would they be sent to a gulag? How should we contact our embassies?

Faced by a situation for which I could only foresee negative issues, feeling my anxious mind, emotions and tense body, I decided to completely let go of my thoughts and anxiety. I closed my eyes to reach within myself the initial vibration of life. It took me into a deep inner quietness and, after some time that could have been minutes, I heard a voice gently say, "Call him by his Christian name."

I searched my mind for his name that would not come. How strange when I knew him so well. Knowing from experience that not finding the name can create anxiety, I stopped looking for it and went back into my inner quiet space. Still sitting next to my friend, I began to sing – actually it was more like chanting. It was as if I was calling the heavens and offering the whole situation to the source of life. The chanting amplified, and I witnessed my soul expanding outside the room, then outside the building. My consciousness was now high up over Moscow and I saw the presence of many angels. I recognised the very fine inner feeling I had experienced before when driving the car on the motorway. I understood that they were there to help. The awareness was most refined, and I heard a soft voice coming from the pure space: "Alexander!"

The rhythmic melodious chants now included his name, calling him back to life. After some time, I realised that the angels were only a necessary step to open the way to a higher source of consciousness. There was now only awareness, in this refined order of consciousness; the 'me', the 'myself', had completely dissipated and was replaced by a pure state of being.

Archangel Michael appeared suddenly in my consciousness. The highly noble being was pure energy and stood gigantic over Moscow, the force filled most of the firmament. Many years before, in the latihan hall in Tunbridge Wells, the Archangel Michael had visited my consciousness unexpectedly in the form of a very large winged being in golden fish scale armour holding a glittering sword.

This imagery, I understood at the time, was only a symbolic language adapted to my artistic nature. The Italian Renaissance painter Raphael's representation of Archangel Michael is the closest similarity I can give you, but this is only an image. Being aware of the archangel was like a kind of confirmation of the level reached by my consciousness.

I am trying to share with you a powerful experience with only the use of words about something, which actually happened beyond words. This is probably a reason why so little has been shared or written about what lies in the spiritual world.

Still in this state of awareness, as if my consciousness had become one with the Archangel life force, I saw myself taking the inert body, that seemed to carry no weight, and lifted it on to the double bed, his dangling knees bent over the edge. I stood by the side of his feet filled with an immense living power and light. Without the use of any word, I found myself commanding inwardly that the breath of life be given back to Alexander. I felt great energy flow all around us. Then in the silence, I heard again the laughter coming through the plywood door. I was back in my earthly ordinary self again and now looked at my friend's grey face to witness the vibration of life flowing back into his body. His eyes flickered several times and then slowly opened. At first, they were looking into nowhere, then looked round the room and finally settled on me. His breathing, although still imperceptible, was coming back as his skin regained colour. I was filled with immense joy and a deep feeling of thankfulness and gratitude for having witnessed what earthly mortals would call a miracle. But from what I had just experienced, I realised that transcendence was the way to access higher degrees of consciousness, where what seems impossible becomes possible.

I looked at my watch to find that we had been 35 minutes instead of the 10-minute latihan announced, and immediately wondered, after what we had just been through, whether it was wise to ask Alexander to participate in Igor's first latihan. I quickly turned to my soul and the answer came back: "Yes, it's fine." I looked at my friend who was now sitting on the edge of the bed looking at the blood on his hand with surprise.

"During your latihan, you fell down and your hand must have hit the corner of the bedside table. Do you remember anything? Are you feeling okay?" I asked with much curiosity and wonder.

"No, I do not remember falling. Yes, I feel okay but a little tired," he answered slowly. I reminded him that it was time to fetch Igor who was waiting to do his first latihan.

I have to tell you that I never told Alexander what I witnessed and experienced during that most unusual latihan. Somehow, I felt that it would not have been right, as what mattered was that my friend stayed close to his own reality. After all, what I described was my experience; although I witnessed that he had died and come back to life after some 35 minutes, Alexander himself had not been aware of it.

Still vibrating with the power of this extraordinary time spent with Alexander, I opened the door into the sitting room in search of Igor.

"We were wondering what was happening to you guys – you were such a long time, we almost came in to see what was going on!" said

Rosalind laughingly, as she came up close to me and whispered in my ear, "Tell me, what happened? You're looking radiant, full of light; it is extraordinary." I said I would explain later and called Igor to join us for his first latihan.

The opening latihan that followed was light and profound; I noticed that my host, Alexander, was now for the first time, moving and emitting sounds as if something had been unblocked and had freed him.

I have not shared this story before except with my wife Mélinda, with Rosalind in answer to her query and to my co-International Helper Dr Hernando Cacho to see if medically this story was credible. He told me that in certain heart conditions the heartbeat can slow down so much that it finally stops, but this is for a maximum period of a few minutes. A longer time would damage the brain irreparably. So, let me tell you that, medically this story would not stand.

The all-embracing life force

As I am on the subject of transcendence, angels and archangels, I will tell you of another out-of-the-ordinary experience which happened one evening on a visit to Cherkassy, Ukraine.

In the early 90s the people of Ukraine were, on the material plane, suffering from the transition from communism to democratic capitalism. The most basic materials and food for daily needs, that one took for granted in the West, were simply not available or if so, in very small quantities and at high prices. Transport, petrol and electricity were in short supply and in the evenings there was no public transport, the streets were not lit and one could not find petrol easily in the rare petrol stations that were still the property of the state.

One late afternoon, the International Helpers and our hosts went by foot from the centre of Cherkassy to a large communal building that stood a few kilometres on the outskirts of town. It had been an intense evening with general latihan followed by questions and explanations. When we came out we felt tired, but welcomed the quietness of the streets and the cool refreshing night air.

I needed to be by myself for a while and decided to leave my chatty friends and take another way home. I was born with a good sense of direction and enjoyed letting my legs and feet carry me home. The streets were wide and long. I was in a suburban part of town, with a few small private properties but mainly large high grey blocks of flats surrounded by vast green spaces and empty car parks. At that time of night most of the inhabitants were in bed, and only a few of the apartments gave enough light to show my path.

I came to the end of the road, and my feet promptly turned left. I followed without resistance; my consciousness was in a deep peaceful state, my thinking inactive; I was enjoying just being. We, my feet and I, came to a T-junction and turned left again. In the city's silence I heard a lamentation, or was it more of a groan? I walked on; to my left was a grassy bank on which stood a partly destroyed rusty wire fence which separated the pavement from pine trees and dense bushy shrubs.

The moaning was now right next to me. I saw in the semi-obscurity an old drunken woman sitting, resting her back against the rusty fence and holding, in the cradle of her crossed legs, an unconscious younger woman. Against the hip of the ragged drunken woman lay an empty bottle of vodka. She was crying, her face disfigured by the suffering probably caused by her incapacity to deal with the situation.

I knelt down by the two women and took a closer look at the seemingly unconscious woman. She was in her 50s, wearing a finely knitted cardigan over a white blouse. Her closed eyelids gave the impression that her evenly shaped black eyebrows were about to fly away. The skin was taunt over the roundness of her high cheekbones; her well-defined unpainted lips hardly touched each other, as if she was about to say something.

I noticed that she was not breathing. My ear against her heart revealed no beat, and her body lay cold and motionless, her hands crossed over her solar plexus. I lifted my head and looked around into the darkness to see if I could find help. There was no one around. To the right across the wide avenue was a large building from which the first floor corner flat gave us a little light. I remembered the incident in Moscow, the call for higher help, the transcendence ...

Letting go of the dramatic situation I found myself in, I went into that space where there is no plus nor minus, just stillness. I followed the chanting that came from within, and once again it took me to what I will describe as the angelic level. We were surrounded by the presence of many angels and I asked them, without the use of words, just by presenting the need, "What is her name?"

"Anna Maria, Anna Maria, Anna Maria ..." my lips rhythmically pronounced the sounds into her ear. I was now moved to gently hold her chin with my left hand, my right hand on her large forehead and tried to give her the kiss of life for some time, while my consciousness was expanding into a wider realm of reality. As I travelled out, I became aware that Anna Maria was out of her body, as if in waiting, appearing lost, not knowing where to go. Awareness grew finer as I came into the consciousness of Archangel Michael again. I understood that this level of consciousness was a part of the whole of the potential of a human being's consciousness; it was an all-embracing force, the life-giving power. It was now flowing back and I felt the fine vibration filtering gently back into Anna Maria's body. I heard voices and realised that now people surrounded me. As I looked up and around, I recognised my group of Subud friends who had taken a longer route. "Léonard, what on earth are you doing here with this women? Who is she?" I heard Kadariyah say in a somewhat alarmed voice.

"I gather that her name is Anna Maria. Quick! Please get someone to call an ambulance! And can someone, in Russian, ask this dear drunken old lady if she knows the person whom she is holding?"

A Cherkassy member ran off to find help while another tried to communicate with the vodka lady. I listened to Anna Maria's heart to hear faint erratic beats and noticed that she was now breathing imperceptibly. The old lady was trying to stand up, leaning against the rusty fence post. She did not know the name of the lady. She had found her unconscious on the pavement and had not known what to do.

I stood close to Anna Maria while the others stood quietly around us. It took 20 minutes for the ambulance to arrive with its lights flashing. Two male nurses rapidly pulled out a stretcher that they laid alongside the unconscious woman. Another arrived with a bottle of oxygen and a mask, which he promptly put over her nose and mouth. She was whisked off to the local hospital still unconscious. The next day Vladimir, who had been present the night before, went to see Anna Maria and told her the story of how she had been found.

Problems at Kinshasa airport

Well before I took on the duties of being an International Helper, in my latihan I often would make sounds and dance to the rhythm of different ethnic groups of the African people, feeling in my whole body the movement of being African. My tongue would be trained in forming the sounds that expressed a feeling. Actually, these experiences were not only related to Africa but to many other cultures and languages of the world, so that when I arrived in a faraway country, I would already feel as if I had been there, whether it was Japan, the Slav countries, Indonesia or north Africa, and therefore their cultures felt familiar. This short explanation about my experiences in the latihan will somehow, I hope, help you to comprehend my behaviour in the many different situations that I found myself in.

It was in late September 1989 when, for the first time, I visited what was then called Zaire, ruled under the iron hand of President Mobutu. My mother had brought my sister and me up with homeopathic remedies, and when Mélinda and I started our own family, we carried on with the tradition of not using allopathic medicine. So before leaving for Kinshasa, I asked our homeopathic doctor to give me a certificate of health and to state that I had received the necessary injections for the tropics. She also gave me different types of vitamins and homeopathic remedies, including one for malaria, to bring with me in case I fell ill. When obtaining my visa, a secretary at the embassy told me that the doctor's certificate I possessed was fine to enter Zaire, now called the DR Congo (Democratic Republic of the Congo).

Lusiyah Bassi and I were very fortunate, on our first journey to central Africa, to have a remarkable woman companion with us who could not only speak French, English, Spanish, Portuguese and many other languages, but who also had visited Kinshasa and the lower Zaire regions several times before as a previous International Helper. She was named Rachmaniyah Bowden and originally came from Hungary, although at the time she lived in Portugal with her English husband.

Once sitting comfortably on the aeroplane next to my Hungarian friend, I listened with great pleasure and interest to the many stories of her life and adventures in central Africa.

An hour or so before our aircraft was due to land, without thinking I took a $50 bill out of my wallet. I carefully folded it, and slipped it into my shirt pocket. "What have I done that for?" I wondered to myself without bothering to look for an answer. I stopped on the platform before descending the aeroplane gangway: the air was hot, humid and dense with a particular rich smell that I find hard to describe. "Ah, the odour of tropical Africa," I thought as I allowed all the pigments of my skin to become one with it. I recalled the first time I arrived at Jakarta airport in 1970, where the humid air carried the particular smell of Indonesia, reminding me of clove cigarettes and sweet rotten tropical fruit. Here, it was quite different. There was no sweetness to it, as very few people smoked. It was more like mushrooms that have gone beyond their edible state. It was not unpleasant but intriguing, unknown.

I could now distinguish in the distance a group of about 30 men and women waving welcomingly and smiling at us. Rachmaniyah had gone through customs with no problems, but a small man wearing a doctor's pale green overall unexpectedly stopped me; he asked me for my medical papers. I opened my passport in which I had slipped the medical certificate and gave it to him. He promptly gave it back to me saying, "What's that? I want your yellow card! Medical card!" He ordered brusquely.

When he realised that I could not produce the document, he asked me to follow him. We went along a dark corridor that led to a metal door, then down some steep steps that took us under the many labyrinths of the airport. We entered a small room. To the left was an old-fashioned fridge standing on tall splayed legs. At some time it had been painted a Nile green colour, but was now mostly covered in rust. Two lanky young male nurses, equally dressed in scruffy Nile green overalls, were leaning on either side of the fridge. They gave large greedy smiles as I entered the room.

A cold shiver went down my spine in apprehension of what might be the outcome of this strange situation. To the right was a rusty metal desk flanked by two metal chairs. The work surface was completely clear; the solemn-looking doctor sat down and while inviting me to do the same said, "I have the authority to send you back to England by the next flight, you know. If you want to enter Zaire, I will have to ask my male nurses to give you all the necessary injections, including yellow fever!" He said it with severity, staring at me with eyes that showed too much white.

As he finished his sentence, the taller nurse, grinning to his ears, opened the fridge door and pointed to the only syringe that lay on the metal grill shelf; it was surrounded by a few mysterious brown flacons.

"But I already have had all the injections needed for the tropics, including yellow fever," I protested strongly, my throat now becoming tense from the lie.

Things were getting out of hand and I decided to find quietness inside. I looked at the doctor, kindly. My anger and fears dissipated and were replaced by a peaceful sensation, a feeling of compassion flooding my heart as I realised that these guys were probably pushed by hunger more then by nastiness. I remembered the $50 in my shirt pocket. In this blissful state I inwardly saw many people who surrounded the doctor, and became aware that they were all members of his family and that they depended on him for their livelihood. I reached for the $50 bill, which I pulled out discreetly between my index and middle finger and curved it into the palm of my hand, thus hiding the green note. Sliding my hand towards the doctor, I lifted the side slightly so that he could see what I was hiding.

"Then, we are going finally to come to some agreement I see!" he exclaimed, bubbling with excitement as he pulled opened the metallic drawer of his desk and brought out the desired little yellow medical book with an array of stamps together with an ink box. "I think that with this, I will put all of them, even a few more if you wish?" he added jokingly as he took the money, taking care that the male nurses did not see the unofficial transaction.

There was now a light, positive atmosphere in the room, and a deep silence pervaded as the doctor carefully inscribed all the diseases and stamped each vaccine in the book with great application.

Abruptly, the door of our now quiet doctor's office burst open. "What on earth are you doing to my brother?" shouted the short man who had just entered. He was called Ruagasore; I had met him at the previous World Congress in Australia, where I had been the translator for the representing group of Zairian members. He was a national helper for his country and was devoted to his role, which he took very seriously. We were close friends.

"What do you mean? How can he be your brother? He is a white man!" retorted the doctor, exploding into a raucous laughter.

I immediately got up and went to hug Ruagasore affectionately. Although he did not give the appearance of being a strong man, as I hugged him, I could feel his steel muscles on his lean body. The doctor neatly inscribed and duly stamped each certificate of the little yellow book, gave it to me, and allowed us to leave. I suddenly felt free and light as a bird as I followed my friend's fast footsteps through the dark corridors of the underworld of Kinshasa airport. As Ruagasore and I came up the aisle that led to the retaining barriers smiling and relaxed, the large group of Subud members gave us a loud cheering welcome; the joy expressed by the gesticulations of our friends on our reappearance sounded as if we had just won an important football match.

Following the ululating dance

My sensitivity and attentiveness would always heighten when I left my home on international journeys, but going to tropical Africa, for some reason, raised my level of awareness to its highest degree. All my senses – hearing, seeing, smelling, receptiveness through feelings, thinking and soul awareness became more intense, sharp and clear. Was it because everything was so different? Was it because I was taken out of my usual routine and had placed myself in a completely different environment, that I felt so complete in my being?

I found that I had a great affinity and much love for the people I was meeting. Secretly inside myself I felt like an African; although I knew of course that my appearance to most of them was that of a true white man. I experienced, as I felt at one with the local people and my Subud friends, how the simple difference of skin colour can be such a barrier by waking up preconceived ideas, which always blur all our human similarities.

The contrasts and colourful diversities of tropical Africa, its luxurious vegetation, flowers and fruit, its bright, brick-coloured earth together with its handsome people, reminded me of the paintings of Douanier Rousseau. It was as if I was part of the living painting but without the four-legged carnivorous animal life.

On our previous trip to Poland, the Polish members had suggested we hold, in their lake district, an international Subud youth camp. Young Subud members from all over the world would spend two weeks together camping around a most beautiful lake not far from Olsztyn, where there was a group of Subud members. We suggested that they send an invitation and information about the camp to all the chairs of the countries where there was a Subud organisation. The idea was enthusiastically accepted and invitations were sent all over the world.

At that time in Zaire, there were between 600 and 700 members practising the latihan, mostly from the lower basin of the River Congo. On the road south of Kinshasa were the towns of Inkisi, Matadi, Boma and finally Muanda, which was right down near the mouth of the River Congo and where a small group had grown around the house and school of Kiti Ki Menghi and his wife Marie Claire. The story I am going to tell you now actually happened when Lusiyah, Rachmaniyah and I visited Inkisi, where there was a large group including many youths. The night was moonless, and we left our host's house to go to the meeting of local Subud members. A kind young man took our arms with great care to lead us the 20-minute walk in the pitch darkness. Over ditches and potholes, round muddy puddles and bumps we finally arrived. I admired our host's ability to see so remarkably well in complete darkness. We were led to three folding chairs on the wooden platform. The low ceiling was made of a large kind of chipboard that partly hung unevenly where the attachment had given way. It looked like a frozen upside-down wavy sea. As the room filled up, the air became more dense, and everybody seemed to be talking excitedly with each other.

RDC Congo visit with Rachmaniyah and Lusiyah

Finally, the chair of the Inkisi group came out of the rowdy crowd and walked up the three steps on to the stage. The audience instantly quieted into just a murmur. He looked severe, moved slowly and solemnly to the centre of the stage and spoke a few words of welcome. I could feel that the words did not come from his heart, though he tried to give the impression that they were. His face was tense and his mouth found it difficult to smile. He could not hold his cool any longer, and came to the point raising his voice and allowing his feelings to express the anger that he had been holding back during the welcoming words.

"Speaking on behalf of the Zaire Subud youth, of their parents and grandparents, I have to say how angry we all are with the World Subud Organisation that calls itself a brotherhood!" He paused and gazed haphazardly to find support in the eyes of the indignant audience. A freezing silence pervaded. He continued, gravely weighing his words. "Our young people received the invitation to go to the youth camp in Poland. They used all their savings, including that of their parents and grandparents, to have photographs taken so as to obtain their passports, and have waited patiently for the tickets that will enable them to obtain the visas required for Poland. But nothing! Do you hear me? Nothing more was heard from the World Subud Organisation, nor from the Poles! Now it is almost too late; they will never get there in time. Where are those tickets so that our youth can respond to the invitation with their presence?" He then stared across in our direction, expecting an explanation.

In the heavy stillness, I could hear angry murmurs coming from the floor. The tension had reached an explosive state. I glanced at Rachmaniyah and Lusiyah; they seemed petrified and I knew that their wish was that I would do something to answer what seemed to be an impossible situation.

Slowly I rose to my feet, and walked to the centre of the stage. All I could see in the badly lit room were the whites of the many eyes that were staring at me. The chairman left and went back to his seat. Standing up on the stage in front of the angry crowd, challenged by this unforeseen dramatic situation, I breathed quietly and deeply, then abandoned my fears together with my ego and came close to my soul ...

Instantly, to my great surprise, and I suppose to everybody else's as well, I started an unusual dance. My stomach violently contracted, bending my body at a right angle to my pelvis as my throat and tongue started ululating loudly in a high-pitched voice, while my legs in a stumping rhythm took my body dancing in large circles on the wooden platform.

"Have you gone crazy? What on earth are you doing?" I asked myself while vaguely remembering that, several years previously, something similar had happened during a latihan. A voice came unperturbed from the depth of my being: "Continue the dance until the atmosphere changes." This strange dance went on for some time and I wondered when it would ever stop.

Each time I passed my two lady companions, I could see from the corner of my eye their horrified faces, but I carried on as I felt that the dance I was performing was an expression of love.

The intensity of the dancing and ululating slowly decreased. I straightened my body and stood there a few seconds, catching my breath and dripping with sweat. I opened my eyes to see an amazing scene: the enthusiastic audience was standing in an overjoyed ovation, gesticulating and shouting, showing full approval of my performance.

I smiled to my ears and when the hyper atmosphere settled down, a flash of understanding came into my heart as I said, "My very dear brothers and sisters, we, my two international helper sisters and myself, understand the reasons for your great disappointment and even anger that you have expressed regarding the invitation that has come via the international channels from the Polish chair of Subud Youth. Having travelled to many parts of the world I realise that, although a given word may be seemingly the same from one country to the other, its content and meaning can differ greatly according to the culture, tradition and ways of life of each nation. This reality has many times in the past and again today in our situation led to great misunderstanding amongst people often resulting in suffering.

"How can a word such as 'invitation', which contains such a positive feeling, lead to so much suffering and confusion? To help you understand, I will ask you to imagine that you are with me in a very northern country, like say, Norway. A brother might say, 'I invite you to visit me.' To a Norwegian it means 'You are invited to pitch your tent at the bottom of my garden for one day or so in order that we can see each other. He might even join you into your tent with a bottle to share a drink with you. An Englishman might say: 'I invite you to drop in for a cup of tea.' When a German invites you he actually means: 'Come for a bite.'

"When a Frenchman or Italian invites you, not only will he give you a big meal which might last half the day, but he will make sure that you taste his preferred wine.

"When a north African or say, an Algerian invites you, he will usually mean: 'Come and share my house, you can stay one or two days if you wish, at my expense.'

"But, I now fully realise that when a Zairian invites you, he actually not only invites you to his home, but he will also send you the travel ticket with the invitation! The same word, invitation, a completely different content!"

By now everyone was laughing without refrain. Some had found the last comment so funny that it brought tears to their laughter. The chairman came back to the stage and said with much amusement in his voice, "Thank you, thank you, Léonard for the clear explanation. Now we understand the reasons for the great confusion. It is true, in Zaire before we invite someone we have to first look into our purse to see if we can afford their ticket!"

Everyone laughed again. Now the meeting had become harmonious, we felt as one with the group and shared our international experiences and also listened to their many stories. We came out late that evening, and the nice young man who had taken our arms led us through the dark paths where we were to stay and asked me, "Léonard, where did you learn to dance like that? Do you realise that never has a white man done an ululating dance for black Africans? This dance is our traditional way to express the highest love and respect to someone for whom we have high esteem, maybe a king or a highly respected being. That's why we were so touched, so moved when you showed your respect using our own traditional language."

I replied, "I did not learn the dance. The dance was already within me. I experienced it during a latihan a few years ago. When I stood on the stage, I went quiet inside and felt much love towards all of you in the room and then I just followed the dance, the movement and sounds that spontaneously came from within."

Receiving guidance from any part of your body

I have to remind you, reader, that what we call testing is often used amongst the people who practise the latihan to bring us to a place of understanding, not through our mind as is normally the case in ordinary life, but via our whole being through experiencing a reality without the use of thought. That is why, when I personally use testing, I always make sure that I haven't used my mind to come to the question and bring clarity to the problem, but that I have listened objectively to the person's problem and then completely let go of what I have heard. In the short latihan that usually follows, comprehension of the whole situation may arise and the appropriate words that follow usually lead the 'receiver' to experience his/her reality and thus to find his/her way.

The story I'm about to tell you illustrates, not without some humour, what Bapak meant when he said when explaining testing: "You can actually receive an answer through any parts of your body and being." I can remember that at the time I had not understood clearly what he meant.

On this occasion we were in Kinshasa. The man I was about to listen to could have been in his mid-50s. He was short, slender and had fine features that somehow amplified his shyness. My friend Ruagasore presented him to me saying "Léonard, for reasons we do not understand, André has stopped receiving in his latihan for quite some time now. Before, his latihan was loud and very powerful. Now he says that he does not feel anything anymore."

André acknowledged his approval by moving his head up and down. I suggested that he come with me to my bedroom to do latihan together. I was staying in the Catholic Centre. We stood opposite each other in the fair-sized bedroom. I explained that we would do a short latihan together first, maybe following it by doing some testing.

We started the latihan. I soon saw that although he was standing peacefully with great sincerity, he was completely motionless and silent, as if totally absent. My own latihan amplified, a gentle tune unfolded out of my mouth while, at the same time, my awareness grew to include André into my field of presence. After a short time, to my surprise, I felt awareness in my genitals. I opened my inner eyes to observe, not without some embarrassment, that the continuation of my semi-erect penis turned into a darker colour as if it was linked as part of André's.

"Léonard! You are truly a strange weirdo, what's all this about now?" As I questioned myself about this most unusual situation, I understood now why André was so blocked in his latihan.

"André," he was obviously faraway into himself, as it took him some time to open his eyes and focus into my mine.

"Yes?" he replied quietly.

"Did you feel anything particular during this short latihan?" I asked.

I immediately felt his embarrassment as his eyes rolled around without him being able to answer.

"Did you feel something down below?" I continued more precisely.

"Yes, I did," he answered in a low voice, feeling now relieved.

"Tell me, are you married? And if so do you have a sex problem with your wife?"

He proceeded to tell me the painful story that had led to the blocking of his feelings and expressed his great distress. "I have been very much in love, for some time now, with a young woman called Felicity. Six months ago, I went to her father to ask for her hand and, after some lengthy negotiations, we agreed that I would give him one cow and two goats for the hand of his daughter. The wedding took place, all was going well although it had been a colossal financial effort for me to gather enough money to honour the wedding agreement; you see, I am a very poor man ... Felicity seemed to love me too and we were happy living together in my small house.

"We had only been married for a week or so when her angry father came back to the house and threatened to kill me if I tried to stop him taking her back. His reason was that I had swindled him in the negotiations with my clever words and that she was worth much more than a cow and two goats."

His voice was now trembling, stirred by his fears and emotions.

"You are frightened of Felicity's father?" I asked gently.

André replied, looking at the floor and putting his hands wide apart, "He's big, he's strong and violent. It is impossible for me to go and fetch her as I am too terrified!"

"Did your latihan become blocked after the father took Felicity away?" I asked in a monotone, closing my eyes.

"Yes," he murmured.

"Close your eyes and relax. Find, through a total letting go of your ordinary self, the place within you where there is neither positive nor negative, just simply peace ..." I waited until I felt that he had reached a neutral peaceful inner state.

"Now, letting it come from deep inside, show how you would be presently if you came across Felicity's father."

Instant fear suddenly possessed André, his body started to tremble and then to shake, his face contorted, expressing panic. There was no need to let this agony prevail, so I said, "That's enough, let go of that fear now ... Come back to your previous inner state where peace resides," as I waited for his breathing to quiet.

"Now, only follow the movements and sounds that come spontaneously. How should you be, if you are close to your soul, when you come to the door of your father-in-law's house to claim your wife back? Receive now."

Slowly André's face lifted as if pulled up by his thin eyebrows, and looked as if light came from inside him. His mouth was now smiling gently, his arms apart ready for an embrace, and he stepped forward.

"That's enough for now, finished," I said softly and waited for his ordinary self to return.

He looked very happy, relaxed and was smiling. "Thank you, I understand now," he said.

"To get Felicity back home, you know what to do now. Stay close to your soul," I concluded as we parted.

A week later we were back in Kinshasa from our trip to the south-west and during a latihan in the Salembao group, I found myself next to André. I had not at first recognised him but had noticed that this man's latihan was free and expressive. I was surprised when I realised it was my friend who had come to see me at the Catholic Centre. After the latihan, he came up to me to tell me the latest developments.

The day after the testing session he had had with me, he went to his father-in-law's house and before knocking at the door remembered the testing, letting go completely of his ego and fears. They were instantly replaced by a feeling of love towards the man whom, in the past, he had feared. He knocked at the door and to his amazement his father-in-law came out, his arms wide open to welcome him and give Felicity back. He had also apologised for his bad behaviour, and said that all he wished now was to be on good terms with his new son-in-law.

"And your latihan is better now?" I said, knowing jolly well that it was.

"Yes, marvellous and free."

Dealings with the ancestry

The story I am about to tell you now shows how the practice of the latihan trained not only my physical body to move more freely in all its hidden parts, but also brought an awareness of the spiritual worlds, worlds that I cannot see with my ordinary eyes. I use the word 'worlds' in the plural form because I have noticed that each world is relative to its own reality and to my own level of awareness. In other words, the relativity of one world has its own truth and that is not really applicable to another.

This experience occurred during a latihan with the male members of the N'djili group not far from Kinshasa international airport. About 15 men were present, mostly under 40, in a small furniture-less room. I had previously suggested to them that, after a short latihan, we would proceed with some general testing.

At some time during the latihan, I found myself close to a very young man. He was motionless and did not seem to be in latihan like all the others. I opened my inner eyes to see a colourful queue of what seemed to be his relatives standing close behind him. My attention was specially drawn to a well-built old woman who was gripping his shirt and pulling him backwards with one hand while holding a long stick in the other. The queue was long as it went out of sight; they all looked sad, I noticed that none of them were smiling.

After 20 minutes, the latihan stopped naturally and I suggested that the men sit on the floor with their backs to the walls, leaving a space in the middle. I shared with them my understanding and experience of what we call 'testing' and then offered the space to whoever felt the need to share their latihan experiences or ask to clarify some point through testing.

A substantial silence pervaded and I felt there was shy hesitation about breaking the silence. To my surprise, Daniel, the young man I had seen during the latihan held back by his ancestry, spoke with a touch of anger in his voice. "I have been doing the latihan for over 18 months. I don't see why I should go on as I don't feel anything, nor move nor emit sounds like the others."

"Shall we see if testing can help?" I suggested.

He agreed and I asked the others to sit quietly round the room while we tested. Daniel and I stood in the middle opposite each other, and when I felt that we were absolutely quiet inside, I said, "Daniel, relax completely in all parts of your being, let your feelings be still like the waters of a lake when there is no breeze. Now, show through your latihan how is it for Daniel when he meets his grandmother, your mother's mother?"

Within a few seconds my young friend screamed, putting his hands and arms over his head as if protecting himself from the blows of a stick. His whole body was shaken by fear; he fell to the ground in the foetus position, his hands protecting his head and face. With agonising yells mixed with tears he was shouting, "Oh no, no! Don't do that, stop, please stop!"

His receiving was intense. We all felt his agony and pain.

"Quiet now, Daniel. Stand up and return to the quiet place inside yourself," I said softly. As if still full of bruises, he slowly rose to his feet and stood quietly in front of me.

"You have just shown us how it is in your relationship with your living grandmother. Now, receive how your relationship with your grandmother could be, if you stayed close to your soul."

While searching within himself for something to hold, Daniel came across the feeling of love for his mother. His face turned beautiful expressing that feeling, his hands alongside his body opened out.

"Yes," I said gently, "that is the loving feeling you have for your mother, but now, so as to find harmony within yourself and within your family, experience the correct feeling to have towards your grandmother."

It took longer for my young friend to receive this, as there was a struggle inside. Finally he abandoned the resistance, his arms came forward and lovingly he embraced his grandmother.

"And again, Daniel, relax completely. Where is that fear that inhabits you? Express it ..."

The trembling in his body came back and his face expressed the fear.

"While continuing your receiving of this fear, what must you do within your being to find the loving feelings where there is no room for fears?"

Rapidly Daniel expressed and showed that it was possible for him to let go of his fears when they arose.

On my following visit to the Congo, a year later, Daniel came up to me to say that his grandmother had stopped beating him with a stick since that testing session and that he did not fear her any more. She had become sweet and nice to him. Also, I noticed that his latihan was now completely loose, free and powerful.

You may wonder how it was that I knew that the first expression of love was for his mother? It is because when I do a testing session with a member, my awareness goes into my finer inner feelings that are attentive to what the person who is testing is receiving. So it becomes clear to me as I myself go through the experience, but to a less intense degree, of what the person is feeling. For the person who is not accustomed to this latihan practice, it may sound strange, almost magical, but in truth, it is as real and logical as the equation two plus two equals four is in the material world.

I have used this form of testing innumerable times to help a person connect to their own truth, to find what they are capable of doing within themselves, to improve the way they are so as to find harmony in themselves and with their family and fellow men. When I connect to my soul, my consciousness does a transcendent action. The latihan has trained my consciousness to use transcendence to reach the soul.

In some of his talks, at the time when he travelled from country to country, Bapak would often explain, not without humour, how the situation of our soul was for most of us: it was that our souls only possessed parts or bits of a spiritual body. He would at times radiate into laughter when he described that someone might only have two spiritual legs up to the waist, but no body on top. Or just a mouth, a stomach and feet. His descriptions were funny and reminded me of some of Hieronymus Bosch's characters. He would say to us that by practising the latihan regularly, we would eventually achieve a complete spiritual body.

To be honest, at the time I did not really understand what he was talking about. It seemed completely weird, yet I loved him so much and, realising that I knew so little about the spiritual, I accepted what he said without judgment as I hoped that, one day, I might come to understand.

In all simplicity I can say now, that within my own reality, I recognise what Bapak was talking about many years ago. Of course, as the latihan comes with no teaching, the language I use is derived only from my own experiences; in that sense I do not use a 'taught' religious language to express my spiritual understanding.

It was an extraordinary opportunity for me to become an International Helper and have the chance to travel to such diverse parts of the world, not only to meet and be with people of all nationalities, but also, in complete trust, to be able to let go together with indigenous people in the training of the latihan. From Scandinavia to Russia, Ukraine and central Europe; from southern Europe, north Africa, from central Africa to South Africa, for four years we were able to travel to all these areas and do the latihan together. There was something beautifully comforting in experiencing, without the use of words, the closeness and similarities between all us human beings. The experience of the latihan, in whichever continent of the world one practices it, seems to bring you close to your fellow humans with a feeling of love. In the latihan, while everybody has completely let go of their egos and desires, without teaching, rules or codes, the divine life force unites the ones who are able to follow the movements initiated from their souls.

Unblocking what is stuck through sound and movement in the latihan

I was surprised when we visited Nigeria, in the autumn of 1992, to notice when I did my first latihan with the Lagos men, that the 11 or so men present were completely motionless, nor did they utter any sounds. Surprised to find myself the only one who moved and sang, I asked them the reason for this. The chairman of the group explained, "Our latihan used to be with free movement and sound, in fact it used to be very noisy. A few years ago something unfortunate happened that could have ended in tragedy.

"We used to do our latihan on the first floor of a large warehouse in a huge market near the centre of Lagos. Once, one of our ladies had rather a powerful latihan where she yelled and screamed. The strong purifying sounds were heard in the market below by a group of men who immediately thought that there was a rape party going on in the warehouse. A few of them had seen some men and ladies go up the staircase sometime before and had deducted that they should go and 'save' the ladies from the barbaric men.

"Fight and chaos followed, some of our Subud brothers got hurt and we could not do the latihan in the warehouse any more. We were troubled by this misadventure and asked our national helper of the time what we should do. He replied that Bapak had once explained that when we do latihan in a room, which is not soundproofed, if it disturbs the neighbours, we should ask to do a quiet latihan. Since then, we do

Visit to Nigeria 1992

not move nor make sounds." He ended with a large smile.

It was now around 9pm and as we had been doing our latihan in an office, I asked David, "Is there anyone under or above us or next to us at the moment?"

"No, no one," he replied.

"So, that's great. I propose that we now test those of you who feel that they are not satisfied with their latihan. Firstly, how is your latihan at present? Followed by, how is your latihan if you are totally free from any sort of conditioning?"

Each man came up for testing one at a time, and the result was a revelation to each when they received, through sound and movement, the expression of their true nature. One of them mentioned that he felt as if he had been in a long sleep since the day of the big fight in the market.

Latif, the national chairman at that time, had kindly taken us to visit the four other main groups and, in each of them, we encountered the same situation: tightness, silence and no physical expression in the latihan. Each time we tested one member at a time and each time their latihan unblocked and they refound their freedom of movement and sound. Unfortunately, many members had stopped doing their regular practice during this long 'quiet latihan' period, discouraged by the feeling that they were not progressing in their spirituality.

The last few days of our visit were spent at their National Nigerian Congress in Ijebu-Ode. It was held in the large house of a local Subud doctor, and was just big enough to contain the many Nigerian members who had come. The latihans were powerful, and it was pleasing to see how each member had been able to let go of the 'quiet latihan' period and were now letting go fully into their own unrestrained latihan.

An encounter with black magic behaviour

While we are in Nigeria I will share with you a strange experience that happened in Enugu. Samson, a young member of the Enugu group, had asked if he could take me, early the next morning, to see the premises in which he hoped to develop his new graphics and advertising enterprise.

He turned up in a small white van in which the windows of the two front doors were missing. Leaning over, he pushed open the creaky door inviting me with a lovely welcoming grin to take the passenger's seat. Samson was extremely happy to have me sitting next to him in his van and his bubbly joy was contagious. We both enjoyed each other's company and set off with large smiles on our faces. He was feeling talkative. I just listened.

"It's a bit on the outskirts of Enugu. You'll see, it's got great potential. My first job is to repaint it all white, at present, you'll see, it's rather grubby. It's amazing what a bit of paint can do ... We are entering a rough part of the city now. If anything happens, let me do the talking," he warned me as if he'd had a premonition.

My young friend suddenly became tense and serious. I looked ahead of us and saw that we were coming up to a crossroad when, to my consternation, a tall man appeared from a side street and ran to the middle of the intersection. He was holding a bow and a few arrows in one hand, his face hidden by a large aggressive-looking painted wooden mask, his ribcage painted in white lines; a short raffia skirt round his waist was his only clothing.

Samson stopped the car within five or six metres of the menacing man who was now standing straight in front of us, his arms stretched out, forearms bent up, pointing to the sky. Both legs far apart, knees bent at right angles, feet pointing out, his whole body was shaking violently.

Passers-by had stopped to watch the scene. Talking quietly between his teeth, without moving his lips nor his head, my young friend said, "Look down, do not react or move, this is bad omen."

The masked man, in his war-like dance, was talking loudly in an unknown African tongue. I just recognised the words 'white man' coming up every so often.

An unpleasant freezing feeling wriggled down my spine when I realised, looking from the corner of my right eye, that a rusty, poisonous-looking metallic arrowhead was pointing only a few inches away from my temples.

By now Samson was trembling with fear, and his face had turned grey. I felt that the best place for me to be was close to my inner universe, and I completely let go of my fears and reached a state of deep peace. As soon as I totally abandoned my ordinary self, I imperceptibly moved my head to focus on the small bow that was fully drawn. I very slowly ventured to look to my right to see who was at the end of the weapon.

The bowman must have been about 17, the strong and steady hands that were gripping the bow and pulling the arrow back had bitten fingernails and traces of white chalk on them; the young face that was staring at me was white with chalk and deadly serious. The once-generous lips of his youthful face had contracted into a small tight circle through which the pink head of a pointed tongue appeared. In the small, sunken black eyes I was now looking at, I could only decipher the look of a huntsman about to shoot his prey.

Although I could hear the tall war dancer coming closer, I allowed an unfamiliar expression to take possession of my face. My tongue pushed the left side of my lower lip upwards, my prominent cheekbone went up closing my left eye while my nostrils widened. My hands with erratically splayed-out fingers joined in the grimace to amplify the effect.

The young bowman literally exploded into loud uncontrolled laughter, his bow and arrows fell on the side of the road, while he hit his knee with delight at the comical scene. I slowly turned my funny expression in the direction of the dancer who, upon seeing my face, equally went into a loud laughter, which we could hear from behind his aggressive mask. Samson, on the alert, saw the space for escape and accelerated away, leaving the passers-by and our aggressors in their bubble of laughter.

Once the crossroads were out of sight, Samson looked at me and asked, intrigued, "This could have become a tragedy you know. How did you manage to turn it into a comedy?"

"I just surrendered, let go of my frightened and nervous self, and followed what came, just like in the latihan, Samson," I replied, feeling quite relieved to have been once again saved from an awkward situation in a completely unexpected way.

Developing soul awareness

I find the word training extremely appropriate to explain how we understand the Indonesian word latihan.

The outcomes of the many experiences I describe in this book were possible because of this spiritual training. It was only gradually that I was able, first of all, to unblock the consciousness that seemed to reside only in one small part of my being. And then, hesitantly, to venture it into other parts of my whole. I understand the soul to be like a divine cosmic vessel in which consciousness can travels to the different parts of one's universe.

Bapak often used another analogy, one's inner being could be seen as a castle in which there are many levels and rooms. He would tell us also that most of us inhabit only one or two rooms and that if we progressed with the latihan, it would gradually free us to discover all the rooms in the different levels of our inner castle.

I understand the training as being the ability to let go of one's egocentric self and to place one's awareness in the cradle of one's soul, so that it is not self-interest that guides us, but the divine order which always harmonises and keeps perfect universal balance.

Coming back to Bapak's explanation about the soul, the more its spiritual body is complete, the further it will take us into our inner universe. I am at the moment sharing with you where I am in my understanding of the link between the material and spiritual worlds. The process of the latihan, over many years, has taken me through a myriad of different phases, each time widening my understanding and consciousness.

In my case, it was the state of fear: fear of the unknown space and fear of finding nothing in the beyond that had blocked my spiritual development. Now, I've found that the term 'nothing' is not applicable where there is spiritual consciousness.

Coming close to my soul in complete trust, and allowing it to live through me in all parts of my earthly activities has become my priority, as I found that living through my ego, wants and desires alone was living horizontally without much depth.

Of course, I cannot detach or separate my life experiences from the latihan. It has been my only spiritual practice, but I hope that some of the readers, who have not practised the latihan of Subud but have used other ways, will have had similar experiences and recognise my language.

Chapter 6

Moving south to Provence

Leaving England after 26 years

Bassetts Oast House

Bassett's Oast House had been a wonderful stage in our family life. The house was large enough to house the 11 of us – that is, including my mother Olivia and her partner, Marcus Hamilton. The unusual distribution of spaces inside, and the land that surrounded the property, gave each of us room to develop freely our own individualities, offering the children a stable environment to evolve in and therefore facilitating the discovery of their own characters.

The antiques and interior design business had fully contributed to the material needs of the family, and our English property represented, at the time, a relative material security. But these were not enough to give Mélinda and myself a cosy retirement.

Family Lassalle at the Oast House 1988

Through the shop, I discovered in myself many talents and was able to use them by creating lucrative activities, as you read in the first and fourth chapters. In the depths of my heart, I always intended, one day, to express myself through the fine arts. I felt that now was the time for me to apply my whole being to pure artistic expression.

Mélinda and I both had a strong desire to return to the south of France, where we had begun our lives together when we were in our 20s. Five of our seven children, Lucianne, Miriam, Richard, Pamela and Hermas, had started their own lives, and the two youngest, Dahlan and Laurence, were studying in London, Dahlan at the International Film School, and Laurence at a graphic design school. They were sharing a small house near Hammersmith Bridge and seemed relatively happy there, discovering and somehow struggling to deal with the big wide world that surrounded them.

Two years previously, in 1988, Richard, who at the time worked with me in the shop, knew of our secret wish to return to live in France. He suggested that Mum and Dad take a week off, go to Provence, and look for a house.

"But darling, we have no money for this!" I exclaimed, wondering where the money would come from. "Never mind, Dad, we will find it somehow," he replied positively, in a manner I seemed to recognise in myself.

Following our son's suggestion, we set off in March that year, having decided to search in the Mont Ventoux region, the Fujiyama of Provence. We booked a hotel room in the medieval part of Vaison la Romaine, which spreads at the foot of the beautiful mountain, and went straight to the nearest estate agency.

Moving to France with Pamela and Laurence

We were looking for an old house that had not been converted, preferring to do the conversion ourselves. It had to be stone built, with a few acres of land within a 10km radius of Vaison la Romaine. The agent proposed three houses, and with much keenness, took us in his car to visit them.

First he showed us the property furthest away, then a smallish house among some vineyards and, noticing our lack of enthusiasm, finally said, "Well! I am taking you to this one last because I thought it highly unlikely that you would want it; although experience shows me that one never knows what is in a client's heart ..."

It was the end of winter. Rain was falling and low clouds still stretched halfway up across the hills. The road took us through narrow gorges, when suddenly the landscape opened up, revealing a delightful small hidden valley, nestled between Mont Ventoux and a smaller mountain called La Platte.

The agent drove rapidly past two hamlets, and a kilometre further up the valley, through an orchard of apricot trees, we turned right on to an old unused lane. We were instantly charmed by the small, very old farmhouse that flanked the rock of the oak- and pine-forested hill.

Although it was raining, we found the old building completely free of damp. Some obviously very poor farmers had built it into the rock with only local materials. It originally possessed a small spring, which was now dry and therefore the property had no water or drainage. The site had no direct access to electricity. It was surrounded by acres of mature apricot trees, truffle oaks and pine woodlands.

Les Mûriers in 1992

It had not been inhabited for over 100 years and was used now by the local farmer for keeping his farm implements. Old dried leaves and ancient animal dung were still thickly carpeting the rocky floors of the three different stables. The dry dung probably came from a pair of oxen, a horse, a herd of sheep and goats. The windows and doors were gone, but the roof was kept in fair condition by the farmer, which helped to keep the walls from crumbling,

On our way back to the hotel, I unfolded a local map and said competitively to Mélinda, "One, two, three! Let's point our fingers at the house we love best." Amongst much laughter our hands met each other while our fingers struggled for the same spot on the shiny and colourful map. We had both chosen the old farm that had no water, electricity, toilets or drains, but was set amongst the woodlands of the magical valley.

Now that we had made the decision that this was the house we wanted, it was up to me to find a way to finance it. I will not bore you with the whole story of how I convinced the bank, but finally, on the guarantee of Bassett's Oast House, my bank manager willingly gave us the money needed to purchase the property.

For the next two years we spent our holidays camping in the house and organising basic alterations to make it relatively comfortable. A diesel generator provided us with electricity while I arranged a 200-metre long hosepipe to siphon water from the stone well, which stood further up in the forest. This water served as an outdoor shower and for general use.

Richard and I drew up all the plans necessary for the main alterations: where to put the kitchen, bathrooms, sitting rooms and bedrooms, and so on. Then we employed a young Englishman to do the basic upgrades from the plans. We built an outside stone shed in which to keep the generator – actually, mostly to dampen its loud monotonous sound. The rest of the work would have to be done by me once we'd moved in.

England was going through a deep depression at the time of our move and the housing market had completely crashed. I had hoped that the sale of our large property would have been sufficient to start a new life in France, and planned to invest the rest in creating a small income for us. But we were not able to sell our house nor pay back our debt to the bank. So we rented out Bassett's Oast House until the situation improved.

Melinda knew how strong was my desire to paint and I remember asking her, "Darling, would you be ready to move into our rough old farm in France, where I would take up my brushes to paint, with no security of income?"

She replied, "There is nothing I would love more than for you to start painting again. Never mind the financial aspect – we have always managed in the past!" Her love and trust gave me the strength to face our new future. My mother confirmed the decision by saying that, as soon as possible, she would like to join us in Provence.

The financial crisis in the UK was felt markedly, especially in the sales of luxury goods like antiques and property. I had difficulty recuperating part of the money the business had invested in stock. Had it been two years before, the material situation would have been much more favourable.

The shop had looked after us for 24 years and provided a wonderful vessel for my talents to unfold; I felt some nostalgia mixed with much gratitude for what it had given us. I sold the lease to an enthusiastic antiques dealer. The separation from the shop created an immense vacant space, which suddenly appeared ahead of us. Now I could fully plan our future.

In the summer of 1991, after having temporarily placed my mother and Marcus in an old people's home in Devonshire, very close to where my sister lived, we felt ready to leave England to prepare our new home.

Two days before our move, we organised a small 'roses and chocolate' party for family and close friends. Unexpectedly and to our great surprise, generous gifts were given to us: a Bramley and a Cox's Orange Pippin apple tree, a set of beekeeping equipment, plus a generous envelope containing a cheque that would greatly help us towards the move.

A few tears were exchanged with our three children present: Dahlan, Laurence and Pamela, who had come down from London to help us pack, load the 40 ton lorry and trailer, and also tidy up the house after our departure.

So it was in mid-summer that we left the Oast House in the fully packed safari car, together with our two very surprised-looking cats, Tequila and Hercules. It was the first time they had been in a car.

Driving on Kent's tortuous roads towards Dover to catch the hovercraft ferry, our ears were filled with the sound of Tequila's nervous mewing. Each one of us was floating in his own world. Mélinda, probably with a heavy heart, was thinking of her children left in England. I myself was feeling strangely free from the shop and all the life responsibilities that had accumulated over the years since our original move to Tunbridge Wells.

I felt like a horse that had been freed from his cart. I thought of my many clients who would not any more be able, just by picking up the phone, to make use of my artistic advice and talent. Twenty-four exciting years had been spent at 21 The Pantiles. Many of my clients had become keen collectors in 17th-century furniture and early collectable articles ...

I suddenly realised that I had been driving automatically for tens of miles; I decided to focus all my attention on the circuitous roads.

Work follows on ...

How wonderful it was to find, on our arrival at the house, a warm welcome from our son Richard and his pregnant wife Miranda. They had been staying in the old farm preparing it for us and were now ready to move to a town named Forcalquier, 100 kilometres further east.

I think I remember telling you that I had been brought up on a wild desert island in the Mediterranean where water was scarce and comfort most spartan. Well, our first year of living on the old farm, at the end of the world, as it is called, reminded me of my early years as a child living on the Ile du Levant with my mother and sister. Water was once again scarce, we had no electricity, and so on ...

There was an enormous amount of practical work to do. The first thing was to bring a water main to the house. Then, to install the piping to all the places where water was needed in the house. Then to fit the bathrooms, toilets, and arrange the kitchen with all its fittings, build chimneys and all the millions of things a house needs to become relatively comfortable.

We named the property les Mûriers, after the two ancient white mulberry trees on the terrace, which gave us plenty of cooling shade during the hot season. Settling ourselves comfortably in this cosy peaceful valley, we started to attend to the many tasks we had to do since our arrival.

My Subud obligations as International Helper still took much of my time and I had not as yet been able to do any painting or promote myself locally as an artist. We had come to the end of our financial reserves and I wondered how we would cope in the months to come.

One afternoon, the day before I was to fly to Moscow, a Norwegian client telephoned and asked if I could advise him on the purchase of a large luxury flat in the ski resort of Méribel, in the French Alps. Would I also let him know, if I found the project desirable, whether I could design its interiors and see it through to completion? I asked him to fax me the plans at once, as I would have to see them before I could give him an answer.

The large chalet was built at the base of the renowned ski slope. It housed three large luxury flats plus parking spaces. The project was appealing and I saw that it was possible to turn it into a beautiful space; I gave him my approval and left for Moscow.

The client wanted me to design and have made the entire contents of the large flat, from furniture to bedlinen and cutlery, even down to choosing the crystal glasses! I decided not to charge my client for my time and design, but to pay myself on the difference made between wholesale and retail prices on everything that was bought or made for the flat. When I painted special effects myself, I charged him an hourly rate.

This job coming out of the blue, at a time when our financial situation was at its lowest, reinforced my confidence that being in a positive place inside myself was all that really mattered; the rest would follow harmoniously.

Méribel was only four and a half hours drive from les Mûriers; this enabled me to supervise closely the interior design plan that I proposed to my client. After several months of intensive work, the whole flat was completed and the client was delighted; although he never really believed me when I explained that my design and work had not cost him any money!

I will enumerate a few more propositions of work that will show you how one job threaded through to the others, although they were very diverse in character.

Diana, an architect friend who had moved with her husband to Jakarta a few years before, rang up one day asking if I would be willing to paint a series of large murals for an international hotel in the super-active Indonesian city. I immediately asked her to send me the square footage of the hotel's fitted carpets together with descriptions of the walls and rooms where the murals would be hung.

The colours and fan symbols that decorated the carpets of the Mandarin Oriental Hotel gave me the colour scheme for the large paintings. I sent seven gouache-painted samples of my propositions. They were accepted and now all I had to do was find a place to paint them, as they were too big to paint in our small house. I had not yet built my large studio in the stables of the old farm.

Artist friends in the village kindly offered me the use of their studio, which happened to be close to the mayor's house and church. One day, as I was painting one of the murals from the top of a stepladder, the mayor of the village walked into the studio and stared at my work. "Hey Léonard! I did not know that you could paint like that." He was obviously very impressed and suggested that, before the murals were sent to Jakarta, we organise an exhibition in the town hall to display them for local people to see. He would arrange the whole thing and tell the press.

The show was a success and the next day photos of the murals and of me were in all the local press. The mayor invited the four directors of the Provence Electricity Board to the exhibition and they decided that an artist of such calibre should be able to see properly in his house. They organised that we be linked to the main electricity supply for an extremely reasonable amount of francs.

In the drive of his enthusiasm, the mayor asked me whether I would be willing to restore the 17th-century dry frescoes on the ceilings and walls of the local church and also to create a new mural to honour St Roch, its patron. I accepted the large project and immediately set to work. Most of the original frescoes had flaked away with time, but I managed to pick up the essentials of the designs and repainted whole parts of the ceiling and walls using the egg tempera natural pigment technique.

I worked for eight weeks with inspired gusto, up and down the scaffolding, making my egg mixtures to use as a binder, adding it to the appropriate colour pigments, then allowing my sable brushes to dance freely on the prepared surfaces. I found that I did not have to think what to do or how to do it; it was as if it was already inscribed in my feelings, I had just to follow the movement and passively watch my hand holding the brush doing the work.

Sniffing the continuous flow of salt water drops presenting themselves at the end of my nose, due to the cold damp atmosphere of the church, my consciousness would at times broaden to embrace, in my feelings, some of the painters of the Italian Renaissance. I felt an affinity with them – Giotto, Fra Angelico, Mantegna, Simone Martini, not to mention Leonardo da Vinci and Michelangelo. Not that I compared my creativity to the Masters, not at all. But the inner and outer atmosphere they must have experienced in the deep neutral silence of the churches where they worked must have been similar.

That particular smell of the egg tempera – a mix of linseed oil, egg yolk and distilled water – plus the still and peaceful feeling felt during the times of concentration when the breathing comes to a standstill while waiting for the hand to finish its brush stroke, these were powerful moments that they must have experienced. Although most of them actually used the wet fresco technique, painting on a freshly laid lime mix.

I did not charge for my work, only a small sum to pay for the cost of the materials. I felt that it would be our contribution to the community of Beaumont du Ventoux. The local population greatly appreciated having their church restored, and demonstrated it by bringing us bottles of wine, broad smiles and warm handshakes.

Also, it had the effect of teasing up my desire to paint again. I immediately started to restore the stables of the old farm and turned them into a fair-sized studio.

Returning to oil painting

Our financial well was once again almost dry, yet I knew that it was a grand time for me to start painting, now that my studio was ready. Not being able to afford canvases yet, I prepared three large panels of plywood that I primed with a self-made mix of rabbit skin glue and gesso. Having recently finished the mural paintings in the church, I used the same egg tempera technique with natural pigments.

I had been wanting to re-actualise the life of Jesus and thought of making a triptych of three famous scenes: the baptism of Christ, with St John the Baptist and Jesus in one of our local rivers; Mary Magdalene putting ointment on Jesus' feet in the house of Lazarus; and Jesus on the cross with the three thieves in the distance. In each panel was represented Mont Ventoux and local scenery; my characters were dressed in today's clothes, Jesus being baptised in his Y-fronts.

What an extraordinary experience it was, after so many years, to be in the silence of my new studio, in front of a large white board that demanded to be painted on. I found myself standing there, crying, tears rolling down my cheeks, filled with feelings of thankfulness for having been able to come back to this magic instant of pure creation. It was not long before my artistic passion took over my being. I was back in the world of feelings, dealing with form, space and colour.

Painting and creativity had come back to life in me and, as I worked, I felt as if I was conceiving other paintings to come. As they appeared in my mind and feelings, I discreetly stored them somewhere in my being. I felt almost embarrassed with myself to be using all that precious time of life for my own self-expression; but I knew there had to be a certain amount of selfishness involved if I wanted to return to my initial talent.

It was interesting to notice that, as I painted, my canvas became a kind of inner mirror reflecting my understanding about what were to me the basics of life: the theme of Adam and Eve, the male-female relationship within oneself; and the creation of the world in Genesis where the elements, through their mix, created life.

I wanted to express through my painting how I understood and lived these realities. To me, Adam and Eve were not over there, in the far past history of man, but were actually present in every moment of my life.

As I went on painting, my artistic eyes and feelings slowly woke up from a long sleep, showing me that the immaculateness of nature was simply surrounding me. The luminescent light of Provence has that particularity of enhancing the inherent beauty of creation. Everywhere I looked, I felt inspired to paint, whether it was landscapes, flowers or still lives. As soon as my eyes rested on a chosen subject, the dancing interplay of the light bringing life to the sculpted forms and colours brought about in me a state of communion, where I felt truly one with the subject.

I found that, although I had not been painting on canvas for over 30 years, I had matured in my art. Yes, it was as if my artistic creativity had continued silently, deep down inside. There was a big difference from when I painted in the late 50s and early 60s: probably due to the continued practice of the latihan together with living fully, I was able to reach a place of consciousness that I did not know when I was a younger man.

I continued to paint almost all the time, building up enough work to put on my first local exhibition. I was encouraged by the reaction of visitors, although I found that I only sold paintings to people I already knew. The following year, I put on another exhibition and again found that, although the local French population admired my work, the only paintings sold were to people I knew who had come from abroad.

It was not long before the material world caught up with me again and put its demanding hand out. The only way for me to go on with painting was to sell half of my private life insurance. I was therefore able to carry on with my work, freeing myself from the immediate worries of money.

Then, an unexpected challenge

While I painted I did not refuse the few jobs that came along whether designing furniture, altering a house, designing fireplaces, helping a client with an interior ... They all contributed to our small income. Late in June 1995, I received a phone call from Diana Wildsmith, the lady architect who had given me the mural job for the Mandarin Oriental Hotel. It was pleasant hearing her voice coming all the way from Indonesia ... She asked whether I felt capable of designing a gigantic crystal clock for a shopping centre in Jakarta. The demand was challenging and I asked her to fax me immediately her plans for the interior of the large project.

It was for a 32-storey building in the centre of the Indonesian capital. The three lowest levels were to be an immense shopping centre comprised of banks, high-quality shops, coffee shops and restaurants. A large atrium would connect the three levels that would be accessible via escalators. The lower floor would have fountains, and in the middle of that enormous space, the wealthy Indonesian family behind the project desired a large suspended crystal clock.

Looking at Diana's drawings, her choice of materials, red and dark green granite plus the bulbous design of the impressive granite columns that supported the floors, reminded me of the time of the Pharaohs, in ancient Egypt. Right away I set myself to work by opening my sketchbook to a virgin page. I closed my eyes, aware of the need, yet emptying my mind of thoughts, and instead inwardly visualised myself in the middle of this empty space.

It was not long before the whole design came into my inner vision: on the lower floor, in the middle of the large atrium would be a circular plan of water. In its centre would rise a round block of black granite surrounded by water jets to form a circular fountain. In the middle of the black granite block would stand red granite panels forming a box without its lid. Inside pink and green moving spotlights would be directed to the high ceilings. Resting on the red granite box would be a 10 metre-tall obelisk made of four panes of crystal glass, illuminated by moving lights below. Inside the two-inch thick crystal glass there would be a golden ball, the size of a basketball, within which would be a small trolley activated by a computer somewhere in the secretariat offices of the building. At 1am the golden ball would slowly start to come down on an invisible copper wire, which brought power to the motor of the trolley inside the ball. Each left side of the four panes of crystal glass of the obelisk would have incised gilded Roman letters giving the time of every hour from one through to 24.

I set to work on my drawing board and, following my inspiration, rapidly came up with a scaled drawing of my propositions and faxed it over. It was not only well-received and accepted, but I was then asked to create designs for two other fountains, sculptures and four large frescoes. The project was enormous and I needed to organise myself methodically so as not to be overwhelmed.

Never had my artistic and engineering talents been challenged on so many fronts at once. It was stimulating and reassuring to discover that I had no problem finding the necessary inspiration. So once again, I temporarily put aside my white canvases, brushes and oil paints, sat at my old architect's table and started drawing.

On the granite base of the crystal obelisk, the Indonesian client wanted to see an ordinary clock. So, on the red granite panel of the square base, the one that faced the escalators to the three levels, I designed a perfectly circular clock of which the thick glass of the face would come flush with the polished stone.

For the next fountain, I designed a long narrow pool in the shape of an ‘i’, its 'dot' being a large round pool, in which four goose-sized bronze female ducks and nine little ducklings would swim around four static male ducks, their necks stretching up to the sky making a fountain of four jets. The long pool was dotted by 12 large water lilies made in celadon stoneware clay, the centre of which would be an

Kreshno – Jakarta project

umbrella-shaped fountain, which would be lit from underwater.

And the third fountain at the top of a large main staircase would consist of a round Carrara marble bowl resting on a crystal column, through which bubbly waters would rise all the way up to the flat top of the marble bowl. On it would stand a life-size Javanese mythological gilded bronze figure called Kresno (Indonesian for Krishna), in a classic Javanese dance position, his right foot squashing the head of a black demon.

The old Indonesian director of the company also wanted four paintings, each representing the four stages of the development of man. From birth to puberty, from puberty to student life, from student life into the business world, and from the business world to retirement and death. This indeed was an exciting project. They also asked me to create a few other designs for the shopping centre.

I found an engineering firm, near Marseilles, to make and put together the different mechanical elements and store them before shipment. A famous French glass manufacturer made and engraved the crystal obelisk. A local stone merchant provided all the granite and marble parts made to my design. The clock was made by Omega. The mechanics and software for the golden globe would be made in the UK and included a short, modern gamelan tune that would briefly come on at every hour throughout the 24. The bronzes of the Kresno dancer and ducks would be cast in Germany near Stuttgart. And, finally,

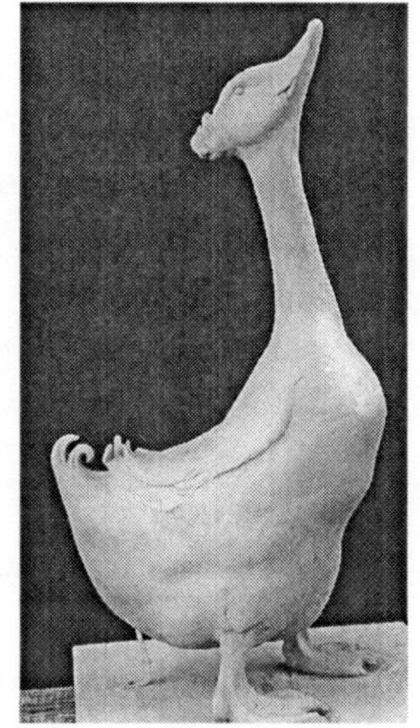
Male duck fountain
Jakarta project

a Paris firm would make the pumps and water jets.

All this work had to be co-ordinated on a schedule. I decided to develop the project in three main stages. The client would have to pay in advance the amount spent on each of the stages. The Indonesian family responsible for the large scheme came to my studio, not only to meet me but also to assess my ability to design and run such a project. During our three-day meeting I took them through all the stages of the development and took them to the engineering firm I had selected near Marseilles. They were impressed by their visit and we got the go-ahead to start immediately.

I worked on all fronts, including making the clay sculptures that would be turned into bronze, then gilded, coloured and patinated. I had not sculpted before, except a little at art school, and I found the challenge greatly enjoyable. When finished, a courier who specialised in works of art came to collect the four statues and take them to the bronze foundries in Germany.

Sometime in late April 1997, while working on the project, a strong clear feeling arose from my inner self: "This project will not come to term. You must tell all the manufacturers and people involved absolutely not to spend any more of their time on the project beyond what they have been paid so far." The warning was so clear that I immediately responded by writing to all the parties concerned and asking them to stop work up to what they had already been paid for and only continue when the second payment arrived.

I had been too busy to give attention to the large paintings, and decided to use that time to start working on them. Using natural pigments bounded by an acrylic medium, I painted on special rot-proof canvases. There was a lot of work to do, and it took me up to the end of August that year.

In the meantime, I found that my Indonesian partners were communicating less often and had not sent the second payments, although I had told them they were due. Then, one day, listening to the news on the radio, I heard that the whole of the Indonesian economy was collapsing and that the country was completely bankrupt! All the banks had to close; the economy was at a complete standstill.

I contacted Diana who confirmed the political and financial crisis, and told me that the project would not be able to continue, as the bank financing the project had gone bankrupt. After that phone call, I felt deep gratitude to my Source of Life for having guided me in good time, protecting me from having enormous debt. At the end, I did not owe one dime to any of the firms that worked on the job except to myself, as I had used the time while waiting for further funds to paint the four murals.

Some months later, in 1998, the Indonesian family offered to buy the paintings that they very much wanted to possess, but they offered to buy all four for the price of two. I refused, preferring to keep them in my studio.

This experience broadened my self-confidence in my inventiveness and creativity; it also pulled out of me a capacity for design I did not know I possessed. I left the crystal clock to the engineers in Marseilles, I asked the foundries to destroy the clay statues, as I could not afford to have them cast into bronze. I was left with the four circular plaques of marble on which the male ducks would have stood, plus the base of the fountain for Kresno; it is now standing as a marble table out in our herb garden, reminding me of a challenging adventure.

There is no doubt that I would have preferred to see the exciting project through to completion, but I felt that the whole exercise had been a very positive one. It stretched my creativity to new frontiers, and gave me the opportunity to work with talented engineers on problems that occurred while developing the many aspects of the project. Last, but not least, it brought Lassalle Art and Design, my company, a good income during those two and a half years.

The tragedy of the 11th of September 2001

At around 4pm on the 11th of September 2001, I was painting in my studio, fully absorbed by a bouquet of flowers and Frédéric Chopin's piano concerto that was playing on a classical music radio programme. Suddenly the music was interrupted, followed by an announcement: "We have just heard from our correspondent in New York, that one of the Twin Towers has been hit by a jumbo jet!"

Stunned by the announcement, I switched on the television I normally keep behind a curtain in my studio. What I saw was incredible. The same commercial tower that I had visited some years previously was on fire. The camera that was filming the horrific scene must have been some distance away. The sky was perfectly blue, except for the dense smoke rising from three-quarters up the building.

I could not believe my eyes when suddenly another aeroplane hit the second tower in a huge explosion of fire and black smoke. The camera zoomed in on the scene; I was now seeing, amongst the debris falling from the impact, some human forms the size of ants, floating as in slow motion down alongside the colossal building.

My heartbeat suddenly increased, pressurising the blood round my body; I was feeling suddenly terribly angry about man's stupidity and criminal behaviour. Had the world gone totally mad? My whole body was shaking due to my greatly disturbed emotions. It was hard to believe that what I was seeing was actually real and happening. Fully aware of how upset I was, I asked my inner self: "Léonard, what is the best state and place to be in during such a dramatic moment?"

Right away I switched off the television and stood up, completely letting go of my upset and indignant feelings, ego suffering, and myself altogether. Immediately I felt a neutral deep quietness inside as my consciousness broadened, while my voice went into powerful melodic sounds. The latihan I was doing was very strong and I was fully conscious. My inner eyes opened while the singing went on and I saw a most amazing scene:

From across the Hudson River I could see the city of New York lit by the golden light of the early morning sun. The wind coming from the north-west was pushing the enormous grey black cloud of dust rising from the collapsed towers towards the light of the sun. I saw, in the dusty cloud, the agony of a suffering humanity, yelling and crying out its profound despair.

Then, I heard harmonious angelic singing. I looked up to the heavens and saw that they were full of angelic beings coming down with their arms forward towards the dramatic scene; their light bodies made golden by the rays of the sun. Although the dark cloud of agony that stretched out from the city carried many faces expressing great confusion and suffering, I could also see, reaching out of the top part of the cloud, upper parts of bodies, arms and hands offering themselves up towards the coming of the assisting angels.

There was a balance between the beauty and the agony. It seemed that the chaos down below was man's creation, the suffering was in the dust and smoke. Souls were being saved by the multitude of angels. They seemed to be there to give assistance and reassurance to the undecided souls that were reaching out of the darkness of the smoke. There was no judgment in their action. Love and care were there to assist the souls who had abandoned their anger and suffering.

9-11 painting

I did not switch the television on again. I felt the need to share the understanding that I gained from this experience; I rapidly took my large sketchbook and started to draw. After a few rapid sketches, I knew that the painting was already waiting in my inner feelings. I took a large white canvas and started to paint. I felt neutral as I watched what I had witnessed reappear on the white linen cloth.

Some days later, the paint had hardly dried when two visitors came into the studio to see my work. Issa, a psychoanalyst and shaman, and her friend Laura, a professional singer. They both lived in San Francisco. Issa went straight to the 9/11 painting and asked how much? I told her and without any hesitation she bought it on the spot.

They both appreciated my work so much that they offered to give me an exhibition in their home on the outskirts of San Francisco. Also, they suggested that I hold an exhibition of my allegorical paintings at the California Institute of Integral Studies.

Just one more story

To tie up with my introduction, I will tell you just one more story that demonstrates how the action of letting go allows other latent powers to come into action – powers which are far beyond those that my ordinary self can access. What I mean is that, when not holding on to the many wants of my ego and self, I become conscious of my true needs – those that are of benefit to my family, myself and surroundings. Knowing of the needs, but not using my will to find a way to obtain them, allows soul action to come into play.

I took up Issa's kind offer and prepared two exhibitions for San Francisco. It was a big job, and over 40 paintings – some of them extra large – were carefully wrapped up and packed in big wooden cases and taken to Paris-Charles de Gaulle airport to be handed to a shipping company.

Mélinda and I went to San Francisco for a month, staying at Issa and Laura's house. Both exhibitions were successful and some 15 paintings were sold. The others were left in storage as I had it in mind to hold an exhibition the following year in New York with the remaining 25 paintings.

We came back in late December, tired from the long journey, and found when we arrived at our house at around 10pm that we could not open the kitchen door. In our absence, torrential rain had flooded the lower floors of the house and workshop, and between one and two inches of water was covering the floors.

The next day I went into my studio to discover I had lost over 200 of my drawings and other artworks. These were works I had done over a period of 45 years, many of them in coloured ink on smooth Bristol paper. The water had stuck them together and it was not possible to salvage them. The house insurance inspector came quickly and, after noting down my claims, told me that there was very little chance of being refunded for the loss of my artworks. The policy would only cover the cleaning of a few carpets and curtains, which they confirmed in writing with a cheque of some €200. I returned the cheque with a letter of protest, and six months later the litigation was still not settled.

Some time later I received a call from a friend in Chicago named Daniel, asking if I was willing to work with others who had experience in social work in Africa. Having been to central Africa on several occasions, I had become quite well-informed about the Subud projects of our friends in DR Congo and Angola. Small clinics, schools, social projects and small enterprises had been backed by the SDIA (Susila Dharma International Association) and by private entrepreneurial Subud members. Daniel was now organising a seminar in his large office to see how we could further help local people develop enterprises in their respective countries. Generously, Daniel offered to cover all costs including flights and I accepted.

The day before leaving for the USA, I wrote a very strong letter to the insurance company reminding them that each of my drawings was worth over €200 and that if they did not partly refund me for their loss, I would put the matter in the hands of my solicitor, adding that I was sending a copy of the letter to him. On the way to the airport I reflected that my car, an old Renault Nevada with over 380,000km on the clock, was beginning to show signs of old age. I wondered how on earth I would be able to afford another car, and how I could pay off the debt that I had accumulated over the last year. I posted my letter to the insurance company before catching my flight to Chicago, having no idea what would be the outcome.

Mélinda at her pots

Although the USA immigration department refused entry to the Congolese, it gave short visitor visas to Angolans. Although we missed the presence of our brothers from DR Congo, we had a very fruitful week working together. On the last day, we felt it necessary to put our hands in our pockets to give our Angolan brothers a few dollars to help them to start their enterprise. I discreetly looked in my wallet where I had exactly $330 left. I pulled out the three $100 bills, keeping $30 for my travel home, and put them in the kitty.

The following day when I arrived back home in France, Mélinda handed me the post and said, "... and there is this strange envelope from the insurance with only a cheque in it. I get confused with all the zeros, is it €3,000?" We looked at the cheque and found to our delight that it was €30,000! We were able to reimburse the debt and purchase a new car, which I'm still using today at the time of writing. There was no explanation from the insurance company, no apology, just the cheque which I cashed the next day. Again, I felt immense gratitude for being so well looked after. It reminded me of the time when I heard Bapak say, "When you give from the right place, you will receive a hundredfold in return."

Since our move to Beaumont du Ventoux, Mélinda and I have been totally accepted by its inhabitants. Painting the frescoes in the church had no doubt been a good move, but it is not all; the locals are now showing us much respect and even caring feelings. I put forward my name for the local council elections a few years ago, and was almost elected but for one vote. The opposition party, to which I belong, decided to start a quarterly paper, it is distributed free to all members of our community. This bulletin reports exactly what was discussed at the council meetings, local news and is open to any articles, providing that they are signed by the authors and are not condemnatory but simply factual reporting. Its creation has bought a unifying and a more democratic feeling into the community. A few locals have started the spiritual training and we are able to do the latihan together.

Last few words ...

As I wrote in the first pages of this book, I started the latihan kejiwaan of Subud when I was 19. My entire life has been informed by its practice; therefore I could not possibly separate it from myself, as it has integrated into my whole. I do hope that you have found the language I have used accessible and that you have recognised some similar unpredictable happenings in your everyday living, which might have originated from your own 'Source of Life'.

Painting of the almond blossom

Glossary

Bapak A respectful Indonesian term to address an older man.

Latihan An Indonesian word meaning training or exercise.

Kejiwaan An Indonesian word meaning spiritual.

Subuh Means dawn. Bapak was born at dawn.

Subud Originally comes from an ancient Asian dialect, meaning 'complete'. It is compiled from three Sanskrit words: Susila, Budhi and Dharma.

Cilandak A suburban village on the outskirts of Jakarta.

Testing Term used to describe a way to approach a question or a situation, so as to experience an understanding, without the use of the heart and mind.

Author's note: I have avoided using religious terms to make the reality of my experiences more accessible to non-religious readers.

About the author

Léonard Lassalle was born in Nice, France, on the 7th of December 1937, to an English mother and a French North African Jewish father; both were painters. For the next six years, with his mother and older sister, Sylvette, he lived on an island off the Var coast. In 1942, in the midst of World War II, the small family moved to a village called Dieulefit, in the Drôme, where the children attended school. Then, interested by A S Neill's alternative method of education, his mother sent the children to England for two years to attend Summerhill Free School.

By the age of 15, Léonard was studying drawing and advertising in Paris, at the Paul Colin Art School. Then, in September 1955, he began studying fine arts at the Central School of Arts and Crafts in London, where he met Jean Orton, the model, who later became his wife and with whom they had seven children.

Shortly after they met, Jean and Léonard started a spiritual training that corresponded to their independent natures; it is called the latihan kejiwaan of Subud.

Léonard had to temporarily stop painting in 1962 in order to provide a better living for his family, and he became a successful antique dealer in Paris.

With their young family, they eventually moved to England where Léonard opened an antique and interior design shop in Royal Tunbridge Wells and raised their seven children.

After 26 years, they decided to move and live permanently in Provence, France, where they each enjoy developing their individual artistic creativity.